Always-On Enterprise Information Systems for Modern Organizations

Nijaz Bajgoric
University of Sarajevo, Bosnia and Herzegovina

A volume in the Advances in Business Information Systems and Analytics (ABISA) Book Series

IGI Global
DISSEMINATOR OF KNOWLEDGE

Published in the United States of America by
IGI Global
Business Science Reference (an imprint of IGI Global)
701 E. Chocolate Avenue
Hershey PA, USA 17033
Tel: 717-533-8845
Fax: 717-533-8661
E-mail: cust@igi-global.com
Web site: http://www.igi-global.com

Library of Congress Cataloging-in-Publication Data

Names: Bajgoric, Nijaz, editor.
Title: Always-on enterprise information systems for modern organizations / Nijaz Bajgoric, editor.
Description: Hershey, PA : Business Science Reference, [2018]
Identifiers: LCCN 2017020970| ISBN 9781522537045 (hardcover) | ISBN 9781522537052 (ebook)
Subjects: LCSH: Information technology--Management. | Management information systems. | Electronic commerce. | Client/server computing. | Business enterprises--Computer networks.
Classification: LCC HD30.2 .A3983 2018 | DDC 658.4/038011--dc23
LC record available at https://lccn.loc.gov/2017020970

This book is published in the IGI Global book series Advances in Business Information Systems and Analytics (ABISA) (ISSN: 2327-3275; eISSN: 2327-3283)

British Cataloguing in Publication Data
A Cataloguing in Publication record for this book is available from the British Library.

All work contributed to this book is new, previously-unpublished material.
The views expressed in this book are those of the authors, but not necessarily of the publisher.

For electronic access to this publication, please contact: eresources@igi-global.com.

Advances in Business Information Systems and Analytics (ABISA) Book Series

ISSN:2327-3275
EISSN:2327-3283

Editor-in-Chief: Madjid Tavana, La Salle University, USA

MISSION

The successful development and management of information systems and business analytics is crucial to the success of an organization. New technological developments and methods for data analysis have allowed organizations to not only improve their processes and allow for greater productivity, but have also provided businesses with a venue through which to cut costs, plan for the future, and maintain competitive advantage in the information age.

The **Advances in Business Information Systems and Analytics (ABISA) Book Series** aims to present diverse and timely research in the development, deployment, and management of business information systems and business analytics for continued organizational development and improved business value.

COVERAGE

- Geo-BIS
- Business Systems Engineering
- Forecasting
- Business Intelligence
- Business Process Management
- Strategic Information Systems
- Data Analytics
- Big Data
- Legal information systems
- Decision Support Systems

IGI Global is currently accepting manuscripts for publication within this series. To submit a proposal for a volume in this series, please contact our Acquisition Editors at Acquisitions@igi-global.com or visit: http://www.igi-global.com/publish/.

The Advances in Business Information Systems and Analytics (ABISA) Book Series (ISSN 2327-3275) is published by IGI Global, 701 E. Chocolate Avenue, Hershey, PA 17033-1240, USA, www.igi-global.com. This series is composed of titles available for purchase individually; each title is edited to be contextually exclusive from any other title within the series. For pricing and ordering information please visit http://www.igi-global.com/book-series/advances-business-information-systems-analytics/37155. Postmaster: Send all address changes to above address.

Titles in this Series

For a list of additional titles in this series, please visit:
https://www.igi-global.com/book-series/advances-business-information-systems-analytics/37155

Smart Technology Applications in Business Enironments
Tomayess Issa (Curtin University, Australia) Piet Kommers (University of Twente, The Netherlands) Theodora Issa (Curtin University, Australia) Pedro Isaías (Portuguese Open University, Portugal) and Touma B. Issa (Murdoch University, Australia)
Business Science Reference • ©2017 • 429pp • H/C (ISBN: 9781522524922) • US $210.00

Advanced Fashion Technology and Operations Management
Alessandra Vecchi (London College of Fashion, University of London Arts, UK)
Business Science Reference • © 2017 • 443pp • H/C (ISBN: 9781522518655) • US $200.00

Maximizing Business Performance and Efficiency Through Intelligent Systems
Om Prakash Rishi (University of Kota, India) and Anukrati Sharma (University of Kota, India)
Business Science Reference • ©2017 • 269pp • H/C (ISBN: 9781522522348) • US $175.00

Maximizing Information System Availability Through Bayesian Belief Network...
Semir Ibrahimović (Bosna Bank International, Bosnia and Herzegovina) Lejla Turulja (University of Sarajevo, Bosnia and Herzegovina) and Nijaz Bajgorić (University of Sarajevo, Bosnia and Herzegovina)
Information Science Reference • ©2017 • 180pp • H/C (ISBN: 9781522522683) • US $140.00

Handbook of Research on Advanced Data Mining Techniques...
Shrawan Kumar Trivedi (BML Munjal University, India) Shubhamoy Dey (Indian Institute of Management Indore, India) Anil Kumar (BML Munjal University, India) and Tapan Kumar Panda (Jindal Global Business School, India)
Business Science Reference • ©2017 • 438pp • H/C (ISBN: 9781522520313) • US $260.00

For an enitre list of titles in this series, please visit:
https://www.igi-global.com/book-series/advances-business-information-systems-analytics/37155

IGI Global
DISSEMINATOR OF KNOWLEDGE

701 East Chocolate Avenue, Hershey, PA 17033, USA
Tel: 717-533-8845 x100 • Fax: 717-533-8661
E-Mail: cust@igi-global.com • www.igi-global.com

Table of Contents

Detailed Table of Contents

This chapter advances the idea that the modern organization can become immune to a full spectrum of risks by re-engineering its organizational capability and culture. Given the accepted role of people in causing or escalating technical risk – the requirement to achieve 'always on' socio-technical protection poses a significant challenge. However, an enterprise's human resources offer a massive potential to detect and report risk and there is also substantial competitive advantage available to the organization which develops, integrates, leverages and acts on intelligence gained from a suite of socio-technical sensors and sense-making processes. The human resources and culture of an organization, properly configured, could comprise a powerful innate (constant) and adaptive (active) immune system. The chapter will provide the reader with a framework for how such an immune capability could be integrated into an organization that takes seriously the requirement to be 'always on' – protected from any form or blend of socio-technical threat.

Considering the expectations of customers on service and information availability 24x7, complete operations suspension in case of adverse events is not an option. Modern businesses have become dependent on their information systems (IS) whose incidents and failures can highly affect business operations. Ensuring continuity in IS is related to the reliable delivery information. In order to lower the negative impact of IS incidents, organizations should get prepared for them. Business continuity management (BCM) is a holistic management approach whose aim is to identify, prevent or mitigate operational risks. BCM consists of business continuity planning (BCP), contingency planning (CP) and disaster recovery planning (DRP). BCP defines the strategies that organizations should implement in order to ensure their survival when a crisis event occurs. The aim of this paper is to identify the relevant elements of continuity in IS.

Multimedia allows and encourages different ways and methods of human sense manipulation using the highest achievement of technological development with the aim of communication, education, or entertainment. The most frequent contents that are transmitted in real time are contents based on voice services, the so-called VoIP services. In order to shed some light to the opportunity of the media delivery of sports content in always-on mode in Croatia the following goals are fulfilled. First, the possibilities of transfer services of multimedia content live via Internet are analyzed. Second, the competitive advantages over the same or similar services and check its influence on the development of society and the general economic activity are examined. Third, habits of potential customers using multimedia services as well as their expectations are analyzed based on the survey research results. Finally, based on this information, the canvas model of providing a service of sport content multimedia delivery in always-on mode in Croatia is developed.

This study aimed to identify to what extent Australian organizations have any plans to manage business continuity threats, and the nature and content of these plans. Sixty-four respondents who were risk management professionals were surveyed to explore the Business Continuity Practices within their organizations. The ANOVA analysis showed 39 per cent of the organizations had developed an enterprise-wide plan of which just over half stated that the plan was tested. However, 36 per cent of respondents had no plan, an "informal plan," were developing a plan, or did not know whether they had a plan. Standardized guidelines for a process to manage risks have been developed across many spheres and countries and are brought together in the international risk management standard ISO31000, which presents a process applicable to all organizations and all risks. Human resource practices that promote consistent communication and an organizational culture that allows business continuity plan values, attitudes and beliefs to become embedded and to move across traditional organizational boundaries are therefore important for gaining the cooperation needed to implement plans in an organization's operational areas pertaining to business continuity.

This chapter presents research results on user requirements related to enterprise risk management software. The authors developed a questionnaire to investigate the standpoints of risk managers, quality managers, and others in charge of risk management regarding the functionality they expect risk management software to support. In today's globalized and volatile world, the recognition, understanding, and management of risks is critical for an organization's survival. Adequate software support enables organizations to take an innovative, risk-based approach to governance and compliance and to gain a holistic, enterprise-wide view of risk exposure and near-real-time risk management and monitoring. Research results show the main attributes that risk management software should have in order to fulfill user expectations. The chapter also provides some important guidelines and suggestions for risk management software development and improvement.

The paper presents two approaches in assessing the business continuity management (BCM) attitudes in the organizational context: qualitative and quantitative. The first approach - case study analysis is based on a series of in-depth interviews with the key people involved in the BCM processes in Croatia (Chief Information Officers – CIOs, Chief Executive Officers – CEOs and BC managers). The second approach is an empirical research that was conducted among companies in Bosnia and Herzegovina based on Confirmative Factor Analysis (CFA) which is used for psychometrically validation of the measurement scale of BCP and Structural Equation Modeling (SEM) and t-test for the hypotheses testing. The empirical research has shown that there is a statistically significant difference in terms of attitudes of respondents regarding business continuity depending of companies' size and sector that company belongs to. Specifically, financial sector is in all of BCM segments more coherent than other sectors.In addition, qualitative research revealed the results showing that business continuity plan (BCP) and disaster recovery plan (DRP) were the only IT governance areas that were implemented in business practice. The reason for that may be found in the fact that BCP and DRP are very expensive to implement especially for small companies.

Foreword

Modern society can't function without the infrastructure provided and maintained by computing and the internet technologies. More physical infrastructures are now integrated with computing infrastructures. However, as people use and depend more on such cyber-physical systems, they operate with the assumption (at least not conscientiously) that these infrastructures are available all the time like air or water. While everyone may acknowledge that this assumption is not automatically guaranteed, in practice, users tend to ignore potential disastrous consequences and disruptions. Ironically, this challenge is getting more difficult as the society embrace the computing and the internet technologies more. Furthermore, the society has to deal with a set of new challenges under cyber-security.

Thus, the notion of "Always-On Information Systems" is becoming more and more critical for today's corporations as well as the society in general. Despite of its importance, the research efforts have been scattered and carried out by a limited number of forward-looking researchers. I am very excited that this new book—a sequel to Dr. Bajgoric's book in 2009—is coming out with a collection of many important research findings on "Always-On Enterprise Information Systems for Business Continuance." I have no doubt that the book will be not only an invaluable contribution to the field but also an important source of information to educate others on this important subject.

I would like to thank all the authors of the articles in the book for their pioneering research works and willingness to share with others. Particularly, I applaud Professor Bajgoric's vision on this topic, insight to select appropriate topics, persistence on working on this topic for decades, and efforts to bring together the leading researchers.

Young B. Moon
Syracuse University, USA

Preface

Modern business computing uses information technologies that are implemented in several forms of enterprise information systems (EIS) such as Enterprise Resource Planning (ERP), Customer Relationships Management (CRM), Supply Chain Management (SCM), Business Intelligence (BI). All these EIS implementations support business processes and make them possible in today's e-business environment. Therefore, there is a high level of dependence between the efficiency and effectiveness of business processes/business operations and organizational performances on one side and availability and scalability of IT platforms that enable them, on the other side.

Several downtime stories from the last couple of years such as application server crashes of stock-exchanges, system outages at the airports, network disconnections, application and storage crashes of cloud providers, and, more importantly, negative financial effects that immediately followed on both provider's and customers side, demonstrate how important is to have the availability ratios of information system platforms as higher as possible. Messages such as "system is down", "service unavailable", "DNS failure", "we want to apologize for the impact this event caused for our customers", and similar, have become common, but frustrating as well.

The book *Always-On Enterprise Information Systems for Modern Organizations* aims at providing a set of high quality chapters describing conceptual, structural and implementation aspects of always-on enterprise information systems, including interrelated concepts such as business continuity, high availability, IT risk management.

Chapter 1, "Always-On Enterprise Information Systems: The Concept, Attributes and Enablers," by Bajgoric, can be considered as an introductory chapter that is aimed at setting the conceptual aspects of „always-on" enterprise information systems. In addition to conceptual dimensions of these information sytems, this chapter demonstrates the shifts in major characteristics of traditional and modern enterprise information systems, identifies their main attributes and enablers, in other words, implementation drivers.

Chapter 2, "The Always-On Business Model and Competitive Advantage," by Romero, contributed to the always-on enterprise information system literature by analyzing competitive advantage effects and presenting arguments affecting strategic advantage on firms adopting and using always-on applications. The article discusses the fact that firms have to see the always-on business model as a life cycle model because technology in general is a very dynamic area and firms have to be continuously innovating in order to differentiate themselves from competitors and use as a strategic advantage the unique characteristics of their business so competitors cannot replicate, or if competitors are trying to replicate, they will have a difficult time replicating it. This chapter will definitely help in understanding how firms can keep a competitive advantage over competitors and its link to the strategy that a firm can have.

Chapter 3, "Always on Guard: How a Concept of Full Spectrum Socio-Technical Sensing Can Build Immunity," by Hills, advances the idea that the modern organization can become immune to a full spectrum of risks by re-engineering its organizational capability and culture. The author argues that the external and internal threats that could conspire to threaten zero downtime can be detected, understood, avoided, treated and learned from early, fast and every time. With an emphasis on cyber and cyber-related risks, a conceptual outline is provided as to how organizations can begin to make themselves immune in this way. This chapter has sought to provide the reader with a stimulating, pragmatic and practical description of the systemic and specific characteristics that a business or public sector organization could adapt from a powerful biological analogy.

Chapter 4, "Business Continuity and Information Systems: A Systematic Literature Review," by Turulja and Bajgoric, aimed at providing a systematic literature review on two interrelated fields "business continuity" and "information systems" being the foundations of the concept of "always-on information systems". The authors argue that modern businesses have become dependent on their information systems (IS) whose incidents and failures can highly affect business operations. Thus, organizations recognize IS continuity as a key information management issue. Ensuring continuity in IS is related to the reliable delivery information. In order to lower the negative impact of IS incidents, organizations should get prepared for them. Business continuity management (BCM) is a holistic management approach whose aim is to identify, prevent or mitigate operational risks.

Chapter 5 is "Always-On Sport Content Multimedia Delivery Over Internet in Croatia," by Kovacevic, Pejic-Bach, and Jakovic. In the digital age, the mobile phones are the devices that everyone has and use regularly on daily basis. Furthermore, many people are always-on either they are working, communicating, browsing Internet or playing games. eSport is the fastest growing entertainment industry and because of its growing popularity it has the same potential in terms of live streaming via Internet, as other multimedia content. In order to shed some light to the opportunity of the media delivery of sports content in always-on mode in Croatia, the canvas model of providing a service of sport content multimedia delivery in always-on mode in Croatia is developed.

Chapter 6, "The Risk Management Profession in Australia: Business Continuity Plan Practices," by McMurray, Cross, and Caponecchia, presented the study aimed to identify to what extent Australian organizations have any plans to manage business continuity threats, and the nature and content of these plans. The study has shown a similar pattern of business continuity plan development in Australia as has been reported in studies in the United States. This study shows there is scope for a more consistent approach to BCP in Australian organizations. Aspects of BCP which relate to the availability of human resources are least likely to be adequately covered even in organizations with well-developed plans and future studies may consider going one step further and uncovering BCP in various organizational contexts and countries. The coordination of resources including staff availability in the event of a business disruption is central to maintaining the capacity, effectiveness, growth and wealth creation of the business. In many instances, when addressing BCP in today's organizations, the importance of the human resource function is overlooked and this poses a concern to the organization's sustainability in today's highly competitive environment.

Chapter 7, "Enterprise Risk Management Software: User Requirements," by Gaspar and Mabic, presents some research results on user requirements related to enterprise risk management software. The authors developed a questionnaire to investigate the standpoints of risk managers, quality managers, and others in charge of risk management regarding the functionality they expect risk management software to support. Research results show the main attributes that risk management software should have in order to fulfill user expectations. The chapter also provides some important guidelines and suggestions for risk management software development and improvement. The results showed that user requirements related to risk management software reached one level of standardization, which could be important for ERM software vendors because, if requirements are known, then they do not have to "waste" a lot of time investigating what to do and can focus instead on how to best to suit user needs.

Chapter 8 is "Two Approaches in Assessing Business Continuity Management Attitudes in the Organizational Context," by Spremic, Turulja, and Bajgoric. The chapter presents two approaches in assessing the business continuity management attitudes in the organizational context: qualitative and quantitative. The first approach - case study analysis is based on a series of in-depth interviews, while the second approach presents an empirical research based on Confirmative Factor Analysis, Structural Equation Modeling (SEM) and t-test for the hypotheses testing. The empirical research has shown that there is a statistically significant difference in terms of attitudes of respondents regarding business continuity depending of companies' size and sector that company belongs to. Specifically, financial sector is in all of BCM segments more coherent than other sectors. In addition, qualitative research revealed the results showing that business continuity plan (BCP) and disaster recovery plan (DRP) were the only IT governance areas that were implemented in business practice.

Chapter 9 is "The Role of Information System Monitoring in Improving System Availability," by Ibrahimovic and Bajgoric. The authors addressed "information system monitoring" and explored the best practices in this field by focusing on different aspects of information system monitoring, particularly network monitoring, server monitoring and application monitoring. They proposed a holistic (top-down) framework which includes the leading industry standards Cobit 5 and ITIL V3 in the layered form as a foundation for monitoring governance and management framework. The chapter presented the current situation and future trends in monitoring tools, as well as main challenges in monitoring modern information systems based on new IT-platforms such as cloud computing, hybrid environment, containerization and DevOps.

Chapter 10, "Always-On Enterprise Information Systems With Service-Oriented Architecture and Load Balancing," by Serdal Bayram, argued that offering a continuous service is of utmost importance for today's businesses where undisruptive service means lack of failure of IS on which the services depend. However, due to the inherent fragility of IS, there are myriad of factors that have the potential of disrupting the smooth running of these systems. This chapter proposes a model that aims continuous EIS operation in terms of hardware and software components where these components work in tandem. The model uses Service Oriented Architecture (SOA) as an important component of the software side of the model.

I would like to thank to all the authors whose manuscripts made this book possible.

A further special note of thanks goes to Ms. Courtney Tychinski, Assistant Managing Editor – Book Development, for her continuous help during the process of working on the book and to the managerial, acquisition, editorial, publishing and marketing teams at IGI Global.

I am grateful to my wife, Ermina, and son, Adnan, for their understanding during this book project.

Nijaz Bajgoric
University of Sarajevo, Bosnia and Herzegovina

Chapter 1
Always-On Enterprise Information Systems:
The Concept, Attributes, and Implementation Drivers

Nijaz Bajgoric
University of Sarajevo, Bosnia and Herzegovina

ABSTRACT

The chapter presents conceptual aspects of "always-on" information systems as well as the main attributes and implementation drivers. In addition, HP's HP-UX server operating environment which provides a possible solution platform for "always-on" information system is presented as a case.

INTRODUCTION

Modern businesses today tend to "keep business in business" and stay "always-on". Not only businesses, most organizations in today's digital age seek for such a kind of information infrastructure that is based on the "continuous computing" platform (Bajgoric, 2005, 2008) which is supported by "always-on" enterprise information system (Bajgoric, 2006, 2010). Such an information system provides, theoretically, an IT platform for a "%100" business continuance or "always-on" business. However, achieving a "%100 uptime" or "zero downtime" is not an easy task, therefore, most organizations tend to reach more realistic, but still high availability ratios in terms of "number of nines", e.g. 99,999% availability, or "near-zero downtimes", in terms of "five minutes per year" downtime. This kind of requirement is valid for all today'

DOI: 10.4018/978-1-5225-3704-5.ch001

client/server architectures that are in use such as "on-premises" and "cloud-based" infrastructures.

Forrester (2013) noted that "across all industries, there is less and less tolerance for any kind of downtime. According to Aberdeen Report (2014) the average cost of downtime for large companies is $686,250 per hour, $215,638/hour for medium companies and $8,581/hour for small companies. Gartner (2014) noted that, with regard to downtime costs, "Based on industry surveys, the number we typically cite is $5,600 p/minute". IDC (2015) reported "... for a large firm, the mean cost of downtime per hour is nearly $1.7 million across industries, with some specific industries approaching $10 million lost per hour of downtime."For the Fortune 1000, the average total cost of unplanned application downtime per year is $1.25 billion to $2.5 billion (IDC, 2014). Martin (2011) stated that the average data center downtime event lasts 90 minutes, and every minute the data center remains down, a company is effectively losing $5,600. The Veem Data Availability Report (2014) revealed that "...there are clear demands for 24/7 access to IT services and applications."

Table 1. presents some reports that demonstrate the downtime costs

Leitch (2016) argued that downtime has reached an estimated cost of $700 billion per year to US businesses in 2016. Ponemon Institute and Emerson Network Power (Ponemon Institute Report, 2016) reported that the average cost of a data center outage has steadily increased from $505,502 in 2010 to $740,357 today (or a 38 percent net change). However, as IDC stated (IDC, 2016) "... Business cannot tolerate the same levels of planned and unplanned downtime that they could before they started on their digital transformation journey. Niemimaa (2015) found that

Table 1. Reports on Downtime Costs

Report	Findings
Butler (2013)	A 49 minutes failure of Amazon's services on January 31, 2013 resulted close to $5 million in missed revenue.
Aberdeen Report (2014)	The average cost of downtime for large companies is $686,250 per hour, $215,638/hour for medium companies and $8,581/hour for small companies.
Gartner (2014, a)	Based on industry surveys, average downtime is $5,600 p/minute.
Avaya Report (2014)	80% percent of companies lose revenue when the network goes down.
IDC (2014)	For the Fortune 1000, the average total cost of unplanned application downtime per year is $1.25 billion to $2.5 billion.
Veem Data Availability Report (2014)	68 percent of those organizations modernizing their data centers are doing so in order to enable 24/7, always-on business operations.
IDC Report (2015)	For a large firm, the mean cost of downtime per hour is nearly $1.7 million, with some specific industries approaching $10 million lost per hour of downtime.
Ponemon Institute Report, (2016)	The average cost of a data center outage has steadily increased from $505,502 in 2010 to $740,357 today (or a 38 percent net change).

leading IS-journals provide little contributions on this perspective. He identified the IS-BC relationship as "a timely question".

The paper aims at developing a conceptual framework for "always-on" enterprise information systems. Always-on information system is identified as a business computing model for "always-on" business in the e-business age. In addition, in order to demonstrate an integrated operating platform as a core component of such an information system, HP's HP-UX server operating platform is presented (www.hpe.com). Several continuous computing technologies, utilities, techniques, integrated tools as well as advanced system administration activities and features of HP-UX platform are identified and presented in the form of a business case in order to illustrate possible ways of practical implementations of the "always-on" information system concept.

LITERATURE REVIEW

Over the last 5-10 years, several authors researched this and similar topics. Aktas (2010) presented some principles and experiences in designing and building enterprise information systems from the always-on perspective. Bayram, Kirlidog and Vayvay (2010) presented a model of an always-on enterprise information systems with service oriented architecture and load balancing. Varga (2010) discussed the challenges of data management in always-on enterprise information systems. Pejic-Bach, Draganic, and Jakovic (2010) elaborated some aspects of implementing always-on it-solutions and standards in banking sector. Spremic (2010) presented some IT governance and it risk management principles and methods for supporting 'always-on' enterprise information systems. Tomic and Markic (2010) discussed aspects of continuous database availability. Delic and Riley (2009) noted that high availability anddependability are necessary engineering features for such global, always-on, always-available systems. Nollau (2009) introduced the term of "enterprise business continuity". Speight (2011) defined business continuity as "a management process that identifies potential factors that threaten an organization and provides a framework for building resilience and the capability for an effective response. This response must safeguard the interests of its key stakeholders, as well as the organization's reputation, brand, and value creating activities". Jarvelainen (2013) focused on a framework for business continuity management and extended it to the context of information systems. The results suggested that the embeddedness of continuity practices in an organisation has perceived business impacts. Saha (2013) noted that enterprises are no longer grappling to have access to the latest technologies; harnessing technology to enable business outcomes is a given. Buckl and Schweda (2013) provided a systemic view of enterprise architecture management. Rabaey

(2013) proposed a new concept of enterprise architecture, namely Complex Adaptive Systems Thinking – Enterprise Architecture.

Several authors addressed issues in transforming or adapting current models of doing business and (re)organizing business information systems. Chalupnik, Wynn and Clarkson (2013) presented a framework for comparing the relationships among reliability, robustness, adaptability, resilience in the context of system design. Bharosa, Lee, and Jansen (2010) considered issues in sharing and coordinating information during disasters, within the concept of disaster management. Lee, Thomas, and Baskerville (2015) emphasized the need to " restore the idea that the study of design in IS needs to attend to the design of the entire IS artifact, not just the IT artifact. Several concepts of business models developed over the last three decades have been created under the impact of IT trends. Typical examples of such trends are the concepts such as cloud computing and business continuity. Sahebjamniaa, Torabi, and Mansourib (2015) presented a framework for integrated business continuity and disaster recovery planning with a mathematical model to determine required resources to cope with disruptive events.

Turban et al. (2010) identified a set of "business pressures" related to modern business environment: market pressures, technology pressures and societal pressures. They argued that businesses employ information technologies in order to provide responses to business pressures and business risks.

However, in today's e-business environment, an additional pressure which relates to business continuity/business continuance or "always-on" business can be identified (Figure 1).

As shown in Figure 1, business continuity/always-on business relies on "continuous computing" – an information system infrastructure which is expected to be "always-on", and with "zero downtime".

Today's enterprises are exposed to several types of business risks, either from outside or from inside the system. They implement several information technologies in order to mitigate these risks. However, some IT-related business risks such as: technical glitches, physical damages, natural disasters, operating system crashes, application bugs, operational mistakes, human errors, logical threats can be seen in practice (Figure 2).

Physical threats result from any kind of physical damage that may occur on IT centers, servers, hardware components, communication devices, etc. Natural-catastrophic event such as fire, lightning, flood, earthquake, hurricane, can damage IT-centers and cause applications/data unavailability for some time. Logical threats may have different forms such as deleted system files, corrupted files, broken processes or programs, corrupted file system, crashed operating system. Technical glitches relate to the hardware component failures that may occur on computer components/devices within the IT infrastructure (memory chips, fans, mainboards,

Figure 1. Business continuity (always-on business): An Internet era's requirement and business pressure

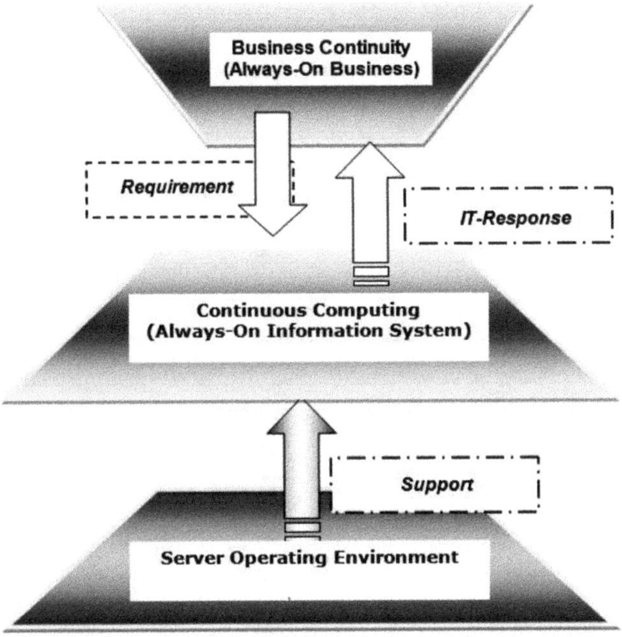

hard disks, disk controllers, tapes or tape drivers, network cards, switches, routers, communication lines, power supply units). System crashes are the situations that make all applications and data stored on enterprise server which underwent the crash unavailable for end users, e.g "BSOD" on Windows Servers.

Application software defects, failures and crashes may have different forms such as bugs in programs, badly integrated applications, and file corruptions. LAN/WAN/ Internet problems, in addition to hardware glitches on data communication devices, include the problems such as those with Domain Controllers, Active Directory, DNS configuration files, DNS servers, network configuration files. Stanton (2005) stated that it can take less than 60 seconds for a company's reputation to be ruined and its business to be crippled. In just one minute a server failure or hacker can knock out vital applications and lead to a catastrophic series of events. Sumner (2009) unveiled the results of a study of top security threats perceived by organizations with over 500 employees, as (1) deliberate software attacks, (2) software failures or errors, (3) acts of human error or failure, (4) deliberate acts of espionage or trespass, and (5) deliberate acts of sabotage or vandalism.

Human errors comprise of accidental or intentional file deletion, unskilled operations, intentional hazardous activities including sabotage, strikes, epidemic

Figure 2. Major threats that cause downtime
(Bajgoric, 2008)

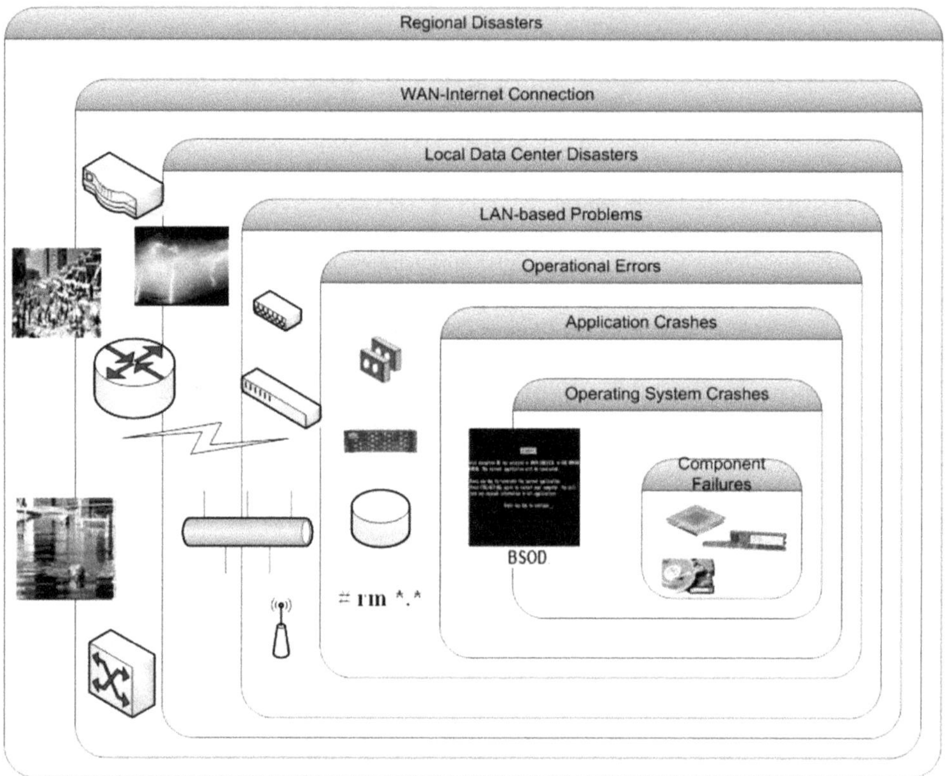

situations, vandalism. Accidental or in some cases intentional removing system file(s) by system administrators can shut down the whole operating system and make applications stored on the server unreacheable/unavailable. Another example is loss of key IT personal or leaving of expert staff due to several reasons, e.g. managerial bad decisions on IT- staffing policy.

A number of IT-related problems that cause downtime may occur within all types of information architectures that are in use today such as hardware glitches on server components, operating system crashes, network components' malfunctions, WAN/ Internet disconnections, application bugs, system or network administrator's errors, natural disasters that hit main computer center organized on the on-premises basis or cloud-provider's site. Some critical points or locations at which a downtime may occur can be identified (Figure 3).

These downtime points are considered critical points of action in creating continuous computing solutions for enhancing business continuity, such as: hardware glitches on client devices, crashes on the client operating systems level (desktop/

Figure 3. Major downtime points in c/s architecture
(Bajgoric, 2010)

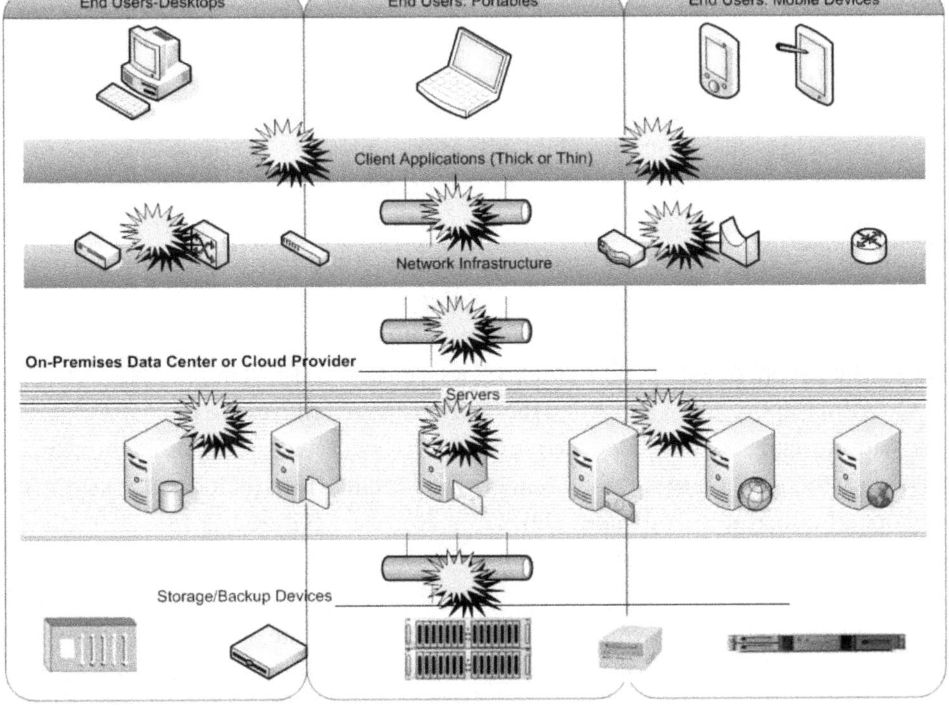

portable/mobile), client applications, LAN/WAN/Internet – disconnections from servers, crashes on server operating platform (dump on core operating system, application protocol, library, network protocol, security intrusion, etc.), problems with data storage (hard disk crash, file/file system corruption, tape broken, etc.).

In the cloud computing model, which tends to replace previous concepts of information architecture and becomes a platform of choice for many businesses, these kind of downtime points can be identified as well. As reported by CIO (2013), "Web-based services can crash and burn just like any other type of technology". Marshall (2013) provided a story about the cloud service provider Nirvana that "... has told its customers they have two weeks to find another home for their terabytes of data because the company was closing its doors and shutting down its services". Brende and Markov (2013) considered the most important risks inherent to the cloud computing and focused on the risks that are relevant to the IT function to be migrated to the cloud. Aberdeen Group (Csaplar, 2012) found that between June 2010 and February 2012, the cost per hour of downtime increased on average by 65%. Forrester predicted that the global cloud computing market will grow from

$40.7 billion in 2011 to more than $241 billion in 2020 (Dignan, 2011). Martin (2011) cited the results of the study by Emerson Network Power and the Ponemom Institute which revealed that the average data center downtime event costs $505,500 with the average incident lasting 90 minutes. Every minute the data center remains down, a company is effectively losing $5,600. The study took statistics from 41 U.S. data centers in a range of industries, including financial institutions, healthcare companies and collocation providers. Some examples of CC outages such as those of Amazon and Google from April 2011 (Maitland, 2011), showed that even within "by-default" highly availably infrastructures such as the cloud providers' data centers downtime is still possible and requires attention. Butler (2013) reported that a 49 minutes failure of Amazon's services on January 31, 2013 resulted close to $5 million in missed revenue. Similar failures happened in January/February/March 2013 to Dropbox, Facebook, Microsoft, Google Drive, Twitter.

Quorum Report (2013) unveiled that the hardware failures are the most common type within small and mid-sized businesses with thepercentage of 55%, while in 22% of thedisasters, reason was the human error. Human errors include the system and network administrators' mistakes and errors. Software failure has 18% according to the report with operating systems' failures mostly being the reason contributing to software problems. The Report states that "Flood, earthquakes, tornadoes etc. are common natural disasters which can physically damage the system components. In spite of the fact that natural disasters happen very frequently, this cause merely takes 5% of the overall reasons." Venkatraman (2013) noted that "More than a third of respondents viewed human error as the most likely cause of downtime. Equipment failure and external threat of power outages were the second and third likely causes cited by respondents." Clancy (2013) noted that "Hardware failure is the biggest culprit, representing about 55 percent of all downtime events at SMBs, while human error accounts for about 22 percent of them .... ". According to Information Today Report (2012), network outages (50 percent) were the leading cause of unplanned downtime within the last year. Human error (45 percent), server failures (45 percent) and storage failures (42 percent) followed closely behind. An example of human error is an accidental or intentional operation of removing files by system administrator on any server. By using a very simple command **rm** on UNIX or Linux servers on the root level, system administrator can remove all the files (Bajgoric, 2010).

ALWAYS-ON EIS AND ALWAYS-ON BUSINESS: CONCEPTUAL FRAMEWORK, ATTRIBUTES, AND ENABLERS

Today's businesses operating in the e-business environment are in most cases run by different forms of business-critical applications. These applications are hosted by application servers and accessed by end users over the network based on the client-server architecture (c/s). Such an architecture consists of one or more servers hosting applications and a number of clients accessing them. Depending on the server infrastructure's availability, reliability and scalability, the whole business operates with more or less downtime which, in turn, has more or less impact on its financial performances. Information technologies are implemented within the information systems that are characterized by different levels of availability, scalability, reliability, with the main objective of achieving "always-on" computing. (Bajgoric, 2006).

In addition to availability, both scalability and reliability of e-business application platforms are business-critical as well as modern e-businesses are expected to be "always-on", with zero or "near-zero" downtime. Such businesses aim at providing products and services on continuous basis as each hour, even a minute, of downtime can be easily expressed as financial losses. As shown in Figure 4, "always-on" business relies on continuous computing technologies that should be implemented in a specific form of an "always-on" information system or, "highly available" IS - IS having a "near-zero-downtime". In other words, this can be translated to: available data, always-on application platform, and consequently always-on information system.

Table 2 demonstrates the shifts in major characteristics of traditional and modern enterprise information systems.

Figure 4. Always-on business: A digital age's requirement and business pressure

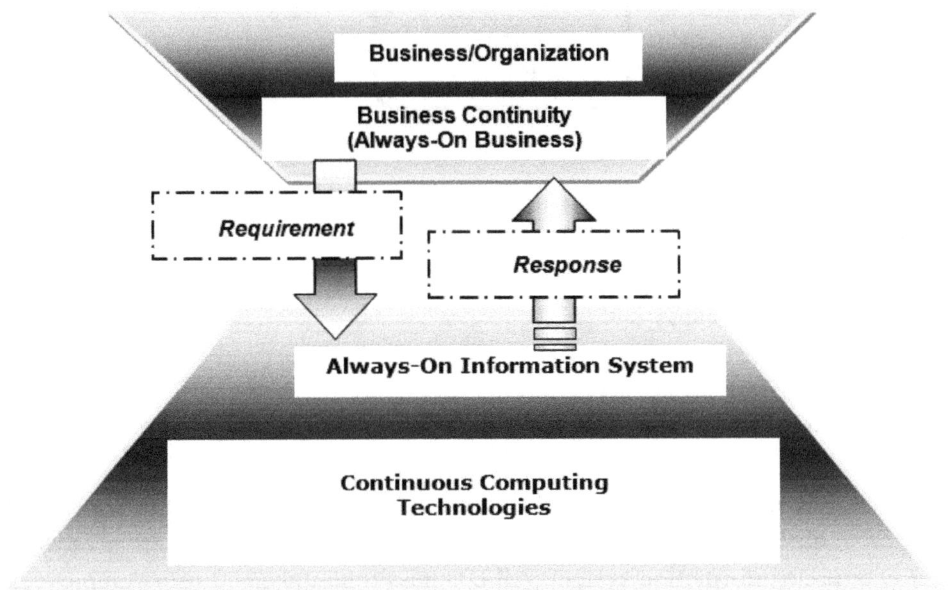

Table 2. Traditional versus current focus on enterprise information systems

Traditional EIS – *Focus On:*	**Current focus of EIS (A-on EIS):** ***All Traditional EIS-Features, Plus:***
Transaction processing Reporting and decision support Integration Efficiency Information Technology	+ Availability Scalability Reliability Effectiveness Business technology ....

Figure 5. The core concepts of always-on IS

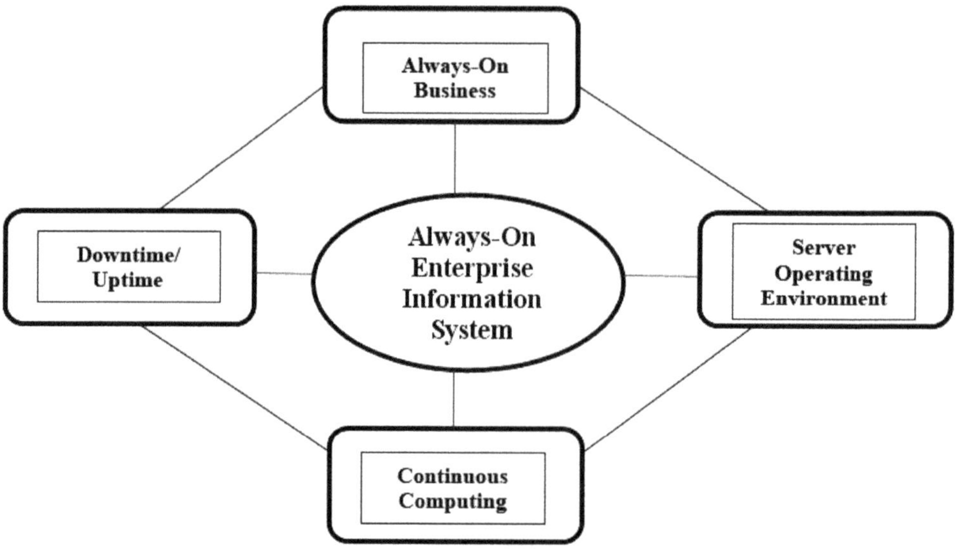

The model presented in Figure 5 includes the core concepts that form an Always-On Information System, namely:

1. Always-On Business
2. Downtime/Uptime
3. Server Operating Environment
4. Continuous Computing Technologies

- Always-On Business is in the same time the main requirement from environment (business system) and the main objective of an always-on enterprise information system. All business functions, end-users/employees, customers, and suppliers, are expecting such a kind of information infrastructure (information system) which will be available on continuous basis and with zero downtime, in other words - “always-on”. The messages such as: “system is down, please try later”, “something went wrong”, “DNS error occured”, simply are not an option from end-user perspective, be it regular employee, CEO, CIO, customer, or supplier.

- Downtime/Uptime is a measure of performace of an always-on enterprise information system. The goal is to have a “100%” uptime or “zero dontime”, however, given the fact that it is not easy to achieve such an availability, the uptime objective is usually expressed by so called high availability ratios and in terms of “number of nines” (e.g. four nines - 99,99%, five nines - 99,999%, ...), or in nubmer of minutes/hours of downtime per year (e.g. ¨five minutes per year”, “five hours per year”).
- Server Operating Environment represents a set of server and server operating system features that are used to install and implement application servers. These application servers host most of business applications particularly those characterized as “business critical” or “mission critical”. Server operating environment (SOE) can be installed “in-house” or within so-called “on-premises” model, as a server side of typical client-server architecture. However, it can be implemented and used within so-called “client-cloud” architecture, where server operating environment resides on cloud provider’s site. No mather which model is used, SOE plays a critical role in achieving high availability and scalability ratios of business applications. Advanced server operating system features include featre such as: online upgrade, reloadable kernel, fault rolerance, system recovery, virtualization, snapshot, HA file systems, dynimic root disk, mirroring.
- Continuous Computing Technologies are an additional set of information technologies that are implemented in order to reduce downtime or enhance uptime. These technologies include:
    - Advanced server hardware such as 64-bit processors, ECC/MEC, crash handling, redundant technologies (RAID/RAIM), fault tolerance, hot swappable components, automatic failover,
    - Advanced application server features such as: VLDB, in-memory databases, crash-handing, application recovery, vendor-specific technologies such as: SAP HANA, Oracle MAA/RAC, IBM HARD,
    - Advanced strage technologies: RAD, storage arrays, unified storage systems, onlien backup, shadowing, snapshooting, clusterng, vitualization,
    - Advanced network technologies: SAN, NAS, virtual networks, software defined networking, reduntant multipaths, IP multipaths, dual home links etc,

The main attributes of an always-on information system are as follows (Bajgoric, 2008):

- Availability
- Reliability
- Scalability

High availability refers to the ability of a server operating environment to provide end users an efficient access to data, applications and services for a high percentage of system uptime while minimizing both planned and unplanned downtime. As said before, the more "nines" in availability ratio, the higher availability is provided, the better business continuity is served.

High reliability refers to the ability of a server operating environment to minimize (reduce) the occurance of system failures (both hardware and softeare related) including some fault tolerance capabilities. Reliability goals are achieved by using standard redundant components and advanced fault tolerant solutions (hardware, systems software, application sofwate).

High scalability refers to the ability of a server operating environment of scaling up and out. Servers can be scaled up by adding more processors, RAM, etc., while scaling out means additional computers and forming cluster or grid configurations.

A conceptual model has been developed, as shown in Figure 6, to illustrate the enablers of always-on EIS. As can be seen from Figure 6, different enablers of Aon EIS are overlapping each other. Therefore, all the enablers/tools should be integrated to achieve an effective integration and management of all kinds of continuous computing technologies.

Further details on the enablers of the always-on enterprise information systems are presented in the following section.

Continuous computing technologies comprise information technologies that are aimed at enhancing the availability, reliability and scalability ratios of information infrastructure. The mission-critical component of such an infrastructure in today's dominant client-server or even cloud computing architecture is a server operating environment as a collection of server, server operating system and serverware features that are aimed at enhancing the ratios/dimensions of system uptime. Server operating environments include core and advanced built-in features related to continuous computing such as: automatic failover, system recovery, fault-tolerance, reloadable kernel, online upgrade, 64-bit computing, crash-handling techniques, memory mirroring, workload management, high-availability clustering, TCP/IP failover, storage scalability (Table 3).

The continuous computing technologies are explored here within an integrated IT-platform called "server operating environment" which is considered a core

Figure 6. A Conceptual model to illustrate the concept and enablers of Always-on EIS

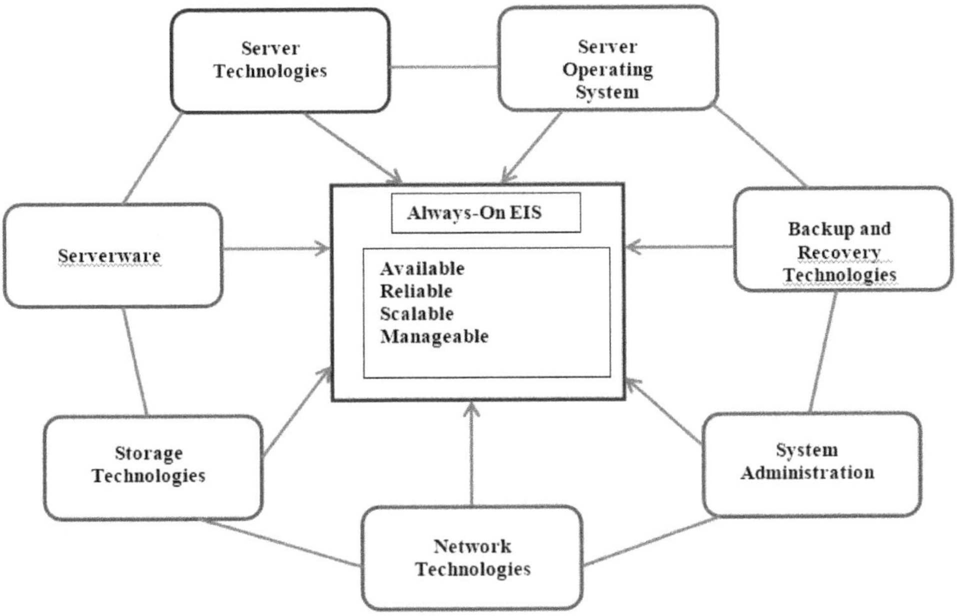

Table 3. Continuous computing technologies

CONTINUOUS COMPUTING TECHNOLOGIES					
Server Hardware	Server Operating System	Application Servers	Network T echnologies	Storage Technologies	System Administration Technologies (HP-UX)
• 64-bit processors • L1, L2, L3 cache • Online upgrade • Crash-handling • Hardware mirroring • HA clustering • Dynamic Root Disk • Automatic Failover • Fault-tolerance • ECC, MEC • RAID • RAIM • Hot-swappable hardware • Redundant units ...	• 64-bit OS • Reloadable kernel • Online upgrade • Crash-handling • Mirroring • HA clustering • Dynamic Root Disk • Automatic Failover • System Recovery • Fault-tolerance • Virtualization • Snapshot • HA Filesystems, LVM, JFS • NFS, CIFS/SMB • ...	• 64-bit applications • VLDB • In-memory database • Online upgrade • Crash-handling • Application Recovery • Virtualization • Oracle MAA • Oracle RAC • Recovery Manager • IBM HADR • MySQL DRBD • SAP HANA • ...	• Virtual networks • SAN, NAS • Resilience-to-link-failures • Fibre channel failover • Software-defined networking • Redundant components • Redundant paths • IP multipath • VPN devices • Dual Home Link • Cluster Switching • IDS/IPS • TCP/IP failover • ...	• RAID • Storage arrays • Unified Storage Systems • Online backup • Virtual tapes • Data vaulting • Mirroring • Shadowing • Snapshoot • Hot sites • Clustering • Disaster recovery sites • Storage virtualization • OLARD ...	• High availability monitors • Compartments • Fine-Grained privileges • Role-based Access Control • Hardware mirroring • Software mirroring • Veritas'VxFS JFS/Online JFS • Bastille security tool • Dynamic Root Disk (DRD • Serviceguard Extensions • ...

technology layer of a continuous computing platform. It contains the technologies related to server hardware, server operating system, server applications, and, in broader term, storage and network technologies. Managerial aspect is seen as a set of system and network administration and business continuity management. System and network administration represent a set of operations on operating system and network layers, including the role of system and network administrators in ensuring business continuity.

Modern server configurations are designed and configured in the form of integrated hardware platforms and implemented in order to enhance availability ratios. Some of the HA-enabling technologies include: 64-bit processors, multi-core processors, L1/L2/L3 cache, ECC, MEC, memory double-chip spare, automatic deconfiguration of memory and processors, hot-swappable components, fault-tolerance, redundant units, etc. Server platforms are run by server operating systems that are expected to provide high ratios in terms of availability, reliability, and scalability. They do it by supporting the following features: automatic failover, system recovery, reloadable kernel, online upgrade, crash handling, SMP, VLM/VLDB, virtualization, etc. Modern server operating systems provide several additional components (software modules) called serverware solutions, in addition to the core operating platform.

Technologies used for data storage, backup and data recovery play crucial role in data management in the form of a secondary layer, in addition to primary data storage (hard disk). The technologies that are used include both local storage and backup technologies such as RAID, tape, virtual tape, D2D, DAS and off-site technologies (online backup, data vaulting, mirroring, shadowing, snapshoot, hot sites, clustering, disaster recovery sites, storage virtualization). Moreover, even on the DBMS level there exists a number of solutions aimed at enhancing availability ratios. Some examples of business continuity – oriented serverware solutions based on DBMS level include: Microsoft SQL Server's component called "SQL Server 2005 Always On Technologies" with features such as: database mirroring, failover clustering, database snapshots, snapshot isolation, peer-to-peer replication, log shipping, and online operations, Oracle's Maximum Availability Architecture (MAA), IBM DB2 feature called HADR (high-availability, disaster-recovery), MySQL's Master/Slave Replication and Distributed Block device (DRBD) and MySQL Cluster.

Several advanced network technologies are used in order to minimize network downtime such as: resilience-to-link-failures, network virtualization, virtual application networks, fibre channel failover, software defined networking, redundant components, redundant paths, IP multipathing, virtual network devices, Dual Home Link, Ethernet Ring protection, Bi-directional forwarding detection, Virtual Cluster Switching, Firewall, IDS/IPS, Malware/SPAM filtering.

In addition to standard continuous computing technologies, IT vendors developed new technologies such as snapshoot mirroring, data vaulting, virtual tape backup, online backup.

System administration knowledge and skills are related to the operating system troubleshooting and system administration as a whole, and they are very important in reducing the time of system recovery. System administrator has a critical role in keeping server operating system up and providing troubleshooting solutions when system goes down. A skilled and experienced system administrator can resolve most of the problems that occur on server or server operating system level when server shuts down or server operating system crashes and reduce significantly the time of system recovery in terms of RTO and RPO. However, system administrator's privileges (data access rights) should be implemented by following the compliance regulations such as FDCC, Sarbanes-Oxley, PCI, HIPAA, GLBA, including solutions such as: Fine-Grained privileges and Role-based Access Control.According to IDC's White Paper (2009),by adopting industry best practices compliance regulations (e.g., ITIL, CobiT), companies can lower annual downtime by up to 85%, greatly reducing interruptions to daily data processing and access,supporting business continuity, and containing operational costs.

CASE: SERVER OPERATING ENVIRONMENT FOR ALWAYS-ON EIS

In order to demonstrate aserver operating platform that contains several continuous computing technologies for building an always-on enterprise information system, HP's HP-UX server operating system has been selected (www.hpe.com) and presented in the form of a case.

HP-UX works on several models of HP servers, including entry-level, midrange and high-end servers. HP decided to rename its HP-UX operating platform from "HP-UX Operating System" (up to version HP-UX11.0) into "HP-UX Operating Environment" (HP-UX11iv1 – HP-UX11iv3). Two major components of this operating environment: High Availability OE and Data Center OE are intended to achieve the highest levels of uptime, availability and flexibility.

Some of the high-availability oriented technologies, security features and system management options of HP-UX operating system are listed below:

- Journalized File System for high reliability and fast recovery
- JFS snapshot technology
- System recovery image
- Hardware mirroring
- Software mirroring
- Hot spared disk technology
- Data encoding
- High Availability Storage Systems
- High availability monitors
- Dynamic Root Disk

- Clustering
- HP Serviceguard Extensions for SAP
- Compartments
- Fine-Grained privileges
- Role-based Access Control
- Bastille as a security tool
- Built-in native multi-pathing and load balancing
- Automatic detection and auto configuration for new storage devices
- Resilience to link failures
- OLARD (online addition, replacement, deletion) of I/O interfaces.
- Device data repository (DDR) name generation.
- Fibre Channel failover optimization, etc.

All these features represent an integrated set of capabilities on the server operating environment level that are aimed at enhancing the levels of availability, reliability and scalability of an always-on information system. This set of features includes not only operating system-related features but the server hardware, network infrastructure, storage systems and integrated solutions for system management as well.

With regard to storage, backup and recovery, in addition to standard features, HP's platform include the following advanced HA/BC-related capabilities: automatic detection and auto configuration of new mass storage devices, SAN - agile addressing of devices, resilience to link failures, native multi-pathing, immense scalability, load balancing, deferred path recovery, device data repository, Fibre Channel failover optimization, Dynamic LUN expansion for improved manageability and to minimize downtime, support for online disk replacement, performance improvements (scan time, activation time), support for storage array snapshots and clones (volume group quiescing), support for striped mirroring providing increased availability, no single point of failure - separate controllers/power supplies, disk mirroring, on-line backup, root disk mirroring, split brain avoidance for high availability.

In addition to standard data communication and networking technologies (devices, media, software) the networking layer in the HP-UX operating environment contains several advanced technologies that are aimed at enhancing availability, scalability and reliability, such as: FlexNetwork architecture, software defined networking, Federated software-defined networking, network virtualization, virtual application networks, NFS v3, NFS v4, redundant NFS server, client side failover.

CONCLUSION AND FUTURE RESEARCH DIRECTIONS

Traditional business requirements towards information system identified in the IS literature over the last 30 years such as efficient data processing, reporting and decision support, in today's digital age are extended by a requirement that relates to always-on business. Therefore, there exists a need to redefine the concept of enterprise information system in order to include the attribute "always-on". A conceptual model and implementation framework have been proposed for an "Always-on" Enterprise Information System that enables both continuous computing and business continuity.

Future research directions with regard to always-on enterprise information systems can be identified around the following research topics:

- Developing new methodologies and/or methods, or redefining the existing approaches in designing, developing and implementing always-on enterprise information systems.
- Developing frameworks for implementing several types of information technologies as business continuity drivers.
- Implementing always-on enterprise information systems in both "on-premises" and "cloud computing" environments.
- Integrating information system management, business continuity management, security management and organizational management.

REFERENCES

Aberdeen Report. (2014). *Preventing Virtual Application Downtime*. Available at www.aberdeen.com

Aktas, M. S. (2010). Principles And Experiences: Designing and Building Enterprise Information Systems. In N. Bajgoric (Ed.), *Always-On Enterprise Information Systems for BusinessContinuance: Technologies for Reliable and Scalable Operations* (pp. 58–77). IGI Global. doi:10.4018/978-1-60566-723-2.ch004

Ashurst, C., Freer, A., Ekdahl, J., & Gibbons, C. (2012). Exploring IT-enabled innovation: A new paradigm? *International Journal of Information Management*, *32*(4), 326–336. doi:10.1016/j.ijinfomgt.2012.05.006

Avaya Report. (2014). *Network Downtime Results in Job, Revenue Loss, March, 2014*. Available at: http://www.avaya.com/usa/about-avaya/newsroom/news-releases/2014/pr-140305/

Bajgoric, N. (2005, October-December). Continuous Computing Technologies for Improving Performances of Enterprise Information Systems. *International Journal of Enterprise Information Systems*, *1*(4), 70–89. doi:10.4018/jeis.2005100105

Bajgoric, N. (2006). Information Systems for E-Business Continuance: A Systems Approach, Kybernetes. *The International Journal of Systems and Cybernetics*, *35*(5), 632–652. doi:10.1108/03684920610662377

Bajgoric, N. (2007). Toward Always-On Enterprise Information Systems. In A. Gunasekaran (Ed.), *Modeling and Analysis of Enterprise Information Systems - Advances in Enterprise Information Systems* (pp. 250–284). IGI Global.

Bajgoric, N. (2008). Continuous Computing Technologies for Enhancing Business Continuity. IGI Global.

Bajgoric, N. (2010). Server Operating Environment for Business Continuance: Framework for Selection. *Int. J. Business Continuity and Risk Management*, *1*(4), 317–338. doi:10.1504/IJBCRM.2010.038622

Bajgoric, N. (Ed.). (2010). *Always-On Enterprise Information Systems for Business Continuance: Technologies for Reliable and Scalable Operations*. IGI Global. doi:10.4018/978-1-60566-723-2

Bayram, S., Kirlidog, M., & Vayvay, O. (2010). Always-On Enterprise Information Systems With Service Oriented Architecture And Load Balancing. In N. Bajgoric (Ed.), *Always-On Enterprise Information Systems for Business Continuance: Technologies for Reliable and Scalable Operations* (pp. 91–108). IGI – Global. doi:10.4018/978-1-60566-723-2.ch006

Bharosa, N., Lee, J. K., & Jansen, M. (2010). Challenges and obstacles in sharing and coordinating information during multi-agency disaster response: Propositions from field exercises. *Information Systems Frontiers*, *12*(1), 49–65. doi:10.1007/s10796-009-9174-z

Brende, N., & Markov, I. (2013). Risk perception and risk management in cloud computing: Results from a case study of Swiss companies. *International Journal of Information Management*, *33*(5), 726–733. doi:10.1016/j.ijinfomgt.2013.05.004

Buckl, S., & Schweda, C. M. (2013). A Systemic View on Enterprise Architecture Management. In P. Saha (Ed.), *A Systemic Perspective to Managing Complexity with Enterprise Architecture* (pp. 237–254). IGI Global.

Butler, B. (2013). Amazon.com suffers outage: Nearly $5M down the drain?. *Network World*. Available at: http://www.networkworld.com/article/2163191/cloud-computing/update--amazon-com-suffers-outage--nearly--5m-down-the-drain-.html

Butler, B. S., & Gray, P. H. (2006). Reliability, Mindfulness, And Information Systems. MIS Quarterly, 30(2), 211-224.

Chalupnik, M. J., Wynn, D. C., & Clarkson, P. J. (2013). Comparison of ilities for protection against uncertainty in system design. *Journal of Engineering Design*, *24*(12), 814–829. doi:10.1080/09544828.2013.851783

CIO Report. (2013). The Worst Cloud Outages of 2013 (So Far). *InfoWorld*. Available at: http://www.cio.com/slideshow/detail/108561/The-Worst-Cloud-Outages-of-2013--So-Far-?source=CIONLE_nlt_cloud_computing_2013-07-08

Clancy, H. (2013). Most common cause of SMB downtime? The answer may surprise you. *ZDNET*. Available at: http://www.zdnet.com/most-common-cause-of-smb-downtime-the-answer-may-surprise-you-7000011137

Csaplar, D. (2012). *The Cost of Downtime is Rising*. Available at: http://blogs.aberdeen.com/it-infrastructure/the-cost-of-downtime-is-rising/

Delic, K. A., & Riley, J. A. (2009). Enterprise Knowledge Clouds: Next Generation KM Systems?. *International Conference on Information, Process, and Knowledge Management*. IEEE Computer Society. doi:10.1109/eKNOW.2009.28

Dignan, L. (2011). *Cloud computing market: $241 billion in 2020*. Retrieved from http://www.zdnet.com/blog/btl/cloud-computing-market-241-billion-in-2020/47702

Forrester Report. (2013). *How Organizations Are Improving Business Resiliency With Continuous IT Availability*. Available on http://www.emc.com/collateral/analyst-report/forrester-improve-bus-resiliency-continuous-it-avail-ar.pdf

Gartner. (2014). *The Costs of Downtime, July 2014*. Available at: http://blogs.gartner.com/andrew-lerner/2014/07/16/the-cost-of-downtime

IDC Report. (2015). *High-Value Business Applications on x86: The Need for True Fault -Tolerant Systems*. Available on: http://www8.hp.com/h20195/v2/GetPDF.aspx/4AA5-8631ENW.pdfaccessed

IDC Report. (2016). *Cut costs, reduce complexity and drive availability for the always-on enterprise*. Available on: https://go.veeam.com/wp-2016-idc-executive-brief.html

IDC White Paper. (2014). *DevOps and the Cost of Downtime: Fortune 1000 Best Practice Metrics Quantified*. AVAILABLE on: http://www.idc.com/getdoc.jsp?containerId=253155

Information Today Report. (2012). *Enterprise Data And The Cost Of Downtime: 2012 IOUG Database Availability Survey*. Available at: http://www.oracle.com/us/products/database/2012-ioug-db-survey-1695554.pdf

Jarvelainen, J. (2013). IT incidents and business impacts: Validating a framework for continuity management in information systems. *International Journal of Information Management*, *33*(3), 583–590. doi:10.1016/j.ijinfomgt.2013.03.001

Lee, A. S., Thomas, M., & Baskerville, R. L. (2015). Going back to basics in design science: From the information technology artifact to the information systems artifact. *Information Systems Journal*, *25*(1), 5–21. doi:10.1111/isj.12054

Leitch, G. (2016). *The True Cost of Downtime in 2016*. Academic Press.

Maitland, J. (2011). *A really bad week for Google and Amazon*. Available on: http://searchcloudcomputing.techtarget.com/news/2240035039/A-really-bad-week-for-Google-and-Amazon?asrc=EM_NLN_13718724&track=NL-1324&ad=826828

Marshall, D. (2013). *Cloud storage provider Nirvanix is closing its doors*. Available at: http://www.infoworld.com/d/virtualization/cloud-storage-provider-nirvanix-closing-its-doors-227289

Martin, N. (2011). *The true costs of data center downtime*. Available on: http://itknowledgeexchange.techtarget.com/data-center/the-true-costs-of-data-center-downtime/

Niemimaa, M. (2015). Interdisciplinary Review of Business Continuity from an Information Systems Perspective: Toward an Integrative Framework. *Communications of the Association for Information Systems*, *37*, 69–102.

Nollau, B. (2009). *Disaster Recovery and Business Continuity*. ABI/INFORM Global.

Pejic-Bach, M., Draganic, M., & Jakovic, B. (2010). Some Aspects of Implementing Always-on IT-solutions and Standards in Banking Sector: The Case of Croatia. In N. Bajgoric (Ed.), *Always-On Enterprise Information Systems for Business Continuance: Technologies for Reliable and Scalable Operations* (pp. 149–174). IGI Global. doi:10.4018/978-1-60566-723-2.ch009

Ponemon Institute Report. (2016). *Cost of Data Center Outages*. Available on: http://www.emersonnetworkpower.com/en-US/Resources/Market/Data-Center/Latest-Thinking/Ponemon/Documents/2016-Cost-of-Data-Center-Outages-FINAL-2.pdf

Quorum Report. (2013). *Quorum Disaster Recovery Report, Q1 2013*. Available at: http://www.quorum.net/news-events/press-releases/quorum-disaster-recovery-report-exposes-top-causes-of-downtime

Rabaey, M. (2013). Complex Adaptive SystemsThinking Approach toEnterprise Architecture. In P. Saha (Ed.), *A Systemic Perspective to Managing Complexity with Enterprise Architecture* (pp. 99–149). IGI Global.

Saha, P. (2013). Preface, Systemic Enterprise Architecture as Future: Tackling Complexity in Governments in the Cusp of Change. In P. Saha (Ed.), *A Systemic Perspective to Managing Complexity with Enterprise Architecture* (pp. xix–xxiv). IGI Global.

Sahebjamniaa, N., Torabi, S. A., & Mansourib, S. A. (2015). Integrated business continuity and disaster recovery planning: Towards organizational resilience. *European Journal of Operational Research, 242*(1), 261–273. doi:10.1016/j.ejor.2014.09.055

Speight, P. (2011). Business Continuity. *Journal of Applied Security Research, 6*(4), 529–554. doi:10.1080/19361610.2011.604021

Spremic, M. (2010). IT Governance and IT Risk Management Principles And Methods For Supporting 'Always-On' Enterprise Information Systems. In N. Bajgoric (Ed.), *Always-On Enterprise Information Systems for Business Continuance: Technologies for Reliable and Scalable Operations* (pp. 1–16). IGI Global. doi:10.4018/978-1-60566-723-2.ch001

Stanton, R. (2005). Beyond Disaster Recovery: The Benefits of Business Continuity. *Computer Fraud & Security, 2005*(July), 18–19. doi:10.1016/S1361-3723(05)70234-7

Sumner, M. (2009). Information Security Threats: A Comparative Analysis of Impact, Probability, and Preparedness. *Information Systems Management, 26*(1), 2–11. doi:10.1080/10580530802384639

Tomic, D., & Markic, B. (2010). Continuous Database Availability. In N. Bajgoric (Ed.), *Always-On Enterprise Information Systems for Business Continuance: Technologies for Reliable and Scalable Operations* (pp. 129–148). IGI Global. doi:10.4018/978-1-60566-723-2.ch008

Turban, E., & Volonino, L. (2010). *Information Technology For Management – Transforming Organizations in the Digital Economy* (7th ed.). Wiley.

Varga, M. (2010). Challenges of Data Management in Always-On Enterprise Information Systems. In N. Bajgoric (Ed.), *Always-On Enterprise Information Systems for Business Continuance: Technologies for Reliable and Scalable Operations* (pp. 109–128). IGI – Global. doi:10.4018/978-1-60566-723-2.ch007

Veeam Report. (2014). *The Veeam Data Center Availability Report 2014*. Available at: https://www.veeam.com/wp-availability-report-2014.html

Venkatraman, A. (2013). Human error most likely cause of datacentre downtime, finds study. *Computerweekly*. Available at: http://www.computerweekly.com/news/2240179651/Human-error-most-likely-cause-of-datacentre-downtime-finds-study

IDC White Paper. (2009). *Reducing Downtime and Business Loss: Addressing Business Risk with Effective Technology*. IDC.

Chapter 2
The Always-On Business Model and Competitive Advantage

Jorge A. Romero
Towson University, USA

ABSTRACT

This chapter discusses the always-on business model of information technology (IT) and how firms can gain a competitive advantage and differentiate themselves from competitors that may be adopting a similar always-on model. The discussion of how firms can get and keep a competitive advantage has been a topic of interest for a long time. An always-on application is a type of IT application; therefore, this is part of a more general research question that has been of interest to researchers that researches have wondered if information system applications actually provide an advantage to firms when firms are getting the same type of IT application. Previous research has concluded that IT improves productivity but the exact mechanisms by which IT increases business value are still not fully understood. One of the mechanism by which IT improves the competitiveness of firms is through the identification of innovative opportunities (Bardhan et al., 2013).

INTRODUCTION

This chapter discusses the always-on business model of information technology (IT) and how firms can gain a competitive advantage and differentiate themselves from competitors that may be adopting a similar always-on model. The discussion of how firms can get and keep a competitive advantage is always a topic of interest.

DOI: 10.4018/978-1-5225-3704-5.ch002

Because an always-on application is a type of IT application, it fits into a more general research question that has been of great interest to researchers who have examined whether or not information system applications actually provide an advantage to firms when competitors are also adopting the same type of IT application. Previous research has concluded that IT improves business value, but the exact mechanisms by which IT increases business value are still not fully understood. One mechanism by which IT improves the competitiveness of firms is through the identification of innovative opportunities (Bardhan, Krishnan, & Lin, 2013). Specifically, it is important to understand how firms can use IT in order to gain a strategic advantage over competitors through improvements in business operations and through the development of unique processes that can differentiate firms in a unique way from competitors. Bardhan et al. (2013) argued that the interaction of IT with other business processes will create more value to the firm, and when these interactions are supplemented with research and development (R&D) investments then the increase in shareholder value is evident. R&D is a firm expense related to activities related to the development of new procedures/products or to improve current procedures/products. It is considered an intangible asset. Bardhan et al. (2013) used Tobin's Q as a proxy measure for IT investments. Tobin's Q is a financial variable that measures future earnings of a firm, while R&D is an intangible variable whose future benefits are uncertain (Pandit, Wasley & Zach, 2011).

The always-on technology is supposed to offer continuous operations, continuous information technology services and permanent support all day long and without interruptions. The fundamental idea of this type of IT application is that information technology applications under the always-on technology offer reliable and constant access and services to clients. This always-on characteristic offered by current information technology services presents a new business model for firms that can help create and deliver value to customers, such as strategic competitive advantage. As firms evolve and implement new technologies and offer a novel service such as always-on, they have to realign their processes and business models in order to remain competitive (Desyllas, 2013). Hence, the business model that has to be in place has to be a life cycle model because especially with IT applications, new systems and new products are being developed at a frequent rate and firms have to be constantly adjusting their strategy (Desyllas, 2013; Chesbrough and Rosenbloom, 2002).

The research question we explore here is: how do firms gain competitive advantage and distinguish themselves from competitors when competitors are also implementing and offering a similar always-on business model? There are two ways to gain a strategic advantage over competitors when competitors are adopting a similar type of IT, either the firm has to adopt and install faster, or the firm has to do it in such a unique way that it is difficult to replicate by competitors (Anderson, Banker, Menon & Romero, 2011). A recommendation that can be provided to firms implementing a new type of IT will be to keep in mind that any competitor can acquire the same type of IT application, but the difficult part to replicate by competitors will be the unique way that the new IT is used within the firm. Moreover, a firm will have to implement an innovative business model that will differentiate itself from its competitors, and keep innovating its business model, thus making it more dynamic and profitable for a firm. Business model innovations are expensive to implement, therefore firms must take this into consideration because they may represent long term investment decision. (Desyllas, 2013).

Specifically, this chapter discusses the always-on business model of information technology. Firms can follow different types of business models. So, what is a business model? A business model is a structure that defines the cost structure, the profit generation mechanism, identifies the market segment, and identifies the structure of the value chain in order to distribute the services (Desyllas, 2013). In a business model, firms need to define the value proposition which is the value of this always-on business model offered to customers, firms need to identify the market segment, because not every firm on every industry will benefit with always-on services and in some industries it is possible that clients may not be interested in always-on services. The firm also has to decide how it is going to implement and support the technology, and finally the always-on services have to represent a profit to the firm because if the always-on services are not going to provide any benefit to the firm then they may not be a good idea to adopt them. There has to be an attractive return on investment in order to implement, maintain and keep expanding the always-on model because the business model should create value for the firm and users (Chesbrough & Rosenbloom, 2002).

This always-on business model is similar to the business model followed by public utility service firms, in that their services are considered essential and that the reliability of the services play a key role to end users (Rappa, 2004). Reliability has to be an important feature of an always-on application in order to avoid any disruption of the services. One way to increase the reliability of the always-on service is to build a redundant network in case of capacity constraints, or in case of failures in software applications or hardware. Redundancy is usually common practice in IT applications, but in the case of always-on application it will play a key role because having a redundant network will guarantee continuous operations and service with no interruptions. Hence, firms have to do a cost-benefit analysis because the question is how much redundancy to include in the network? The more redundant the network, the more expensive the system, and the higher the investments. Especially in IT applications such as hardware and software, we have to consider that IT assets depreciate in a short of period of time mostly because of obsolescence given the fact that it is a very dynamic area where improvements in technology happen at a fast rate. So, firms will not want to compromise much of their capital, cash flow and resources into rapidly-depreciable assets but at the same time they need to have a minimum level of redundancy, so finding the optimal point is not an easy task and is usually a moving target over time because requirements will change based on different market conditions.

While the business model of a typical public utility firm falls under a monopoly model, the business model of a firm operating in an always-on model will fall under high competition. Increased competition should also be favored (Loudder, Khurana & Boatsman, 1996). A main characteristic of the service offered by public utility service firms are that users only pay for what they consume. Some of those essential services are considered a necessity such as water, electricity, phone, and gas among others. A service is considered a necessity when end users depend on that in order to meet their daily needs.

As we may move more towards a utility business model, and when setting usage rates either for pay-as-you-go customers or customers under a specific usage plan, regulators have to take into account investment costs, including cost of capital incurred by firms, and their revenue model that they will follow in order to recover their capital and investment (Louder et al., 1996).

If this new always-on business model is going to be similar to that of a utility business model, then, in order to protect end users of always-on applications against monopolistic manipulations, some regulations have to be in place in order that some minimum standards have to be followed (Louder et al., 1996). In addition to that, utility services are considered commodity business; therefore economies of scale are a factor to consider (Rappa, 2004). If economies of scale are a factor, then larger players may have an advantage over smaller players, given the fact that in order to attain the always-on characteristics, firms will have to make significant investments in infrastructure. Information about which firms benefit from economies of scale is not public information, therefore competitors and regulators will not have access to that data (Calzolari & Scarpa, 2007). Also, when we discuss economies of scale, there are two components to consider: quantities and prices. With regard to quantities, it will take into account the number of always-on clients that the IT system can support simultaneously. With regard to prices, it will take into account the amount of IT investments the company has incurred and the number of IT clients using the system. In both, cases, larger firms will enjoy the benefits of economies of scale.

Larger investments will be required for firms to guarantee an always-on service, and some of these investments will include a redundant infrastructure. As firms move towards a more standard always-on business model, firms will have to invest more money to ensure that their services are always on and fully reliable, given the fact that all related IT services may require planned hardware and software updates, be ready for unplanned hardware and software failure, and human errors that may happen.

The use of IT has become a necessity and an essential tool for everyday business operations of firms and for everyday personal operations of end users. Moreover, connectivity and compatibility among IT applications both play a key role in always-on relations because businesses are challenged to keep up with technology innovations and end users expect to be able to connect at any time during the day. Another factor to consider is that currently end users have access to high speed internet at home, at the office, airports, cafes, and on their personal mobile devices.

There are alternate conclusions about the role of IT in competitive advantage and this question extends to always-on applications as well. For instance, within the same industry, it is possible that any firm can have access to the same type of ERP (Enterprise Resource Planning), the same type of CRM (Customer Relationship Management), the same type of cloud applications, and the same type of always-on applications. Therefore, IT may not matter because if any firm can have access to the same type of technology and resources then there is no strategic differentiation and no competitive advantage that a firm can obtain adopting that type of IT (Carr, 2004; Bhatt and Grover 2005). Other studies have argued that it is not only about the IT being used by the firm, but it is about how it is being used by the firm so that the technology combined with complementary resources owned by the firm are difficult to imitate by competitors, and because each firm has its own unique processes and resources (Bardhan et al., 2013).

Part of the competitive advantage that a firm can gain over competitors when it implements an always-on business model is the fact that some information is still private such as economies of scale, but imitation can play an important role because any company can adopt an always-on model given the fact that there is no intellectual property protection that can protect the firm from imitation. So, if everybody adopts an always-on model, then how do firms can gain a competitive advantage over competitors from using the same always-on model? In addition to that, long term competitive advantage will depend on the company's ability to offer a reliable always-on service; it will depend on a good ERP system that synchronizes and supports all operations in the firm in real time and on a good CRM system. From the point of view of the end users, the theory of consumer proposes that consumers will benefit from this competition of information systems because prices will drop and the quality of the service will increase (Melville, Kraemer & Gurbaxani, 2004).

With the increase in always-on tools and applications, we will see more of these tools and applications that are called network goods, the utility will be more dependent on the connection to a network. The always-on feature will push even more on the digitalization of products and services (Van Hove, 2016). Therefore, always-on applications will be used to control the demands of the job.

Some examples of always-on applications are RSS feeds, push email, instant messaging, and voice over IP applications (Baird & Fisher, 2005; Haverine, Siren

& Eronen, 2007). RSS is the Rich Site Summary technology that follows an XML format and serves as the backbone to publish frequently updated information such as Weblogs, news headlines, community groups, and podcasts among other documents. XML is the extensible markup language which is similar to HTML and where users define their own tags. XML tags describe data that is human-readable and machine-readable. Subscribing to an RSS feed allows subscribers to automatically get updated data in real time (Baird & Fisher, 2005). In the case of RSS feeds, it is an application where subscribers do not need to manually check for updated data, the content is automatically updated in real time and is shown in the feed reader. Users have the option to select and customize the content that they want to be shown in their readers (Baird & Fisher, 2005). Some examples of RSS feeds applications are: Google Reader, Netvibes, Protopage, Good Noows, NewsBlur, FeedShow, and Gritwire among others.

THE SIGNIFICANCE OF THE ALWAYS-ON BUSINESS MODEL

In order to implement a successful always-on business model, the company will have to have a good understanding of its own customer needs. According to previous research, firms may struggle dealing with technological innovations with which they have no previous experience. This struggle may be due to several factors such as the complexity of the technology itself, the complexity to manage the technology, or the resources needed to access the technology. Therefore, these factors could represent a road block for some firms that may want to implement the always-on technology in their everyday activities and in their interactions with clients (Chesbrough & Rosenbloom, 2002).

Under an always-on business model, new services can be provided that not only depend on the information input by a user, but also on their current location, which can be identified by the embedded GPS on their mobile devices or the IP address of a computer. One example is radio-frequency identification (RFID) tags on items in stores for display or RFID tags of items that are already being used by clients at home or at work can provide always-on opportunities for manufacturers and retailers to offer scheduled maintenance or to offer new models to clients (Gershman, 2002). Firms operating under the always-on business model will have to have the infrastructure to support the demand and satisfy their clients and supply chain network. Specifically, RFID stands for radio-frequency identification, which is a technology that relies on electromagnetic fields in order to identify RFID labels automatically. Different RFID applications operate in different frequencies of the electromagnetic spectrum, and depending on the frequency used the distance at which an RFID label can be read will be different. The distance could be a few inches to several feet. The RFID technology usually consists of two components: one is a passive tag also known as RFID label that can be placed in clothing, books, mobile phones, cars and even animals; and the other is an active RFID reader that usually has a power source. Once the RFID reader sends a signal to the RFID label, the information collected could be the serial number of the product, the production date, or some additional data that may have been saved in the RFID label. Lately, information saved in RFID labels is now being encrypted in order to avoid any unauthorized person to access the information saved in the RFID label.

Furthermore, with regard to the value of a network, the Metcalfe's law postulates that the value of a network increases when more users join a network and this increase is proportional to the square of the number of users (Mankins, 2016; Middleton, 2007; Van Hove, 2016). Professor Robert Metcalfe is an engineer that co-invented the Ethernet and postulated the Metcalfe's Law that states that the value of a network is proportional to the square number of users. For instance, if a network grows and triples its size then the value of that network becomes worth nine times its original value because the value will be calculated as the square value of three. Over the years, the Metcalfe's Law has been criticized and other researchers have proposed other calculations related to the value of a network. Weinman (2007) discusses different proposed calculations related to the growing value of a network instead of the square number of users. For instance, the growing value of a network can follow a different pattern such as the logarithm of the number of users, or just equal to the number of users. Also, in any network, there is a limited capacity on the number of users connected, therefore the more users connected to a network, bottlenecks may appear, and the speed to access the network will be reduced as more users join the network. Therefore, the value of each additional connection will not be constant, but it may decrease.

Users that are always-on become active members of a network, and once a user is part of a network there may be direct network effects among users and indirect network effects through the use of complementary services (Van Hove, 2016). Taking a closer look at the Metcalfe's law after a certain number of users that join the network, it is possible to reach a point of decreasing marginal utility in accordance to the Zipf's law (Van Hove, 2016). When we discuss the value of a network, how do we value a network? Do we value a network based on total assets? Total revenue? Revenue per user? or, is it based on network size? Network size can be measured as the number of internet websites, number of internet subscribers, or cellphone subscribers among other metrics that can be used for this purpose (Weinman, 2007).

NETWORK EXTERNALITIES

If we look at a specific industry where several firms are already operating under the always-on business model, then, based on the concept of network externalities it will be better for a firm that is not operating under the always-on business model to adapt that model, otherwise the firm will face a competitive disadvantage. Additionally, as time passes the competitive advantage gap may grow even larger and it will be even more difficult for this firm to compete at the same level.

In the past, always-on services may have not been that important from the point of view of network externalities but as time passes and services spread out, users are already adapted to the new always-on technology. Because more users have started using the technology, the always-on service becomes more important. In addition to that, users will figure out more applications and more ways to make good use of the technology.

In always-on applications, complementary capabilities such as cloud access, CRM, and ERP are important in how they interrelate and support one another. According to theory of complementarity, complementary capabilities of information technology provide positive effects for firms (Bresnahan, Brynjolfsson & Hitt, 2002; Hendricks, Singhal & Stratman, 2007). In the case of complementary IT needed to offer always-on services, such as cloud computing services, ERP, and CRM, we have to understand that services are usually standard services offered to firms; competitors may also have access to exactly the same type of technology and services. Therefore, firms have to be creative in order to gain competitive advantage in relation to competitors using the same type of tools and technology; firms will have to add another layer of unique characteristics that are not easily replicated by competitors.

In the always-on business model, the basic premise is to offer a reliable and constant service with a good ERP, CRM and cloud support. But, from the perspective of a firm and in order to remain competitive, firms have to be careful to avoid overbuilding the always-on infrastructure, otherwise they may have underutilized assets and their efficiency and profitability may drop. Firms have to try to forecast what will be the capacity utilization of their always-on network in order that they offer an optimal size and remain competitive.

CLOUD COMPUTING

In an always-on business model, having cloud computing as part of a firm's operations and services is important because users and clients can get access to services anywhere and they can enjoy real-time data. In addition, having cloud computing as part of operations is key because although firms may not have employees working 24 hours a day and 365 days a year, cloud computing services owned or contracted will provide always-on services to clients. Cloud computing services usually include online storage, virtual servers, CRM and ERP applications (Choudhary & Vithayathil, 2013).

Using cloud computing services is more cost effective for firms because they can lease only what they need in terms of storage and software. Cloud computing could be a good tool for firms in order to get a competitive advantage because firms can reduce costs of online storage and software licenses, and firms can contract only the amount of cloud computing power based on the number of users that they are forecasting will use the cloud computing service, therefore firms may eliminate some fixed costs that are usually associated with IT infrastructure (Chatman, 2010; Choudhary & Vithayathil, 2013). Cloud computing can also help firms achieve competitive advantage through the use of algorithms designed to use real-time data and to identify unique customer needs providing in this way an agile process to firms (Weinman, 2015).

One example of a cloud application is Prezi, which offers presentation tools for end users without the need to install any software. Internet access is required and there is no option to work offline on a presentation. This feature could be considered a drawback, but as more firms adapt an always-on model and as internet availability becomes ubiquitous, we will see more applications like Prezi being available.

Another example is ERP. Nowadays, firms rely heavily on the use of information technology, which is needed in almost all operations including telecommunications, cloud operations, and back office operations. Moreover, with the growing use of ERP systems among firms, firms rely even more on the data generated by ERP systems in order to make business decisions at faster rate. Some of the benefits of ERP systems are that they synchronize all departments within a firm, and synchronize the ERP system of the firm with the whole supply chain including suppliers and customers.

The way that systems will use these types of cloud applications can help them create competitive advantage over competitors. If data is not always-on, therefore not always available then the potential competitive advantage can be wiped out and the negative effects on revenue, income, customer retention may be difficult to quantify.

CRM AND ALWAYS-ON SYSTEMS

The always-on model will also push customer service expectations to higher levels. In order for firms to meet customer expectations, firms will have to have a good CRM system and a good ERP system in place, among other technological capabilities.

CRM focuses on customers looking to retain customers, improve interactions with customers and at the same time maximize profits and competitiveness. It also integrates marketing and sales with other divisions of a firm (Weinman, 2015; Chen & Popovich, 2003). CRM usually helps firms have a better understanding of their customers' needs, what type of customers they have and what is the corporate behavior of them. For instance, Salesforce, one of the software leaders in CRM is a cloud-based application that follows an always-model business model offering data analytics services, marketing services and sales.

It is also important to take into account the expectations of younger users. Younger users are growing up in a culture in which they are always connected to the internet and with constant access to online and digital resources. Younger users may be more inclined to be working or collaborating when they are connected to the Internet rather than just reading a printed book. Especially given the fact that nowadays everybody has easy access to mobile devices, therefore younger users have different expectations and styles than older users (Baird and Fisher, 2005). Therefore, the CRM system should take into account the needs of younger and older users, and the CRM system has to be designed accordingly.

ERP SYSTEM AND ALWAYS-ON SYSTEMS

Enterprise Resource Planning (ERP) systems started to play a major role for firms after a major event such as the year 2000 problem (Y2K) forced firms to start using four digit numbers in order to record the variable year. Before that, firms used to record only two digits in their systems for the variable year. Another major event that has also pushed firms to adopt ERP systems was the Sarbanes Oxley Act (SOX) of 2002 where publicly traded firms were better off adopting ERP systems in order to be in compliance with new SOX regulations.

ERP has replaced legacy IT systems and is considered an evolution of Material Requirements Planning (MRP) (Gumaer, 1996; Yusuf & Little, 1998; Cooper & Zmud, 1990). An ERP system uses a logically centralized database where data needs to be input only once, therefore reducing the amount of errors related to data input. In the past, different departments in a firm were not necessarily synchronized, but with ERP the whole infrastructure can be synchronized within the firm, and firms can synchronize their systems with the systems of other firms in the supply chain. Therefore, this can help firms create operational excellence and business value.

The enormous complexity of ERP systems and the great amount of time and cost of implementation may reduce its strategic advantage in order to create business value for the firm (Bardhan et al. 2013). ERP systems are a type of IT that is very expensive to implement and usually a full implementation of all the modules may take several years, obviously causing disruption in the operations of the firm and in its cash flows. The difficulty is not only about installing and configuring the ERP software, but also about the firm putting the effort adapting the new system to meet the unique requirements of its operations and making sure that the installation is successful (Anderson et al. 2011).

As a way to reduce costs, there are multiple cases where firms have implemented ERP systems using different modules from different ERP vendors. Using different modules from different ERP vendors is usually not an ideal alternative given the fact that the modules from different vendors may not be fully compatible and may cause some errors and delays in the processing of the data and transactions. This would also be true in the case of always-on applications. It will be recommended that firms use modules from the same vendor given the fact that in always-on applications errors or delays may cause a disruption and will have a larger negative effect on end users. The ERP system will play a key role in setting up a successful always-on business model defining the settings of the supply chain needed to offer a reliable always-on service and additional assets needed to have a successful competitive strategy over competitors.

ADVANTAGES AND DISADVANTAGES OF THE ALWAYS-ON BUSINESS MODEL

In addition to the main data processing operations and the electronic data interchange, IT is also an essential personal tool that individuals rely upon to perform their daily activities. The always-on business model presents many advantages but at the same time the technology needed to support this business model may present some disadvantages at the personal level for users because nowadays users are connected through cellphones, tablets and other electronic devices that this may affect their personal interrelations because they may not be completely focused on corporate related tasks during work hours, and their attention may be compromised, and if their attention is compromised then their business decisions may also be compromised. Also, social connections and team work may be affected (Turkle, 2008). Being always-on may improve the efficiency of users or may interfere with the necessary down time that users may need in order to generate ideas and think at a higher level. Moreover, the security and privacy of the corporate data may be compromised because employees can always access corporate data using their personal electronic devices.

EFFECTS ON USERS

Smartphones are devices that are always-on, and create expectations that people are available beyond office hours. Their original design was conceived as a device that will help balance a better work environment where users can have more control over their communications, but on the contrary it may create conflict between work and personal activities. End users will value the always-on access to different applications, but at the same time there is a side effect in the form of intrusion that those connections create because we may see work-family and family-work interference. There is not much academic research on the effects of always-on applications and organizational usage (Middleton, 2007).

A couple of decades ago, information technology applications such as email and teleconferencing applications helped increase the productivity of end users because collaboration and information flows got easier, but currently that is not the case and productivity of end users has even declined in some cases. Setting up meetings in the past was not an easy task and it was even more difficult when the number of people involved increased because electronic calendars were not available, but nowadays it is very easy to synchronize calendars therefore the number of meetings and the number of attendees per meeting has increased exponentially. This has a negative effect on the productivity of end users because a large percentage of their time may be dedicated to attend meetings, and read and reply emails, reducing the amount of periods of interrupted time where end users can think at a more strategic level (Mankins, 2016). Taking this into consideration, does always-on applications help end users to increase productivity and efficiency or will they be another source of distraction?

FUTURE RESEARCH

Always-on applications may not be good for the environment because it requires that the whole supply chain, including ERP systems, CRM applications, and databases have to be on constantly, using energy, and these systems do not go into a dormant stage when there are no users accessing always-on applications. Moreover, these systems do not reduce their energy consumption when fewer users are accessing them, and their energy consumption will remain relatively constant. This is a factor to consider in the development of new systems especially now that there is a movement towards green initiatives and applications that can meet current and future environmental challenges. Therefore, the way that firms design and set up their always-on application will have a great impact on the environment and this has to be part of their corporate social responsibility strategy. For instance, there are some IT vendors already moving in this direction. In the case of Oracle, it has an application called Environmental Accounting and Reporting where it measures environmental performance based on some preset targets and at the same type monitors energy, waste and water usage. It uses the Oracle Business Intelligence module that manages environmental data with cost management tools. In the case of SAP, they are already working on corporate social responsible applications, and they offer a package called sustainability management and environment, health, and safety (EHS) that monitors profitability, and energy consumption among other metrics. SAP is one the major vendors of ERP software and is the market leader in many industries. SAP is a multinational firm with headquarters in Germany. In the last few years, it has been putting a lot of effort toward developing cloud ERP services for firms, and it has partnered with IBM and Microsoft in order to move into that direction.

CONCLUSION

This chapter contributes to the always-on literature by analyzing competitive advantage effects and presenting logical arguments affecting strategic advantage on firms adopting and using always-on applications. Also, it discusses the fact that firms have to see the always-on business model as a life cycle model because technology in general is a very dynamic area and firms have to be continuously innovating in order to differentiate themselves from competitors and use as a strategic advantage the unique characteristics of their business so competitors cannot replicate, or if competitors are trying to replicate, they will have a difficult time replicating it (Clemons and Row, 1991). This chapter will also help us understand how firms can keep a competitive advantage over competitors and its link to the strategy that a firm can have.

IMPLICATIONS FOR MANAGERS AND PRACTITIONERS

This chapter contributes to the always-on topic providing key conceptual knowledge that will help firms, researchers, and managers identify the sources of competitive advantage that will add value to the firm and will help them differentiate from competitors. It will also contribute to the literature on the always-on business model, and strategic investments analyzing models used to measure competitive advantage and providing a better understanding of this new technology.

REFERENCES

Anderson, M., Banker, R., Menon, N., & Romero, J. (2011). Implementing Enterprise Resource Planning Systems: Organizational Performance and the Duration of the Implementation. *Information Technology Management*, *12*(3), 197–212. doi:10.1007/s10799-011-0102-9

Baird, D., & Fisher, M. (2005). Neomillennial User Experience Design Strategies: Utilizing Social Networking Media to Support Always On Learning Styles. *Journal of Educational Technology Systems*, *34*(1), 5–32. doi:10.2190/6WMW-47L0-M81Q-12G1

Bardhan, I., Krishnan, V., & Lin, S. (2013). Business Value of Information Technology: Testing the Interaction Effect of IT and R&D on Tobins Q. *Information Systems Research*, *24*(4), 1147–1161. doi:10.1287/isre.2013.0481

Bhatt, G., & Grover, V. (2005). Types of Information Technology Capabilities and their Role in Competitive Advantage: An Empirical Study. *Journal of Management Information Systems*, *22*(2), 253–277. doi:10.1080/07421222.2005.11045844

Bresnahan, T., Brynjolfsson, E., & Hitt, L. (2002). Information Technology, Workplace Organization, and the Demand for Skilled Labor: Firm-Level Evidence. *The Quarterly Journal of Economics*, *117*(1), 339–376. doi:10.1162/003355302753399526

Calzolari, G., & Scarpa, C. (2007). *Regulating a Multi-Utility Firm*. Centre for Economic Policy Research (CEPR) (No. 5516).

Carr, N. (2004). *Does IT Matter? Information Technology and the Corrosion of Competitive Advantage*. Cambridge, MA: Harvard Business School Press.

Chatman, C. (2010, May). How Cloud Computing is changing the Face of Health Care Information Technology. *Journal of Health Care Compliance*, 37-70.

Chen, I., & Popovich, K. (2003). Understanding Customer Relationship Management (CRM) People, Process, and Technology. *Business Process Management Journal*, *9*(5), 672–688. doi:10.1108/14637150310496758

Chesbrough, H., & Rosenbloom, R. (2002). The Role of the Business Model in Capturing Value from Innovation: Evidence from Xerox Corporations Technology Spin-off Companies. *Industrial and Corporate Change*, *11*(3), 529–555. doi:10.1093/icc/11.3.529

Choudhary, V., & Vithayathil, J. (2013). The Impact of Cloud Computing: Should the IT Department Be Organized as a Cost Center or a Profit Center?. *Journal of Management Information Systems*, *30*(2), 67–100. doi:10.2753/MIS0742-1222300203

Clemons, E., & Row, M. (1991). Sustaining IT Advantage: The Role of Structural Differences. *Management Information Systems Quarterly*, *15*(3), 275–292. doi:10.2307/249639

Cooper, R., & Zmud, R. (1990). Information Technology implementation research: A technological diffusion approach. *Management Science*, *36*(2), 123–139. doi:10.1287/mnsc.36.2.123

Desyllas, P., & Sako, M. (2013). Profiting from Business Model Innovation: Evidence from Pay-As-You-Drive Auto Insurance. *Research Policy*, *42*(1), 101–116. doi:10.1016/j.respol.2012.05.008

Gershman, A. (2002). *Ubiquitous Commerce – Always On, Always Aware, Always Pro-Active.* The 2002 International Symposium on Applications and the Internet SAINT 2002, Nara, Japan.

Gumaer, R. (1996). Beyond ERP and MRPII. *IIE Solutions*, *28*(9), 32–36.

Haverine, H., Siren, J., & Eronen, P. (2007). Energy Consumption of Always-On Applications in WCDMA Networks. *Vehicular Technology Conference.*

Hendricks, K., Singhal, V., & Stratman, J. (2007). The Impact of Enterprise Systems on Corporate Performance: A Study of ERP, SCM, and CRM system implementations. *Journal of Operations Management*, *25*(1), 65–82. doi:10.1016/j.jom.2006.02.002

Liebowitz, S. J., & Margolis, S. E. (1998). *Network externalities (effects).* The New Palgrave's Dictionary of Economics and the Law.

Loudder, M., Khurana, I., & Boatsman, J. (1996). Market Valuation of Regulatory Assets in Public Utility Firms. *Accounting Review*, *71*(3), 357–373.

Mankis, M. (2016, February). Is Technology Really Helping Us Get More Done?. *Harvard Business Review.*

Melville, N., Kraemer, K., & Gurbaxani, V. (2004). Review: Information Technology and Organizational Performance: An Integrative Model of IS Business Value. *Management Information Systems Quarterly*, *28*(2), 283–322.

Metcalfe, R. (1995, October). Metcalfe's Law: A Network Becomes More Valuable as it Reaches More Users. *InfoWorld*, 2.

Middleton, C. (2007). Illusions of Balance and Control in an Always-On Environment: A Case Study of Blackberry Users. *Continuum (Perth)*, *21*(2), 165–178. doi:10.1080/10304310701268695

Pandit, S., Wasley, C., & Zach, T. (2011). The effect of research and development (R&D) inputs and outputs on the relation between the uncertainty of future operating performance and R&D expenditures. *Journal of Accounting, Auditing & Finance*, *26*(1), 121–144. doi:10.1177/0148558X11400583

Rappa, M. (2004). The Utility Business Model and the Future of Computing Services. *IBM Systems Journal*, *43*(1), 32–42. doi:10.1147/sj.431.0032

Romero, J., Menon, N., Banker, R., & Anderson, M. (2010). ERP: Drilling for Profit in the Oil and Gas Industry. *Communications of the ACM*, *53*(7), 118–121. doi:10.1145/1785414.1785448

Turkle, S. (2008). *Always-On/Always-On-You: The Tethered Self. In Handbook of Mobile Communication Studies*. Katz and Castells.

Van Hove, L. (2016). Testing Melcafes Law: Pitfalls and Possibilities. *Information Economics and Policy*, *37*, 67–76. doi:10.1016/j.infoecopol.2016.09.001

Weinman, J. (2007, August). Is Metcalfe's Law Way Too Optimistic?. *Business Communications Review*.

Weinman, J. (2015, November). Digital Technologies and Competitive Advantage. *Research-Technology Management*, 12-17.

Yusuf, Y., & Little, D. (1998). An empirical investigation of enterprise-wide integration of MRPII. *International Journal of Operations & Production Management*, *18*(1), 66–86. doi:10.1108/01443579810192916

ADDITIONAL READING

Agre, P. E. (2001). Welcome to the always-on world. *IEEE Spectrum*, *38*(1), 10–13. doi:10.1109/6.901159

Anderson, B., Gale, C., Jones, M. L. R., & McWilliam, A. (2002). Domesticating broadband—what consumers really do with flat-rate, always-on and fast Internet access. *BT Technology Journal*, *20*(1), 103–114. doi:10.1023/A:1014578227619

Bajgoric, N. (2009). *Always-On Enterprise Information Systems for Business Continuance: Technologies for Reliable and Scalable Operations: Technologies for Reliable and Scalable Operations*. IGI Global.

Cherkasova, L., Staley, L., & Solutions, A. O. I. (2003). Building a Performance Model of Streaming Media Applications in Utility Data Center Environment. *CCGRID*, 3.

De Lange, M. (2009). From always on to always there: Locative media as Playful Technologies. *Digital cityscapes: merging digital and urban playspaces*, 55-70.

Könönen, V., & Pääkkönen, P. (2011). Optimizing power consumption of always-on applications based on timer alignment. *Communication Systems and Networks (COMSNETS), Third International Conference on.*

Moser, D., & Martin, P. (2012). A Broader Perspective on Corporate Social Responsibility Research in Accounting. *Accounting Review*, *87*(3), 797–806. doi:10.2308/accr-10257

Riche, Y., Dodge, J., & Metoyer, R. A. (2010). Studying always-on electricity feedback in the home. In Proceedings of the SIGCHI *Conference on Human Factors in Computing Systems*. doi:10.1145/1753326.1753628

Sadler, K., Robertson, T., & Kan, M. (2006). It's always there, it's always on: Australian freelancer's management of availability using mobile technologies. *Proceedings of the 8th conference on Human-computer interaction with mobile devices and services*. doi:10.1145/1152215.1152226

Tso, M. M., Gillespie, D. J., & Romrell, D. A. (1996). Always on, always connected mobile computing. *Universal Personal Communications, 5th IEEE International Conference*.

KEY TERMS AND DEFINITIONS

Accelerated Implementation: In a ERP implementation, firms have an option to follow an accelerated implementation in order to shorten the amount of time that an implementation may take. It may be more expensive and firms may be looking for an option like this in order to reduce disruption of operations that usually happen during the implementation period. For instance, SAP offers accelerated SAP installations that are a good alternative for firms operating in fast-changing environments where strategic advantages may depend on the speed of the implementation. The disadvantage is that firms have to fit their processes into packaged ERP components, therefore reducing differentiation from competitors and possible reducing competitive advantage. Also, firms may not have an opportunity to reformulate strategies and redesign processes (Anderson et al., 2011).

Corporate Social Responsibility: (CSR): It refers to business practices where a firm takes responsibility for the firm's effects on the environment and society. Being involved in corporate social responsible projects and initiatives will help project a better image of the firm especially when the firm includes its corporate social responsible projects and initiatives in its annual report and press releases. We can find two cases; one of them could be when managers just try to maximize profits and therefore will keep environmental and social responsible initiatives at the minimal level, and the other group of managers that in response to demands of environmental groups and regulators may overspend in social responsible projects reducing corporate profitability (Moser & Martin, 2012).

Enterprise Resource Planning: It is a type of IT that not only integrates and synchronizes all the departments of a firm, but it also can synchronize the ERP system of the firm with the ERP system of suppliers and clients. For instance, with an ERP systems, inventory reorders can be made automatically because when inventories levels are low at the retail store, then the ERP system can check if there is enough inventory in the warehouse, if not, then the ERP systems can send an automatic order to the corresponding supplier. Nowadays, that we live in a global world, many firms have offices and operations in different parts of the world, and having an ERP system help them synchronize easily and in a seamless way all of their global operations. The main ERP modules that represent the core of a full ERP installation are the following: human resources, finance, inventories, sales, marketing, and production (Romero et al., 2010).

ERP Implementation: It is the amount of time that a firm allocates from the beginning of an installation to the moment the installation is declared complete.

Firm Performance: It is a measure of efficiency and profitability of a firm.

Network Externalities: It has been defined as the change in the benefit that an agent can obtain when more agents are using the same type of service or product (Liebowitz & Margolis, 1998). The definition of network externalities is different than the one of economies of scale because in the case of economies of scale a larger number of items produced or traded will reduce the unit cost of the item, while network externalities do not have an impact on prices or costs. In the case where network externalities are robust, connectivity and compatibility are important factors to consider when adopting a new technology. A good example of robust network externalities is industries where SAP has a large market penetration. In the case of those industries with a large SAP market penetration, it is important for a firm to decide about adopting a new SAP because connectivity and compatibility with suppliers and customers will be affected if this firm decides to adopt a different ERP vendor that may not be fully compatible with SAP. If the firm decides to adopt a different ERP vendor then it may have a strategic disadvantage similar to the example mentioned by Liebowitz and Margolis (1998) where if almost everybody has access to a telephone network then whoever does not have access to that telephone network will have a disadvantage.

Chapter 3
Always on Guard:
How a Corporate Immune System Can Engage Full-Spectrum Risks – A Conceptual Framework to Re-Engineer Organizational Capability and Culture

Milyan (Mils) Hills
University of Northampton, UK

ABSTRACT

This chapter advances the idea that the modern organization can become immune to a full spectrum of risks by re-engineering its organizational capability and culture. Given the accepted role of people in causing or escalating technical risk – the requirement to achieve 'always on' socio-technical protection poses a significant challenge. However, an enterprise's human resources offer a massive potential to detect and report risk and there is also substantial competitive advantage available to the organization which develops, integrates, leverages and acts on intelligence gained from a suite of socio-technical sensors and sense-making processes. The human resources and culture of an organization, properly configured, could comprise a powerful innate (constant) and adaptive (active) immune system. The chapter will provide the reader with a framework for how such an immune capability could be integrated into an organization that takes seriously the requirement to be 'always on' – protected from any form or blend of socio-technical threat.

DOI: 10.4018/978-1-5225-3704-5.ch003

INTRODUCTION

This book is charged with providing readers with conceptual and implementational frameworks to enable them to enhance their organizations' ability to deliver 'always on' availability, and (therefore) to avoid economic, reputational, opportunity and other costs. This chapter seeks to make a substantive and pragmatic contribution to the ability of businesses and other institutions to leverage and harden their defense against a significant cause of cyber-security breaches: people. More positively, rather than seeing the employees, contractors, visitors and customers of an enterprise merely and exclusively as a source of insider threat and other risk – and drawing on my background as a corporate and security anthropologist - this chapter suggests that these individuals enmeshed in an appropriate organizational culture can constitute a corporate immune system.

People can avoid risks, detect unusual events, trigger appropriate responses and learn from both past exposures to challenge and developing immunizations to harden protection and evade infection. And, of course, the immense benefit of a biological immune system – which organizations would desire to have – is that all of its actions occur automatically and without the investment of cognitive effort. To adopt a military, doctrinal term – components of the immune system have "mission command" to act in the best interests of the organism. Innate and active structures and systems form a shield and response capability which are always on duty.

Of course, when we as individuals are sick - we seek expert assistance to help aid our recovery (prioritize our survival and wellbeing, prevent us from transmitting our illness to others) and therefore invest cognitive effort to do this. Likewise, in the world of the bureaucratic institution, under extreme circumstances – all efforts should be focused on containing, understanding, recovering from and becoming invulnerable to future occurrences of the cyber risk encountered. In parallel –the organization must continue to deliver its strategic objectives and not let its guard down elsewhere.

Despite numerous surveys and analyses (more or less reliable as the case may be), it is apparent that the human resources of an organization - and those people who have (or can create) legitimate access to its premises, systems and insiders – comprise the most challenging aspect of an organization to secure. Rather than seeing individuals solely as sources of risk, this chapter advances the notion that they can (and should) be seen as a largely untapped security resource.

By extension, the organization(s) and supply-chain(s) which do unleash the protective and responsive potential of their personnel would have significant (and cheap) competitive advantage over others. This cultural re-engineering of values and power is not without its challenges in terms of the courage needed to embrace and make this change –but the rewards would be immense. An always-on enterprise information system implies the need for an always on enterprise immune system. Given that we are in a condition where technical protection alone has almost reached its apogee – we have no choice but to consider alternative options to assure ‘always on’ availability of systems and services (cf. Hills 2016 for more on socio-technical security).

The analogy advanced in this chapter – and that culminates in an initial description of a framework to apply the notion to a real-world organization – works because it equates the corporate body with a mammalian one. The immune system, as with the biological version, is the constituting, communicating and critical set of structures and mechanisms which flow through and around the body and ultimately enable that body to function, repair and sustain itself.

BACKGROUND

In relation to cyber risk alone, all companies are potentially on the target list of focused or diffuse threats. A recent article in the UK newspaper *The Daily Telegraph* summarized the findings of a government-funded survey which revealed that the “number of UK businesses that suffered a cyber attack doubled last year with almost half of firms *detecting* a breach in 2016” (McGoogan 2017, emphasis added). One can only speculate on how many of the fifty-four per cent which did not report a cyber attack have simply not (yet) detected an attack or the damage caused by it.

Many of these cyber attacks involve users being persuaded to click on links in phishing emails, identity theft, impersonation and more sophisticated approaches. Whilst there is always a certain quantity of malicious intent within the staff of organizations (or their authorized visitors, contractors, suppliers) – many such events will be entirely inadvertent and not maliciously-oriented at all. However, with humans being an excellent vector to circumvent physical, personnel and technical security measures – the advantage of being able to rely on one’s people as both first and deep lines of defense would be immense.

Some hard facts make this claim compelling:

When you combine the incidents involving malicious and inadvertent insiders, you will see that they are dwarfing any other computer security threat that your company faces. Among 874 incidents, as reported by companies to the Ponemon Institute for its recent 2016 Cost of Data Breach Study, 568 were caused by employee or contractor negligence; 85 by outsiders using stolen credentials; and 191 by malicious employees and criminals (Tripwire 2017).

There is, then, a full spectrum of threats relating to cyber (and cyber-dependent) risks alone. Ensuring always-on availability of services (and confidence) must therefore be underpinned by a dynamic detection of changes in threat state or the explopitation of an identified susceptibility.

The need for decision-makers in organisations – of any stripe – to be sighted on threats of this character is far from being a uniquely modernimperative, although ensuring that this occurs effectively remains (to say the least) a substantial challenge. In the sixteenth century, for example,the chronicler of muscular statecraft Machiavelli counselled that leaders:

Are extremely well advised to listen closely to all of the signals, however faint, of impending bad news. They are your only lines of defence. You need to constantly scan your Kingdom for signals of bad things that are about to happen, whether they are of your doing or someone else's. This is the only chance you have to gain advantage (Machiavelli, The Prince 1515).

This chapter contends that the promise and the peril of 'signals of bad things' remains elusive, but is very much an attainable capability that can and should envelop the execution of actions as well as the interpretation of signs.

Authoritative sources such as IBM have found, in significantly large surveys, that"60% of all [cyber] attacks were carried out by insiders", where a mere quarter of these were *inadvertent*(van Zadelhoff 2016). Given that these attacks no doubt occurred despite the presence of all sorts of conventional implementations of software, awareness-raising, training, policies and procedures relating to cyber and information security – the need for novel, pragmatic and practical approaches to support organizations that need to assure always-on performance is clear.

From clever but off-the-shelf email ploys leveraging the curiosity of recipients through to social engineering, impersonation, blackmail, inserting agents or scattering USB drives outside of a building – all of these and more could be detected, contained and blunted by an alert, engaged, empowered, self-directed organizational culture. van Zadelhoff (writing as the general manasger of IBM Security) titles his article in the *Harvard Business Review* 'The Biggest Cybersecurity Threats Are Inside Your Company', and whilst this is true – these individuals are also a critical and valuable reservoir of resistance. Activating this potential is a complicated matter that requires more than just 'desk drops' of information, guidance or rules: instead the re-engineering of organizational culture is needed, supported by effective and genuine communications activities. By combining existing technical intelligence with insight provided from human resources, and a constant scanning of new forms of potential data from across the organization and its up and down-stream supply-chain participants the organization can meet Machiavelli's earlier prescription.

This chapter will shortly promote the idea that the detection of, and action on, threats and risks should be expected to be achieved and reported by the lowest possible levels of an organization's hierarchy – with the collation, recording and dissemination and complementary decisions being achieved by a dedicated or re-purpose corporate function. Those ideas will combine to form a framework for how the modern corporate body can achieve immunity, but ahead of that it is necessary to explore prior efforts by academics and others to exploit the concept of immunity.

Prior Attempts to Exploit the Analogy of Biological Immunity

It is not novel to suggest that organizations need to be 'immune' to challenge and to suggest that threats can be seen as akin to diseases. But transitioning from colourful rhetoric to actionable insight is, unfortunately, rare. What is, superficially, an appealing device in speeches and outline policies – with widespread appeal to the public and media – often breaks down in terms of logic. If one labels a complex – even intractable - problem as a disease that needs to be treated and that we should become immune to, the question arises as to what extent the disease and the patient are is actually 'like' the problem at all. In many ways, such verbal and textual flourishes queer the pitch of being able to find and apply genuine analogical power from such parallels.

Politicians are especially fond of likening security challenges to disease: "[t] errorism is like cancer, history won't forgive us if it is not treated" (Prime Minister of Pakistan Nawaz Sharif in 2014, FirstPost 2014). Meanwhile, consultancy-providers such as IBM use the marketing collateral of the 'cybersecurity immune system for business" – but they don't really get the holistic concept either. The utility of the concept (and the opportunities that it raises) are way beyond this sales spiel:

Imagine treating infections with 80 different medications prescribed by 40 different doctors. That's the environment many companies find themselves in when dealing with cybersecurity. Like infectious diseases, cyber threats will never be eliminated entirely. But they can be limited and contained (IBM, n.d. (a)).

On another webpage, they note that: 'IBM has built an enterprise-level "immune system," an adaptive security architecture to battle today's cyber pathogens' (IBM, n.d. (b)). and this integrating 'system' acts 'as connective tissue for today's disjointed cybersecurity infrastructure' (*IBM, n.d.(b)*). Immediately, we see the problem with the ill-considered use of analogies. Connective tissue – in general – has no role in immunity: it is the fibrous structure, such as a tendon, that links bones or the adipose tissue that accommodates fat. Technically, blood is a connective tissue – and would be the smart way to enable and actualize the immune system analogy in this regard. However, this line of inquiry was not pursued.

There is one promising precedent of a good application of thinking of risks as pathogens in the literature, albeit with no exploration of the relevance of the immune system. In a very readable article from a 2003 edition of the *Harvard Business Review*, Mitroff and Alpaslan. report on the utility of companies looking at other industries in an attempt to gain fresh perspective on the risks they were open to. An electronics manufacturer, for example, re-considers how operations and strategy would be different if they were instead in the business of food production focused on the need to eliminate the potential for bacterial contamination. The difference between assuring the quality of hardware and the safety of food "so intrigued executives that they hired an infectious disease specialist to assess how the company could prevent pathogens from contaminating their production systems and infecting their products" (Mitroff et al. 2003: 114).

The high-tech company sought to implement lessons learned, in particular against a:

Pathogen it [had] identified [that] was the possibility that a disgruntled employee or supplier would deliberately introduce faulty components into a product. As an inoculation, the company stipulated that executives must determine if product failures had been deliberately caused, once customers reported a certain number of them. In addition, products that had not been shipped would be quarantined until the inoculation had been administered (Mitroff et al., 2003).

This author appreciates, and finds inspiring, the use of the term 'pathogen' here and the referencing of inoculation – but the potential power of the analogy is hampered. In particular, having a process that depends on receiving alerts from customers who have received faulty products is deeply unsatisfactory. This would not meet Machiavelli's requirement for early warning. Further, the term 'inoculation' is not applied in a reliable way. Inoculation is preventative – and inoculation would not solve the problem of the introduction of faulty components, instead costly re-work or even replacement of existing, unshipped, stock would be needed. In short, the use of the analogy was arguably superficial and lacking in ambition.

Another publication, also from 2003, explored the idea of a corporate immune system (CIS). Simmons, writing in the *Illinois Law Review*, immediately disappoints in stating that 'the monitoring board, compliance and risk management systems, compensation, and an enhanced chief legal officer (CLO) role — [are to be] collectively known as the "Corporate Immune System" (CIS)' (2003: 1132). This use of the analogy does not hold up either. A pot pourri of structures, systems and officers cannot be a corporate immune system because they are not the entirety of the corporate body. They comprise parts of the overall organizational organism, but one cannot have a creature which is both a creature and not and with an immune system that works in the creature 'bit' but not the rest. The whole point of systems of systems is that they are total.

The author continues to run with elements of the analogy proposing, for example, that when corporate governance fails – "external regulation, functioning like drugs and antibiotics, will not have its intended impact on corporate opportunism and malfeasance" (CIS, 2003.: 1133). The discipline of this analogical reference is breaking down – treatments are proposed for bacteria and unspecified other conditions (by 'drugs'). Slightly more usefully, the author finds that, as with "antibiotics and other medicines, corporate regulations are an external treatment to an already-infected system" (CIS, 2003). This makes some sense: regulatory requirements and interventions are imposed on affected organization(s) – yet it is hard (for this reader at least) to logically characterize fines and other sanctions as being in any way 'like' antibiotics, antivirals or anti-inflammatories. It strikes me that such rules would instead be more like an odd clinical setting where physicians demand that a patient refrain from risky behaviors and employs painful punishments to ensure compliance with those strictures. The article continues for many more pages, but there is no concerted or imaginative effort to explore just how such an immune system works (i.e. what are the bacteria, antibiotics, medicine and how would the 'system' function).

Although using the lexicon of diseases, immune systems and pathogens is very attractive to (and colorful for) politicians and marketing professionals, as one can see - it is not a trivial matter to translate a superficially attractive analogy into practical application. Precisely, the terms are usually used as *similes* (terrorism is 'like' cancer) whilst what is really needed is deep exploitation of the *analogy*: corporate security (and its constituent systems) need to be immune, the challenges are pathogens and pathological, the organizational body has critical organs, nerves, dependencies and protective responses need to be passive and reactive, supplemented by conscious and unconscious direction. All biological organisms are fundamentally open to their environment – although with protective mechanisms (skin, mucous membranes, fur, scales) – just is any organization. Some are perhaps less exposed to dependencies, some more so. But all have 'attack surfaces' on their external edges as well as within (e.g. at the level of the cell).

The remainder of this chapter seeks to do what prior efforts have failed to do: to present the constituent and co-operative elements of the mammalian immune system and demonstrate how direct analogies between those and the functioning of a corporate body can drive the development of corporate immunity to a full spectrum of risks pertaining to cyber, blended threats and other forms of challenge to corporate security.

THE AUTHOR'S EXPERIENCE

The author of this chapter has been involved in research and consultancy on cyber, asymmetric and unconventional threats since 1998 (cf. Hills 2017). After academic training – culminating in a PhD in Social Anthropology, the author led research for the Ministry of Defence's scientific laboratory into the individual and organizational cultural defenses and susceptibilities to Information Warfare (IW) as a driver of decision-making. Ultimately heading a national capability in this area for the United Kingdom, the author was later seconded to the Cabinet Office, developing tools and techniques to test, break and refine plans, policies and procedures. A key requirement of those individuals, teams and capabilities tested was to adapt to unexpected, uncertain or very dynamic scenarios, co-ordinate across silos of information and responsibility and run parallel responses, crisis management, media and other operations whilst delivering strategic objectives.

After a number of years running a private consultancy, the author returned to the academic world in 2010, pursuing research, supervision of Masters and Doctoral students and working with government and commercial stakeholders and clients.

TOWARDS IMMUNITY FOR A CORPORATE BODY

How Does an Immune System Provide 'Always On' Protection?

An immune system is a complex and highly effective capability providing constant – 'always on' - protection to the organism which is dependent on it. An immune system is best thought of as a 'system of systems' which generates layers of security to an animal. This chapter advances an even more holistic interpretation of immunity: where the biological or corporate body can be thought of as needing to be *resistant* to a range of forms and strengths of threat. Some of these risks can simply be avoided by smart decisions, some attacks can be shrugged off, whilst still others require more deep and dynamic action to ensure that immunity is available to *expected* microbes (e.g. as we immunize children against or develop immunity to certain diseases) or that the capability exists to understand and counter novel pathogens (bacteria, viruses, fungi).

At this level – the one at which most uses of the term 'immunity' are employed –organisms become resistant to infection (i.e. invasion) by a microbe through two key routes. The first is the ability of white blood cells to deal with some of these invaders that they encounter directly (i.e. these cells literally engulf and digest an attacking cell or parasite). It is this form and this sub-set of 'immunity' which forms the bulk of the analogy used by previous researchers.

However, there is a second function which is also triggered by a body detecting unwanted biological material and that is the systemic response with which we are anecdotally familiar. Here, specialist cells detect, digest, analyze and signal the susceptibility of the attacker. These cells enable the wider cellular immune response to start producing massive amounts of antibodies to a previously or newly encountered pathogen and efficiently prevent systemic attack by preventing the invaders from binding with the body's cells that it needs to hijack and use to reproduce.

Both of these capabilities have, to this author, clear power in how the analogy could map into an organization and drive incredibly powerful and advantageous behaviors and actions (supported by pre-existing and rehearsed capabilities) to engage, contain and mitigate a risk and reduce damaging effects of it in future. In its most fortunate implementation, the employee(s) who function as a white blood cell detect and destroy a threat which is only present in low volume, thereby avoiding the need for any further commitment of cost and resource. Here, say, a savvy worker might see a risk (e.g. someone planting a hidden camera in a sensitive location on a production line), call security and then they and law enforcement responders deal with the individual and the camera.[1] Even beyond that, though, a slightly wider response would be useful to scan for other cameras previously planted, other devices (hardware or software) that this individual (trespasser, visitor, contractor, employee) or someone associated with them could have inserted within the site(s) of the organization.

A more holistic interpretation of the breadth of the immune system, then, contains a good deal more structures, mechanisms, resources and capabilities than might be expected. These include evolved instinctive behaviors which seek to keep the creature away from harm; barriers of skin or fur to protect fragile surfaces and tissues, reflex actions which cover eyes or withdraw from heat, detection of breach and swelling to reduce ability of microbes to spread from a wound, white blood cells which engulf any foreign or unexpected matter; specialist cells which analyze microbes to reproduce or invent antibodies and, of course, systemic responses which enhance disease-fighting capability.

The following sections sets out more detail on the immune system of systems and the parallels in terms of organizational capability that are implied by this broader understanding.

Key Capabilities of an Immune System and the Parallels for Organizations

Behaviors and Cognitive Competence to Avoid Risk and Ensure Fitness

Although – to the author's best knowledge – good decision-making is rarely thought of as part of the immune system, it does make sense to extend the notion of immunity. For example, the organization which is committed to outsourcing – perhaps of payroll or logistics – that does not choose the cheapest provider who has a track record of poor service, data protection breaches and so on, is reducing its exposure to risk and thereby enhancing its immunity.

Equally, the fitter, 'healthier' organization will have fewer unmaintained systems, disenchanted employees, approaches to accounting and legal activities which sail close to the wind, and so on. The company that has a committed, cheerful, empowered workforce is more likely to be able to count on those human resources to detect and report unusual activities as well as have them go 'above and beyond' their formal responsibilities in a crisis situation.

For those reasons, this author holds that decision-making and organizational fitness can usefully be regarded as part of the immune system of systems and a glance at the biological parallels reinforces the value of this. For instance, animals have sets of unconscious (instinctive) and conscious actions which serve to keep them away from many dangers. For instance, some mammals and insects are phobic of water; many mammals will flee from an unexpected sound or movement.

Animals also maintain their physical health (and therefore seek to avoid the situation where the immune system may be subject to depressed effectiveness from micro-nutrient or trace element deficiency, or the breakdown of the ability of skin, fur or shell to be a reliable barrier to the intrusion of pathogens. So too the healthy corporate body should not be deficient in any key and enabling resources and capabilities.

In addition, humans and the animals that we husband, should ensure that they are up to date with immunizations which means that (even with exposure to attenuated live vaccines), the side-effects of the immunization are an order of magnitude lower than the effects and risks of contracting the actual disease. Resistance to infection is assured (whe the vaccination is effective) because, having been exposed to an attenuated version of the pathogen, the body develops antibodies to that infection. When the 'real' infection strikes, the body can generate large amounts of effective antibodies to prevent the pathogen from binding to (and therefore reproducing in and killing) cells in the body.

Perception: Nerves, Senses, and Sense-Making

If one takes a typical mammal - a mouse, say – and places it in a contained space, it is swiftly apparent that such an animal is constantly receiving information about the environment in which it finds itself. The eyes, ears, skin and whiskers sense the space that the creature is in – with the brain processing that information so that the animal is aware of its location, what's happening in it and where, for example, food or an easy escape lies. Similarly, the animal feels whether objects are hard or soft, sharp or blunt, thereby being capable of avoiding creating damage through being cut by, say, a thorn or trapped in too small a space.

The animal is also able to sense changes in the temperature of, smell or hear new entrants into that environment. Driven by instinctive drives and assessments, such animals take risks and take actions to preserve themselves. Some such mammals may also be keyed-into their environment such that they understand the alarm calls of other species and take appropriate protective action.

Hard Barriers

The innate aspects of an immune system run from outer layers of an animal through to white blood cells circulating in its blood. Skin, fur, scales are all a barrier to self-inflicted injury and a barrier that makes penetration by a predator or parasite more challenging. In addition, as well as forming an actual hard barrier – surfaces such as skin and fur are also maintained at a specific pH to make that surface inhospitable to bacteria and viruses to colonize and thereby gain access to the body through any scratch or graze or to just reduce its effectiveness.

Limiting Exposure From Breach

Should a breach of the hard barrier occur, through injury or attack, the mammalian body automatically works to limit the extent of the damage. The blood contains clotting agents which are activated by exposure to the air, whilst other cells seek to prevent further blood loss, consume invading pathogens and understand which pathogens are present. Other mechanisms cause inflammation, where swelling 'walls off' the affected area, reduces the ability of blood to escape (in one direction) and for bacteria, viruses and parasites to enter. Together, these form a series of actions which seek to focus and limit the threat and prevent systemic infection or substantial blood loss.

Contain Obvious Threats Encountered

As pathogens enter the bloodstream, being foreign entrants they are likely to be recognized by white blood cells (sometimes known as natural killer cells) as having characteristics (surface proteins) which mark them as needing to be destroyed. These cells engulf the invaders and digest them. This is very useful, but is quite an inefficient way of dealing with a substantial, growing infection – but will handle a small, focused infection where each cell will reliably destroy those that it detects as 'other'. The same process can work for threats which emerge from within the organism.

Capture and Analyze Threats to Prevent Replication, Produce Countermeasures, and Manage Wider Response

Specialist (T) Cells are a key element of the immune system's ability to generate vast amounts of antigens. These cells encounter pathogenic cells or organisms which white blood cells have not destroyed, engulf them and then deconstruct them in order to indicate to other cells what the nature and susceptibility of the attacker is. The system of systems then either re-produces antigens that have previously been encountered, or generates new antigen countermeasures at speed.

These antigens block receptors on the animal's cells to prevent invading ones being able to bind to the cells, enter them and use them to reproduce, for example, exponential numbers of cloned attacker cells.

In addition, these cells recruit helper cells and activate other supporting (systemic) responses, thereby essentially leading to the co-ordination and management of resources throughout the lifecycle of the infection. The recruitment of helper cells, stimulation of the production of more white blood cells, and the triggering of a fever (to make conditions for the attacking pathogens less benign) has this type of cell as leading a targeted attack on the invader and (hopefully) recovery.

Associated with the defeat of the pathogen, the immune system retains a kind of memory of the effective antigens against that attacker – a phenomenon which is harnessed by immunization.

The author hopes that it is becoming apparent to the reader how the characteristics, automatic responses and effective countermeasures in the biological system would be very desirable to have in a bureaucratic one. The table below sets out an initial mapping between the components of a biological immune system, what these deliver and enable for the organism and the corresponding corporate immune system components and their benefits.

Table 1.

Biological Immune System Component	Actions, Effects & Benefits	Corporate Immune System Analogue Component	Actions, Effects & Benefits
Behaviours & Cognitive Competence To Avoid Risk & Ensure Fitness	(Un)conscious actions to minimize risk (e.g. mammals which are innately phobic of water)	The organization (at all levels) is configured to recognize, avoid or mitigate risk caused by its actions and operations (e.g. avoiding dependency on a single platform or supplier).	Having inherently avoided decisions which would increase risk exposure, the corporate body seeks to ensure that it continues to be mindful of the consequences of poor decisions (at whatever level) which might lead it to be susceptible to avoidable hazard.
	Maintain mental and physical health	Ensuring the corporate body is appropriately resourced, rehearsed and competent in sharing information, escalating reports, communicating decisions.	The socio-technical elements of the organization must be configured to be in a good condition on a daily basis, both leading to avoiding risk but also therefore capable of good performance under challenging circumstances.
	Opt-in to immunizations and guarded exposure at appropriate time to develop resistance.	A organization has ensured that it has practiced response to an identified threat, learned lessons for specific scenarios and enabled use in transferable situations	In learning from incidents, near misses and exercises, any corporate body enhances its ability (at all levels) to have near instant-immunity to many attacks which would challenge the unprotected.
Perception: Nerves, Senses & Sense-making	A suite of sensors to perceive the environment, linked to a sense-making function to detect & avoid risk. Notice changes of temperature or approach of a predator	Business intelligence, health and safety, security and other functions sense the external and internal environment to understand dynamic risks, avoid them and manage protective security levels.	The business or public sector organization is cognizant of changes in its current and emerging environments (inside and outwith the perimeters) that indicate changing status of risks.
	Reflex actions encountering sharp or hot objects	Instant ability to react to a situation which presents unexpected risk, without reference to strategic management, including protective actions in face of detected attempt to exploit.	Good decisions made at the lowest possible level to move away from or deploy shields against a suddenly detected risk or threat.

continued on following page

Table 1. Continued

Biological Immune System Component	Actions, Effects & Benefits	Corporate Immune System Analogue Component	Actions, Effects & Benefits
Hard Barriers	Skin, fur a barrier to injury and a hostile environment for pathogens: Maintain integrity of barriers to damage	Perimeters (or attack surfaces) which may be physical, cyber or human should be maintained as barriers which are inspected, inhospitable and invulnerable.	Existing and well-known perimeters and attendant security technologies and functions should be subject to scrutiny and 'red team' testing to ensure that they are as robust and complete as is assumed. Testing should include conventional and unconventional strategies and tactics.
Limiting Exposure from Breach	Skin mechanisms seek to swiftly close breaches of an outer layer (clotting), use inflammation to 'wall off' exposure to potential infection and attract cells to deal with any microbial intrusion.	Swift detection of any form of breach should lead to an immediate containment of the ability of the threat to propogate. Relevant resources which are held ready deploy to support the response.	Having detected a failure of a perimeter, the extent of the ability of the breach to be exploited should be limited by individuals and teams working to uncover the extent of penetration and impose hard interventions at the margin of these areas. Technical and other expertise should respond immediately to reinforce effort and apply specific counter-measures.
Contain Obvious Threats Encountered	White blood cells (Natural Killer Cells) – automatically recognize, capture and destroy 'foreign' microbes or internal threats	Individual employees or teams automatically identify unusual behavior or phenomena and act locally to prevent further development or exploitation by the threat.	Deviations from accepted and valued behaviors, standards and activity should trigger positive and immediate involvement by employees and others. Reporting should trigger a wider awareness and provide supportive additional assistance.

OPERATIONALIZING THE ANALOGY: ENABLING CONDITIONS AND CHANGES

Changing Corporate Culture

The following section explores how an organization could operationalize the immune system analogy and some critical conditions which need, in the author's mind, to be in place for there to be a functional immune system. In other words, even when an organization has designed how its corporate immune system will work, there are absolutely critical conditions that must exist to ensure that it can work. For instance, the ability of individuals / teams fulfilling anything like a 'white blood cell function' can only be relied upon if those individuals have the ability to operate without reference to middle or strategic decision-makers in the first instance. They would have to be trusted, expected to work (and used to functioning) on their own with appropriate authority and responsibility.

A good parallel of the unleashed human capability in action is the problem-solving expectation loaded into the personnel of leading companies in the automotive and logistics industries, for example, where the fixing of inefficiencies and overcoming of unexpected risks to delivery are identified and resolved at the lowest possible level (the concept of subsidiarity or mission command). Of course, some companies operate a platinum standard here, where making an aspect of a production line leaner, for instance, is rewarded by paying the identifier of the solution a generous percentage of the savings made (or – who knows? – risks and attendant costs avoided).

It goes without saying, then, that the organizational culture and its top-down appetite to rewarding performance dictates whether or not genuine, subsidiarity can helpfully occur and deliver the organization the competitive advantage and fitness that it could access. Organizations must decide how seriously they take (cyber)security and, if indeed it is taken seriously, how much cash and cultural re-engineering will be invested in completely changing how employees are expected and encouraged to identify, engage, report risk. Such a tailoring of the entire corporate culture – not just an effort to change some corners of an organization or the behaviors of some small numbers of staff.

Integrating Functions

From my professional experience, and ongoing insight from my colleagues and contacts in industry and beyond, there continues to be the preservation of silos of expertise, responsibility, budget and influence. Hence, cyber security is divorced from over aspects of corporate security; business continuity preparations, exercises and board interest relate to specific scenarios rather than generic capabilities. In addition, wider corporate functions such as security, health, safety, human resources, reputation and press management, are almost certainly poorly connected to any crisis management activities and unlikely also to be able to sustain support to lengthy (and complex) processes for which there are likely no easy solutions.

Unlocking Vital Security Information

In addition, each (or between) these functions, there is likely to be data that could form vital intelligence for the enterprise. For example, a very junior line manager fulfilling their human resource responsibilities may be aware of problematic behaviors that are not in line with corporate values and standards. Whilst these may be irritating and annoying to deal with, the fact remains that the behaviors and actions could be a sign of something that bears on the security of the enterprise.

For example, an employee who has been reported for sexist and harassing activities should be regarded as a risk above and beyond the specific, and worrisome, behaviors. The author has encountered cases where such an individual (and information about them) has not been treated as indicative of a potential security, reputational and further risk. In one particular instance, a specialist software engineer was arrested in the process of a criminal investigation. All of the code that this person been writing, for a range of clients and with access to an even wider set of work programs, had to be checked at great expense and risking the confidence and contractual peril of several customers. On investigation, it transpired that there had been low-level sexist comments and harassment and, whilst it was not likely that the individual's criminal associations could have been unearthed – the individual should obviously have been regarded as a more significant insider threat than other employees, further information should have been collected on the individual and their access to any or some systems and work programs should have been curtailed.

Unfortunately, handled at the lowest possible level – the organizational culture 'locked up' vital risk profiling information within its system, not recognizing a pathogen and essentially allowing an insider threat to continue working and – potentially – doing great damage. Reflecting back to the biological parallel once again: "in a number of situations in which certain types of cancer take hold, it appears that the immune system might have failed to realize what was going on and in this sense has let us down by exposing us to the ravages that will follow" (Dwyer 1993: 6). Such a failure is extremely unfortunate in the biological context – unforgiveable in the corporate body. As with a late detection of a malignancy in a person, treatment (chemo- and radio-therapy) *can* be effective, but at the same time is damaging to the organism, expensive and reduces the individual to being capable solely of minimal operation during the time of treatment. At worst, this is an existential threat and, indeed, in the software engineer example provided above – this situation could have been an existential one.

Cultural Values and Standards

So, at the tactical level and in the co-ordination of the strategic response to an emergent risk, all organizations must spell out the expectations, authorities, terms of reference, appetitefor risk, budgetary and other responsibilities to all staff. Even the most junior line manager (and their team members) should understand that they have the ability and capability to detect potential breaches of or appearance of internal malignancies in the corporate immune system, and must act to contain, identify and communicate the presence of this adversary.

Any organization must have a clear set of cultural values and standards that relate to security and risk (here a personnel risk that undermines cyber security and exposes financial, reputational and other elements of corporate value in peril). These values and standards must enable, allow, demand and reward certain behaviors. If information could have been known and could have been acted on – then it is absolutely no defense for the organization and its senior officers to whine that they did not have that information.

CONCLUSION

This chapter has sought to provide the reader with a stimulating, pragmatic and practical description of the systemic and specific characteristics that a business or public-sector organization could adapt from a powerful biological analogy.

The analogy advanced in this chapter – and that culminates in an initial description of a framework to apply the notion to a real-world organization – works because it logically and realistically equates the corporate body with a mammalian one. The immune system, as with the biological version, is the constituting, communicating and critical set of structures and mechanisms which flow through and around the body and ultimately enable that body to function, repair and sustain itself.

The framework summarized in the chapter should not be expected to be (nor judged as) a recipe or blueprint that can be lifted from the page, translated into strategic planning and injected into a business or government setting. Instead, any organization which needs always-on capability should review the suggestions provided, extent and tailor them to fit with the characteristics, structures, existing condition and operating environment(s) that it knows better than anyone. The concept of the corporate immune system is a powerful and useful one, but learning points from it cannot just be 'cherry-picked'; immune systems work because they are systems of systems with mutually interdependent elements.

ACKNOWLEDGMENT

This research received no specific grant from any funding agency in the public, commercial, or not-for-profit sectors. The author acknowledges the support in kind of research remission by the University of Northampton.

REFERENCES

Dwyer, J. (1993). *The Body at War: The Story of Our Immune System*. London: JM Dent.

FirstPost. (2014). *Terrorism is like cancer, history won't forgive us if it is not treated now: Nawaz Sharif*. Retrieved April 25, 2017, from http://www.firstpost.com/world/terrorism-like-cancer-history-wont-forgive-us-treated-now-nawaz-sharif-2014153.html

Hills, M. (Ed.). (2016). *Why Cyber Security is a Socio-Technical Challenge: New Concepts and Practical Measures to Enhance Detection, Prevention and Response*. New York: Nova Science Publishers.

Hills, M. (2017). On Her Majesty's Service (and beyond): Anthropology's Contribution to an Unconventional Career. In J. MacClancy (Ed.), *Anthropology and Public Service: the UK Experience* (pp. 61–78). Oxford, UK: Berghahn.

IBM. (n.d.b). *4 Ways to Build Your Immunity to Cyber Threats*. Retrieved April 26, 2017, from https://securityintelligence.com/events/4-ways-to-build-your-immunity-to-cyber-threats/?cm_mc_uid=36931390999714782651689&cm_mc_sid_50200000=1478265168

IBM. (n.d.a). *IBM Threat Protection System*. Retrieved April 26, 2017, fromhttp://www-03.ibm.com/security/uk/en/threat-protection/

Machiavelli, N. (2003). *The Prince*. London: Penguin Classics. doi:10.1522/cla.man.pri

McGoogan, C. (2017). *Cyber attacks hit half of UK businesses in 2016*. Retrieved 15 May 2017 from http://www.telegraph.co.uk/technology/2017/04/19/cyber-attacks-hit-half-uk-businesses-2016/

Mitroff, I. I., & Alpaslan, M. C. (2003). Preparing for Evil. *Harvard Business Review*. Retrieved 15 May 2017 from www.hbr.org/2003/04/preparing-for-evil

Simmons, O. S. S. (2003). The Corporate Immune System: Governance from the Inside Out. *Illinois Law Review*. Retrieved 15 May 2017 from https://illinoislawreview.org/wp-content/ilr-content/articles/2013/3/Simmons.pdf

Tripwire. (2017). *Insider Threats as the Main Security Threat in 2017*. Retrieved 15 May 2017 from https://www.tripwire.com/state-of-security/security-data-protection/insider-threats-main-security-threat-2017/

van Zadelhoff, M. (2016). *The Biggest Cybersecurity Threats Are Inside Your Company.* Retrieved 15 May 2017 fromhttps://hbr.org/2016/09/the-biggest-cybersecurity-threats-are-inside-your-company

ENDNOTE

1. The author is here thinking of the behavior of animal rights activists and extremists who have planted cameras in facilities where animals are trained for entertainment or processed for food. Anecdotal and other evidence has indicated that some such organisations pay insiders to undertake illegal treatment of those animals once the cameras are in place.

Chapter 4
Business Continuity and Information Systems:
A Systematic Literature Review

L. Turulja
University of Sarajevo, Bosnia and Herzegovina

N. Bajgoric
University of Sarajevo, Bosnia and Herzegovina

ABSTRACT

Considering the expectations of customers on service and information availability 24x7, complete operations suspension in case of adverse events is not an option. Modern businesses have become dependent on their information systems (IS) whose incidents and failures can highly affect business operations. Ensuring continuity in IS is related to the reliable delivery information. In order to lower the negative impact of IS incidents, organizations should get prepared for them. Business continuity management (BCM) is a holistic management approach whose aim is to identify, prevent or mitigate operational risks. BCM consists of business continuity planning (BCP), contingency planning (CP) and disaster recovery planning (DRP). BCP defines the strategies that organizations should implement in order to ensure their survival when a crisis event occurs. The aim of this paper is to identify the relevant elements of continuity in IS.

DOI: 10.4018/978-1-5225-3704-5.ch004

1 INTRODUCTION

Information and knowledge are the main sources of firms' competitive advantage in modern digital era. Customers expect service availability 24x7, therefore, system downtime is not an option. Employees, shareholders and customers expect that the services and information are available throughout the day.However, even minor disaster events or business interruptions can cause irreparable damage to the organization and its image.Especially, the business has become dependent on information technology (IT) and information systems (IS) whose incidents and failures can highly affect business operations. Organizations' business continuity is increasingly vulnerable to IS incidents(Niemimaa, 2017). Despite all the advances in the development of IT, it is certain that it will always be subject of failures as well as attacks. Thus, organizations recognize IS continuity as a key information management issue (Järveläinen, 2013). In order to lower the negative impact of IS incidents, organizations should prepare for them. This is why the concept of business continuity management (BCM) gained in importance. It was largely neglected until the moment when the Y2K problem showed the possible impact of infrastructure flaws of information technology. The main goal of BCM is to enable organizations providing an acceptable level of services to all stakeholders, including customers and other business partners, even in the case of certain unforeseen circumstances that can happen. The process itself involves the development, maintenance, implementation and management of business continuity plans. Therefore, many scholars and practitioners agree that BCM should be an essential part of any contemporary organization's information management(Bajgoric & Moon, 2009).

Business continuity management encourages flexibility in the business in terms of responses to operational challenges and threats by ensuring maximum operational efficiency of critical business processes. Organizational culture must encourage employees to be aware of everyday dangers and ensure that each employee is responsible for reducing the risk. Thus, King (2003) introduced a term of *business continuity culture* and highlighted the fact that "*If you fail to plan, you will be planning to fail*".

The main objective of this chapter is to improve the understanding of continuity planning for information systems in organizations. Specifically, the aim is to identify common methodologies, risks, drivers, inhibitors as well as phases of continuity planning for information systems. In this regards, the following research questions are defined: i) What are the most common methodologies of IS continuity?; ii) What are the most common risks of IS continuity?; iii) What are the most common key drivers of IS continuity? iv) What are the most common inhibitors for IS continuity?;and v) What are the stages/phases of IS continuity planning?

In order to address these questions, a systematic literature review methodology will be employed. Similar research has been conducted by Niemimaa (2015) who reviewed the multidisciplinary literature on BC from an IS perspective guided by the question: "*how organizations can prepare for and respond to IS incidents*?". His main conclusion is summarized through four themes: i) social aspects as IS continuity enabler; ii) technology as IS continuity enabler; iii) salience of IS continuity; and iv) models that improve IS continuity.

The chapter is structured as follows. First, the concept of BCM is presented prior to the presentation of the BCP. Second, systematic literature review (SLR) methodology is discussed in regard the conducted steps. Finally, results discussion is provided using narrative method (Wahono, 2015).

2 BUSINESS CONTINUITY MANAGEMENT

Organizations' strategic plans are mainly focused on how organizations can improve organizational performance through clear understanding of their competitive, political and organizational environment. Nowadays, planning responses to the events that could interrupt normal operation and which pose a threat to business are becoming more important tasks. However, given the expectations of customers in terms of availability of services, it is clear that business continuity management should be a part of the firm's strategic orientation. Without the operational continuity, critical business functions may be endangered, as well as the reputation of the organization. Business continuity helps to preserve organizational value. An organization's capability to resist the crisis or to recover quickly and minimize losses is what is called the value preservation(Swartz, Herbane, & Elliott, 2004). Value preservation is background capability of BCM that provides stable operation and affect the competitive edge. Swartz et al. (2004) pointed out that it cannot be suggested that BCM necessarily leads to a competitive advantage, but without BCM, organization is exposed to increased threats and uncertainty. Thus, the potential contribution of BCM in an organization is that it presents an essential item in preserving the values of the organization because it helps organization to mitigate the risk of disruptions in business operations (Peterson, 2009).

BCM should ensure that an organization has response to major disturbances that threaten its survival. It is about managing the processes, resources and systems in the event of a disaster. In addition, it addresses connecting, planning and controlling the various elements of the business practice in a unique way prior, during and after crisis or disaster. This concept offers organizations strategic direction and assumes the operational framework for planning, inspection, testing and improving the business when faced with an incident. Business continuity management refers to the socio-technical approach, in which the emphasis is on preparation for possible continuity problems whose objective is to identify potential risks and avoid, minimize or prepare for them so as to continue business processes and services without interruption (Järveläinen, 2012). BS25999-1[1] defined BCM as:

a holistic management process that identifies potential threats to an organization and the impacts to business operations that those threats, if realized, might cause, and which provides a framework for building organizational resilience with the capability for an effective response that safeguards the interests of its key stakeholders, reputation, brand and value-creating activities.

Herbane (2010) identified the development phases of BCM, from disaster recovery planning (DRP), business continuity planning (BCP) to BCM. Basically, DRP and BCP are elements of BCM together with contingency planning (CP). Botha & Von Solms (2004) explained the relationship between BCP, DRP and CP as it is shown in Figure 1. BCM has evolved from the notion of disaster recovery planning, combining practices from risk, crisis and supply chain management(Järveläinen, 2013).

When it comes to the IS continuity, Niemimaa (2017) identified sometrends in the literature. First group of scholars suggest to utilize technology to improve reliability and availability of technology, thus improving the business continuity of technology supported operations and processes.Second group of scholars suggest approaches of methodological steps for crafting thorough plans that should govern organizational preparations and recovery actions.However, despite the technological improvements and plans, in the end, it is people who deal withbusiness continuity. Thus, social aspect of business continuity is important aspect as well, or the issues related to how the social dynamics shape the IS continuity process

3 BUSINESS CONTINUITY PLANNING

Business Continuity Planning (BCP) is the process of business continuity management (BCM), which defines the strategies that organizations should implement in order to ensure its survival when an crisis event occurs causing disruption of normal business operations and to mitigate the impact on the organization (Swartz et al., 2004). There is no single recommended plan for business continuity. Instead, organizations need to develop a comprehensive BCP based on its unique situation (Cerullo & Cerullo, 2004).

Disasters and crises are a continuous risk for normal operation of the organization. To mitigate the impact of such events, it is necessary to develop different types of scenarios of events that may affect the business continuity and business continuity plans, where for each scenario one or more strategies could be developed.In view of the above explanations, BCP can be defined as the complete process of developing measures and procedures to ensure the readiness of the organization in the event of a disaster. This includes ensuring that the organization will be able to effectively respond to disaster and that its critical business functions can continue to take place as usual.

In order to properly understand the concept of business continuity planning, it is necessary to address the following items:

- Definition of disaster/crisis; and
- The two aspects of BCP: i) contingency planning; and ii) disaster recovery planning;

Crisis can be defined as "*a low probability, high impact event that threatens the viability of the organization and is characterized by ambiguity of cause, effect and means of resolution, as well as by a belief that decisions must be made quickly*" (Taylor, Dani, & Deep, 2010). In other words, crisis relates to situations featuring severe threat, uncertainty, and sense of urgency (Rosenthal & Pijnenburg, 1991). In this regard, it can be concluded that the crisis or disaster event that: a) threaten to some aspect of the organization security and its operations; and b) it requires special measures to be taken to get processes back to normal functioning.

It is necessary to ensure that, in the event of unforeseen circumstances, organizations continue business as usual, or at least at the certain acceptable level. That is the issue of contingency planning. The objective of contingency planning is to define measures for the continuation of operations in the disaster event until it comes to the recovery phase. It can be defined as the process of testing the key organizational functions identifying potential disaster scenarios and the development of methods to solve these problems (Rubin, 1999). Contingency planning represents processes of the organization or business unit that are used in response to the emerging disaster; may include procedures, an alternative location to perform activities or alternative resources.

Finally, business processes as well as information technology should be returned in similar condition that preceded the disaster.Disaster recovery planning is the process of preparing for disaster recovery. A proper DRP will enable the organization to restore operations back to normal after a disaster has struck the organization(Vuong, 2015).Botha & Von Solms (2004) noted that there is no precise and clear distinction between the three processes. However, they offered the inter-relationship of these processes as it is presented in Figure 1. Similarly, Jamieson, Smith, & Jamieson (2005) considered that BCP encompasses DRP and both are components of BCM.

Figure 1. The relationship between CP, BCP and DRP (Source: Botha & Von Solms, 2004)

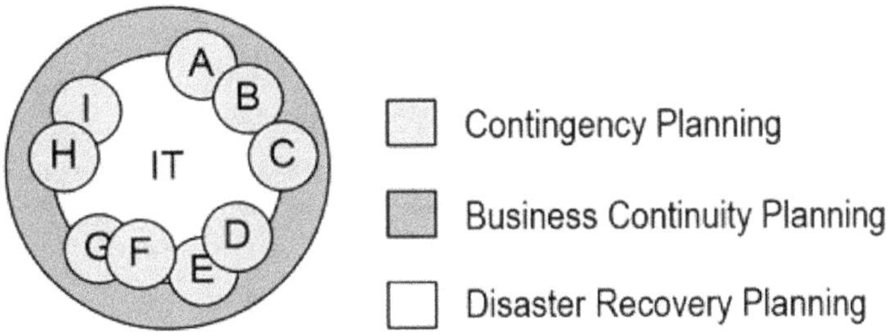

4 SLR METHODOLOGY

This chapter employs asystematic literature review (SLR) in order to address the research topic. . A SLR presents a summary and evaluation of the state of knowledge on a given topic structured to rigorously summarize existing understanding. It involves reviewing studies and papers according to formulated questions and using systematic criteria to select relevant research. In addition, it involves reporting of search terms and criteria for inclusion and exclusion of articles, documenting publications excluded in the analysis along with those included as well as use of quantitative and qualitative analysis of trends in the literature (Ford, Berrang-Ford, & Paterson, 2011).

SLR is conducted in accordance with the steps adopted from Wahono (2015) and depicted in Figure 2. SLR is performed in three stages: planning, conducting and reporting the literature review. At the very beginning, the requirements for a systematic review are identified. The objectives for performing the literature review were presented in the introduction part of this chapter.

After identification of the need for a systematic review regarding business continuity planning regarding information systems, the review protocol was developed. First, research questions are identified. After that, search strategy is developed as well as process of papers selection. Research questions that are identified are:

RQ1: What are the most common methodologies of IS continuity?
RQ2: What are the most common risks of IS continuity?
RQ3: What are the most common key drivers of IS continuity?
RQ4: What are the most common inhibitors for IS continuity?
RQ5: What are the stages/phases of IS continuity planning?

Search strategy refers to the databases as well as search strings that will be used for the publications search. In order to address research questions, ISI Web of

Figure 2. Systematic Literature Review Steps

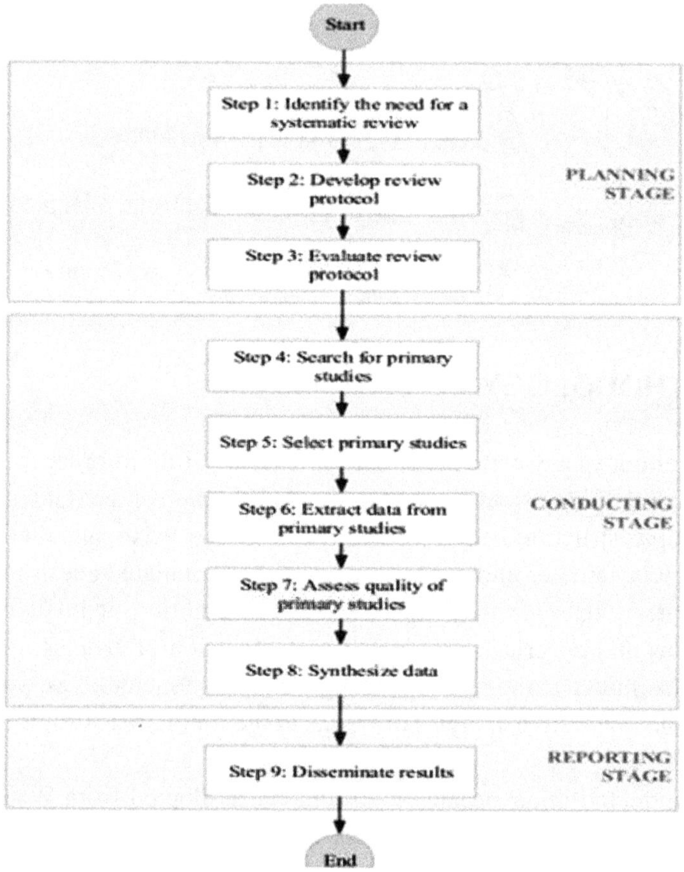

Science, Scopus, Emerald and EbscoHost have been chosen for the search. Relevant publications were identifiedusing the search string "*"business continuity planning" AND "information system*"*". Table 1.presents the search details as well as number of retrieved papers. The search retrieved 49 documents.The search is conducted on April 3rd, 2017.

Finally, the selection of primary papers is conducted taking into account their relevance to the research questions and study similarity. The relevance is assessed by analyzing the papers' objectives and twelve papers are identified: Järveläinen, 2012; Zambon, Bolzoni, Etalle, & Salvato, 2007;Jamieson et al., 2005; Dynes, Pixley, & Madory, 2009; Pinta, 2011; Halliday, Badenhorst, & von Solms, 1996; Ma, Johnston, & Pearson, 2008; Bajgoric, 2014; Bajgoric & Moon, 2009; Singh, Gupta, & Ojha, 2014; Chander, Jain, & Shankar, 2013; Peterson, 2009. The data extraction was conducted to gather data from the primary papers needed to answer

Table 1. Publications Search Details

Source	Search Phrase	Search Filter	Excluded	Number of Papers
ISI Web of Science	"business continuity planning" AND "information system*"	Topic	1 case study	2
Scopus	"business continuity planning" AND "information system*"	Article title, abstract, keywords. Conference papers and articles.	5 medicine articles and 1 case study	25
Emerald	"business continuity planning" AND "information system*"	Articles and chapters		20
EbscoHost	"business continuity planning" AND "information system*"	Academic Search Complete Academic Journals		5
- Duplicates (papers appear in both Scopus and Emerald)				3
			Total	49

the research questions. The goal of data synthesis is to aggregate evidence from the selected studies for answering the research questions. The narrative synthesis method was used (Wahono, 2015) with the descriptive methodology.

5 SLR RESULTS DISCUSSION

All 49 documents were reviewed in terms of objectives, methodology and findings. For some of them, only abstract was available, so conclusion is made based on it. The review is presented in the table which is given in the attachment of this chapter. The main conclusions of the literature review can be presented as follows:

- Papers dealing with this topic are mainly conceptual, or papers whose methodology is based on the literature review, and a number of papers with the case study methodology. Only a small number of papers used other qualitative and quantitative methodology.
- The objectives that dominate in the reviewed papers are: the presentation and explanation of the concept;to offer better understanding;to make framework proposal: or to present or identify methodologies for the issue of IT security, business continuity management etc.

A narrative overview of the primary papers is presented below in order to address the research questions.

5.1 Business Continuity and Information Systems

IT and IS incidents and failures can highly affect business operations which resulted with the higher awareness of IS continuity as a key information management issue (Järveläinen, 2013). Ensuring continuity in IS is related to the reliable delivery of data and information. In order to lower the negative impact of IS incidents, organizations should prepare for them. Zambon, Bolzoni, Etalle, & Salvato (2007) pointed out that BCP for information systems is particularly challenging, because it has to take into consideration the numerous interdependencies between the IT assets present in an organization. BCP in this connection refers to developing and implementing a strategy to manage potential harmful threats to the information systems (Zambon et al., 2007).

Jamieson, Smith, & Jamieson (2005) considered business continuity in relation to IS as:

The protection of information systems against unauthorized access to or modification of information whether in storage, processing, or transit, and against denial of service to authorized users, including those measures necessary to detect, document, and counter such threats.

A BCP refers to the process of planning to create a state of readiness that will provide an immediate response to a disaster affecting a business unit or the IT environment of an organization. An integral part of the BCP is CP as well as DRP which refers to the procedures of management and recovery of the critical IT services of an organization(Jamieson et al., 2005). Zambon et al. (2007) stated that DRP's main task is to define *recovery time objectives* (RTOs) or the maximum acceptable downtime to guarantee the business continuity. RTO should be defined for all IT assets supporting business activities for which is necessary to ensure continuity. The core applications and IT dependent devices needed to be prioritized as well (Dynes et al., 2009). At the other side, *recovery point objective* (RPO)implies the maximum acceptable level of data loss (Pinta, 2011).

Halliday, Badenhorst, & von Solms (1996) citied that the two very important aspects of IT areessential to the successful organization's operation: availability and functionality.Availability enables organization to perform its activities while functionality enables performing its operations correctly.

5.2 BCM/BCP Methodologies

There are several methodologies available to carry out a BCP for IS. Most of them rely on the standard BS25999 that provides guidelines to understand, develop and implement a BCP(Zambon et al., 2007; Pinta, 2011). However, Jamieson et al. (2005)considered the business continuity and information systems issue addressing ISO/IEC 17799information technology code of practice for information security management whichprimarily refers to information and systems security, but it includes sections on BCP as well. Furthermore, Peterson (2009) provides a list of documents that have a greater context of information security but they contain elements that are frequently referenced in regard to BCM: PAS56, BS25999 (1 & 2), NFPA1600, ISO 27001/27001, and NIST 800-34. These documents could make a starting framework or model for BCM planning. In addition, Ma, Johnston, & Pearson (2008) listed GASSP, a joint international effort between ten countries to develop a set of rules, practices, and procedures to achieve information integrity, availability, and confidentiality; as well as FIPs PUBs that that provide guidelines that are mandatory for government agencies, but optional for the private sector.

The main conclusion is that there is no one unique methodology but organizations should choose and develop it based on its size and security issues. The most of the methodologies are based on the mentioned documents and standards with the BS25999 as the most dominant one.

5.3 Key Risks

Bajgoric & Moon (2009)identified following factors affect the level of BC:data availability; application availability;networking reliability;operating system's reliability, availability and scalability; andserver hardware reliability, etc. Furthermore, Halliday et al. (1996)classified risks in accordance with their primary effect on one of the following: availability of information systems and computer resources; integrity of information; confidentiality of information. For each risk, likely causes; expected frequency; impact on a business process; and growth factor should be recorded. In addition, frequency of past occurrences; and probability of future occurrences should be identified, as well as the prioritization of risks and the recommendation and selection of appropriate security controls (Halliday et al., 1996).

Based on this, Halliday et al. (1996) proposed bubble chart with risk/control measures presented in Figure 3.:

- **First Quadrant:** Accept/retain risks presents the risks that normally have a very low frequency and impact.

Figure 3. Recommendation and selection of countermeasures (Halliday et al., 1996)

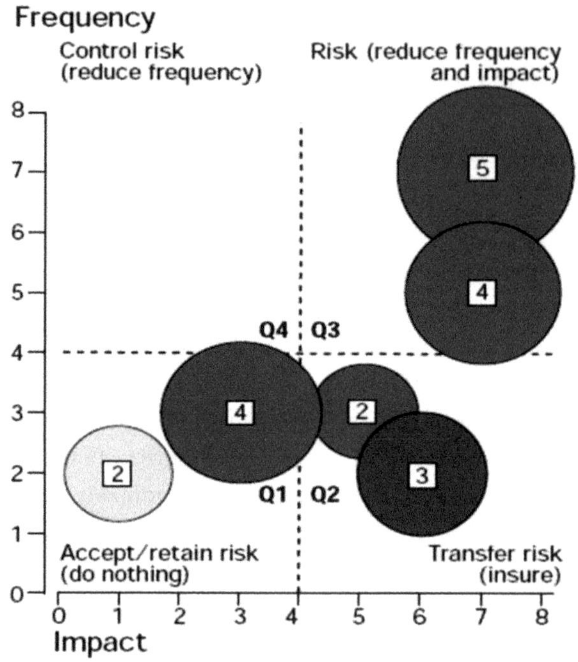

- **Second Quadrant:** Transfer risks presents the risks that have a very high impact and a low frequency and they are totally unpredictable and the losses they cause are generally uncontrollable. The example of these risks are fire, floods, terrorism etc.
- **Third Quadrant:** Avoid/prevent risks presents the most critical risks as they have both a high impact and high frequencyand may be too expensive to insure against. Examples are fraud, theft of hardware or information etc.
- **Fourth Quadrant:** Control risks refers to the risks that normally have a high frequency and a low impact and are management problems. Examples of risks are errors and omissions or virus attacks.

5.4 Key Drivers

Jamieson et al. (2005) identified following key drivers for IS security in relation to BCP: active support of senior management;commitment of funding;protection of information assets; statutory / legislative requirements; staff awareness & training;maintain integrity of electronic records; negative experiences can drive change; andcompliance with standards e.g. ISO/IEC 17799:2001. Furthermore, Singh, Gupta, & Ojha (2014) proposed ten management factors that address organizational information security: top management support; information security policy; information security training; information security awareness; information security culture; information security audit; information security management best practices; asset management; information security incident management; and information security regulations compliance. In addition, Chander, Jain, & Shankar (2013) found very similar drivers of IS security: top management commitment; identification and classification of information assets of organization; technological tools and solutions; providing is policies and procedure; providing is organizational structure and resources; awareness, education and training of stakeholders; motivation, reward and punishment; physical and environmental security of organization; is audit, testing and certification; compliance to legal and regulatory provisions; incident management, business continuity planning and disaster recovery; and developing IS culture in the organization.

Based on this, it can be concluded that the most significant driversof IS security and IS continuity, among others, are:

- Management commitment and support – management should actively support security within the organization through direction, demonstrated commitment, explicit assignment and acknowledgment of IS responsibilities (Chander et al., 2013).
- Policies and procedures – organizations should develop policies and procedures to improve security (Jamieson et al., 2005).
- Awareness – it is important for organizations to make employees realize the importance and benefits of continuity programs. Organisations should communicate to employees about organizational BCP and their roles and responsibilities (Singh et al., 2014).
- Compliance to legal and regulatory provisions – conducting internal as well as external IS audit is important for an organization to check the compliance of its security policies, guidelines and procedures (Singh et al., 2014).

5.5 Key Inhibitors

Jamieson et al. (2005) identified following key inhibitors for IS security in relation to BCP:

- Lack of management awareness;
- Lack of security awareness and training for all staff;
- Lack of allocated funds due to low priority;
- No negative experiences so it is assumed that everything is ok;
- Resistance to set up a uniform user interface across the organization;

- Lack of consistency of risk management processes across the breadth of organization;
- Expectation of users to be able to access all information when they want; and
- Securityperceived as hindering productivity.

In conclusion, the key inhibitors are the opposite behavior of the key drivers: the lack of management commitment, the lack of policies and procedures, the lack of awareness, non-compliance with the legal and regulatory provisions, etc.

5.6 Steps of BCM

Peterson (2009) identified following guidelines for the information systems security management topic of BCP that can be considered as steps: establish business case and business metrics for BCM and DRP;identify, quantify, and mitigate risk;make the DRP/BCM distinction clear to executives;take a combined approach toward the BCM and DRP projects to eliminate rework;include planning for voice and data network survival and an emergency contact as part of the enterprise BCM and DRP;understanding business;formulating continuity strategies;developing the response;implementing an action plan; andtesting the plan, maintenance, and auditing. However, Pinta (2011) addressed the steps and the procedure of BCM in accordance with the BS25999 and the process is called the business continuity life cycle: understanding the organization; determination of BCM strategy; development and implementation of BCM; and testing, maintenance and revision of BCM. Given the importance of BS2599 standard and its focus on the BCM, these steps could be accepted as best practice (citied in Table 2.). That is, BS2599 consists of two parts: *BS 25999-1:2006 Code of practice for business continuity management* that establishes the general principles, terminology and recommendations for implementation of the BCM in an organization: and *BS 25999-2:2007 Specification for business continuity management* that describes the requirements for certification of business continuity management and requirements that can be objectively and independently audited (Pinta, 2011).

In addition to the identified primary papers, Niemimaa (2017) addressed the IS continuity and proposed the three phases of continuity process: preparing for incident; coping with the mitigating impact of incident; and recovering from incident. This process is presented in Figure 4. Preparing for IS incidents is related to the challenges of initiating projects to improve organizational preparations and to motivate employees; to estimating the business impact of IS incidents; to the implementation of agreed measures as well as enhancement of awareness. Coping with and mitigating the impact of IS incidents is related to the detection as well as

Table 2. BCM steps – based on Pinta (2011)

1. Understanding and awareness activities in the organization	Statement and willingness of management to implement the project, determine the structure of the project and way of its leadership.
	Identification of key processes, resources and critical activities of an organization that directly affect business continuity and delivery of products or services to the customer.
	Business impact analyses (BIA) whose aim is to prioritize functions and applications. For each critical function are defined two values: *Recovery Time Objective* (RTO), which represents the maximum acceptable amount of time to restore function; and the *Recovery Point Objective* (RPO) indicating the maximum acceptable level of data loss. In other words, in this phase, *maximum tolerable period of disruption* (MTPD) and *maximum tolerable data loss* (MTDL) will be defined.
	Threat analysis should be conducted in a way to forecast potential threats, along with detailed specifications of the individual steps of recovery.
	Risk assessment is the quantitative or qualitative determination value of risk associated with specific situations and documented threats. Quantitative risk assessment requires calculation of two components: • the risk and size of potential losses, • the probability that the loss occurs.
	Selection of appropriate risk management measures to reduce their probability of occurrence, time minimizing disruption and impact on critical processes of the organization.
2. Determination of BCM strategy	The aim of this phase is to establish such procedures under which an organization would be able in the shortest possible time to react to a certain incident, maintain control over the situation and ensure the required level of continuity of critical activities. Scenarios to consider: • physical presence; • human resource lack; • technology failure; • service provider failure.
3. Development and implementation of BCM	This phase is about establishment and implementation of the plans as well as definition of authorities and responsibilities: crisis team; coordination team; and operational team.
4. Testing, maintenance and revision of BCM	The objective of this step is to create a testing program which is consistent with the subject of business continuity plan.

reaction and contamination of IS incident. Finally, recovering from IS incident is related to the recovery and incidents review (Niemimaa, 2017).

Figure 4. IS continuity process (Niemimaa, 2017)

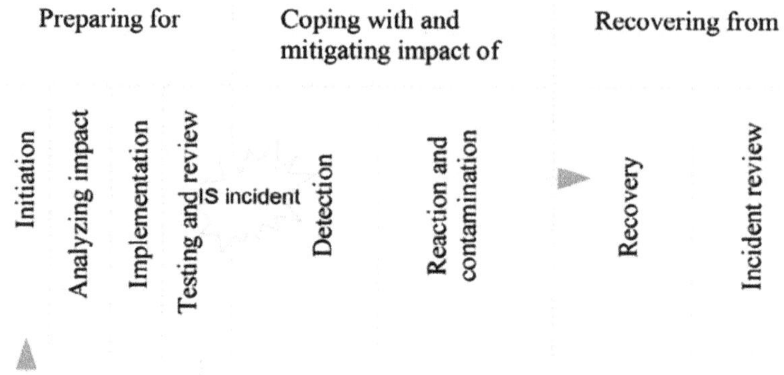

6 CONCLUSION

The purpose of this chapter is to improve the understanding of continuity planning for the information systems (IS) in organizations through critical review by means of a systematic literature review (SLR) methodology. SLR is conducted in accordance with the steps adopted from Wahono (2015). The narrative synthesis method was used with the descriptive methodology. Continuity in IS is related to the security and risk management issues of information systems. It refers to the protection of information systems against unauthorized access to or modification of information whether in storage, processing, or transit, and against denial of service to authorized users, including those measures necessary to detect, document, and counter such threats. This chapter addressed the methodology, risks, drivers, inhibitors and steps of IS continuity planning. The main conclusion on methodologies is that there is no one unique methodology but organizations should choose and implement it based on its size and security issues. The most of the methodologies are based on the mentioned documents and standards with the BS25999 as the most dominant one. Key risks can be analyzed within the Halliday et al. (1996) bubble chart where four types of risk according to needed measures are identified: accept/retain risks; transfer risks; avoid/prevent risks; and control risks. Most significant drivers of IS security and IS continuity, among others, are: management commitment and support; policies and procedures; awareness; and compliance to legal and regulatory provisions. The key inhibitors are the opposite behavior to the key driver activities: the lack of management commitment, the lack of policies and procedures, the lack of awareness, non-compliance with the legal and regulatory provisions, etc. Pinta (2011) addressed the steps and the procedure of BCM in accordance with the

BS25999 and the process is called the business continuity life cycle: understanding the organization; determination of BCM strategy; development and implementation of BCM; and testing, maintenance and revision of BCM. At the other side, Niemimaa (2017) addressed the IS continuity and proposed the three phases of continuity process: preparing for incident; coping with the mitigating impact of incident; and recovering from incident.

REFERENCES

Arduini, F., & Morabito, V. (2010). Business continuity and the banking industry. *Communications of the ACM*, *53*(3), 121–125. doi:10.1145/1666420.1666452

Bajgoric, N. (2014). Business continuity management: A systemic framework for implementation. *Kybernetes*, *43*(2), 156–177. doi:10.1108/K-11-2013-0252

Bajgoric, N., & Moon, Y. B. (2009). Enhancing systems integration by incorporating business continuity drivers. *Industrial Management & Data Systems*, *109*(1), 74–97. doi:10.1108/02635570910926609

Baskerville, R., & Sainsbury, R. (2005). Securing against the possibility of an improbable event: Concepts for managing predictable threats and normal compromises. In *4th European Conference on Information Warfare and Security 2005, ECIW 2005* (pp. 29–38). Academic Press.

Bell, R., & Gomez, E. A. (2011). Business Continuity for Small Business Owners : Do the Tools Fit Their Need?. *Proceedings of the 8th International ISCRAM Conference – Lisbon, Portugal, May 2011*, 1–5.

Beranek, L. (2011). Risk analysis methodology used by several small and medium enterprises in the Czech Republic. *Information Management & Computer Security*, *19*(1), 42–52. doi:10.1108/09685221111115854

Blos, M. F., Quaddus, M., Wee, H., & Watanabe, K. (2009). Supply chain risk management (SCRM): A case study on the automotive and electronic industries in Brazil. *Supply Chain Management: An International Journal*, *14*(4), 247–252. doi:10.1108/13598540910970072

Botha, J., & Von Solms, R. (2004). A cyclic approach to business continuity planning. *Information Management & Computer Security*, *12*(4), 328–337. doi:10.1108/09685220410553541

Braun, T., & Martz, B. (2007). Business Continuity Preparedness and the Mindfulness State of Mind. *AMCIS 2007 Proceedings*. Cerullo, M. V., & Cerullo, M. J. (2004). Business Continuity Planning: A Comprehensive Approach. *Information Systems Management, 21*(3), 70–78.

Chander, M., Jain, S. K., & Shankar, R. (2013). Modeling of information security management parameters in Indian organizations using ISM and MICMAC approach. *Journal of Modelling in Management, 8*(2), 171–189. doi:10.1108/JM2-10-2011-0054

Chen, J. (2009). An exploratory study of alignment ERP implementation and organizational development activities in a newly established firm. *Journal of Enterprise Information Management, 22*(3), 298–316. doi:10.1108/17410390910949733

Choudhuri, B., Maguire, S., & Ojiako, U. (2009). Revisiting learning outcomes from market led ICT outsourcing. *Business Process Management Journal, 15*(4), 569–587. doi:10.1108/14637150910975543

Cigolini, R., Pero, M., & Sianesi, A. (2016). Reinforcing supply chain security through organizational and cultural tools within the intermodal rail and road industry. *The International Journal of Logistics Management, 27*(3), 816–836. doi:10.1108/IJLM-02-2014-0023

Dinnie, G. (1999). The Second Annual Global Information Security Survey. *Information Management & Computer Security, 7*(3), 112–120. doi:10.1108/09685229910693812

Doomun, M. R. (2008). Multi-level information system security in outsourcing domain. *Business Process Management Journal, 14*(6), 849–857. doi:10.1108/14637150810916026

Dynes, S., Pixley, S., & Madory, D. (2009). Managing risk of IT disruptions in healthcare settings: A continuity of operations planning process. In *15th Americas Conference on Information Systems 2009, AMCIS 2009* (*Vol. 2*, pp. 1360–1373). Academic Press.

Fang, L., Zhang, Y., & Ma, Y. (2005). Business continuity management security module and implementation. *Jisuanji Gongcheng/Computer Engineering, 31*(24).

Finch, P. (2004). Supply chain risk management. *Supply Chain Management: An International Journal, 9*(2), 183–196. doi:10.1108/13598540410527079

Ford, J. D., Berrang-Ford, L., & Paterson, J. (2011). A systematic review of observed climate change adaptation in developed nations. *Climatic Change, 106*(2), 327–336. doi:10.1007/s10584-011-0045-5

Foster, S. P., & Dye, K. (2005). Building continuity into strategy. *Journal of Corporate Real Estate*, *7*(2), 105–119. doi:10.1108/14630010510812530

Halliday, S., Badenhorst, K., & von Solms, R. (1996). A business approach to effective information technology risk analysis and management. *Information Management & Computer Security*, *4*(1), 19–31. doi:10.1108/09685229610114178

Herbane, B. (2010). The evolution of business continuity management: A historical review of practices and drivers. *Business History*, *52*(6), 978–1002. doi:10.1080/00076791.2010.511185

Hesson, M., & Al-Ameed, H. (2007). Online security evaluation process for new e-services. *Business Process Management Journal*, *13*(2), 223–246. doi:10.1108/14637150710740473

Hiete, M., & Merz, M. (2009). An indicator framework to assess the vulnerability of industrial sectors against indirect disaster losses. In *ISCRAM 2009 - 6th International Conference on Information Systems for Crisis Response and Management: Boundary Spanning Initiatives and New Perspectives*. Information Systems for Crisis Response and Management, ISCRAM.

Iwatsuki, K. (2016). *Cyber physical system based on resilient ICT, (2011), 97720J.* Academic Press.

Iyer, R. K., & Bandyopadhyay, K. (2000). Managing technology risks in the healthcare sector: Disaster recovery and business continuity planning. *Disaster Prevention and Management*, *9*(4), 257–270. doi:10.1108/09653560010351899

Jamieson, R., Smith, S., & Jamieson, R. (2005). Key Factors in E-Government Information System Security. *18th BLED 2005 Proceedings*, 1–15.

Järveläinen, J. (2012). Information security and business continuity management in interorganizational IT relationships. *Information Management & Computer Security*, *20*(5), 332–349. doi:10.1108/09685221211286511

Järveläinen, J. (2013). IT incidents and business impacts: Validating a framework for continuity management in information systems. *International Journal of Information Management*, *33*(3), 583–590. doi:10.1016/j.ijinfomgt.2013.03.001

King, D. L. (2003). Moving towards a business continuity culture. *Network Security*, *2003*(1), 12–17. doi:10.1016/S1353-4858(03)00112-0

Kwok, L., & Longley, D. (1999). Information security management and modelling. *Information Management & Computer Security*, *7*(1), 30–40. doi:10.1108/09685229910255179

Lawler, C. M., & Szygenda, S. A. (2007). Realities of disaster recovery: IT systems & disaster preparedness. In *WMSCI 2007 - The 11th World Multi-Conference on Systemics, Cybernetics and Informatics, Jointly with the 13th International Conference on Information Systems Analysis and Synthesis, ISAS 2007 - Proc.* (Vol. 3, pp. 33–40). Academic Press.

Ma, Q., Johnston, A. C., & Pearson, J. M. (2008). Information security management objectives and practices: A parsimonious framework. *Information Management & Computer Security*, *16*(3), 251–270. doi:10.1108/09685220810893207

Martin, N. (2007). The Asian tsunami: An urgent case for improved government information systems and management. *Disaster Prevention and Management: An International Journal*, *16*(2), 188–200. doi:10.1108/09653560710739513

McGovern, T. J., & Samuels, H. W. (1998). Our institutional memory at risk: Collaborators to the rescue. *Campus-Wide Information Systems*, *15*(3), 103–107. doi:10.1108/10650749810227170

Mcmanus, D., Carr, H., & Adams, B. (2011). Wireless on the Precipice: The 14th Century Revisited. *Proceedings of the IADIS International Conference Information Systems 2009, IS 2009*, *54*(6), 138–143. doi:10.1145/1953122.1953155

Mitchell, R. C., Marcella, R., & Baxter, G. (1999). Corporate information security management. *New Library World*, *100*(5), 213–227. doi:10.1108/03074809910285888

Naqvi, S., Dallons, G., & Ponsard, C. (2010). Protecting corporate ICT infrastructures by using digital forensics. *2010 International Conference on Computer Information Systems and Industrial Management Applications, CISIM 2010*, 255–258. doi:10.1109/CISIM.2010.5643653

Nicolle, L. (1999). Countdown to disaster? *Computer Bulletin (London)*, *1*(3), 22–25. doi:10.1093/combul/41.3.22

Niemimaa, M. (2015). Interdisciplinary Review of Business Continuity from an Information Systems Perspective: Toward an Integrative Framework. *Communications of the Association for Information Systems*, *37*, 69–102.

Niemimaa, M. (2017). Information systems continuity process : Conceptual foundations for the study of the " social. *Computers & Security*, *65*, 1–13. doi:10.1016/j.cose.2016.11.001

Noguchi, H., Ohtaki, Y., & Kamada, M. (2015). Design and practice of file backup system taking advantage of remotely distributed campuses. *Proceedings - 2015 18th International Conference on Network-Based Information Systems, NBiS 2015*, 694–697. doi:10.1109/NBiS.2015.105

Okuda, K., Ohashi, M., & Hori, M. (2011). On the studies of the disaster recovery and the business continuity planning for private sector caused by Great East Japan earthquake. In *Communications in Computer and Information Science* (Vol. 219, pp. 14–21). CCIS. doi:10.1007/978-3-642-24358-5_2

Paton, D. (1999). Disaster business continuity: Promoting staff capability. *Disaster Prevention and Management: An International Journal, 8*(2), 127–133. doi:10.1108/09653569910266175

Peterson, C. A. (2009). Business Continuity Management & guidelines. In *Proceedings of the 2009 Information Security Curriculum Development Annual Conference, InfoSecCD'09* (pp. 114–120). Academic Press. doi:10.1145/1940976.1940999

Pinta, J. (2011). Disaster recovery planning as part of business continuity management. *Agris On-Line Papers in Economics and Informatics, 3*(4), 55–61.

Rosenthal, U., & Pijnenburg, B. (1991). *Crisis Management and Decision Making - Simulation Oriented Scenarios*. Springer-Science+Business Media, B. V.

Rubin, H. (1999). Bracing for zero day. *IT Professional, 1*(3), 73–79. doi:10.1109/6294.774957

Šimonová, S., & Šprync, O. (2011). Proactive IT / IS monitoring for business continuity planning. *Ekonomie a Management, 14*(3), 57–65.

Šimundić, S., & Boban, M. (2008). Business Continuity management systems - challenges of management on the way to business success in digital economy. In *MIPRO 2008 - 31st International Convention Proceedings: Digital Economy - 5th ALADIN, Information Systems Security, Business Intelligence Systems, Local Government and Student Papers* (Vol. 5, pp. 53–56). Academic Press.

Singh, A., Gupta, M., & Ojha, A. (2014). Identifying factors of organizational information security management.. *Journal of Enterprise Information Management, 27*(5), 644–667. doi:10.1108/JEIM-07-2013-0052

Swartz, M., Herbane, B., & Elliott, D. (2004). *Business Continuity Management: Time for a strategic role?*. Academic Press.

Taylor, P., Dani, S., & Deep, A. (2010). International Journal of Logistics Research and Applications : A Leading Journal of Supply Chain Management Fragile food supply chains: reacting to risks. *October, 5567*, 37–41.

Vuong, J. (2015). Disaster recovery planning. In *Information Security Curriculum Development Conference 2015* (pp. 1–3). Academic Press.

Wahono, R. S. (2015). A Systematic Literature Review of Software Defect Prediction: Research Trends, Datasets, Methods and Frameworks. *Journal of Software Engineering*, *1*(1), 1–16.

Wan, S. H. C., & Chan, Y. (2008). Improving service management in campus IT operations. *Campus-Wide Information Systems*, *25*(1), 30–49. doi:10.1108/10650740810849070

Wester, R. B. (2006). Emergency preparedness, business continuity, and the new normal. In *1st Joint Emergency Preparedness and Response/Robotic and Remote Systems Topical Meeting* (Vol. 2006, pp. 603–609). Academic Press.

Whitworth, P. M. (2006). Continuity of operations plans: Maintaining essential agency functions when disaster strikes. *Journal of Park & Recreation Administration*, *24*(4).

Yao, X., Turoff, M., & Hiltz, R. S. (2010). A field trial of a collaborative online scenario creation system for emergency management. In *ISCRAM 2010 - 7th International Conference on Information Systems for Crisis Response and Management: Defining Crisis Management 3.0, Proceedings*. Information Systems for Crisis Response and Management, ISCRAM.

Zambon, E., Bolzoni, D., Etalle, S., & Salvato, M. (2007). A model supporting business continuity auditing & planning in information systems. In *Second International Conference on Internet Monitoring and Protection, ICIMP 2007*. Academic Press. doi:10.1109/ICIMP.2007.4

APPENDIX

Review of Collected Papers

Table 3.

Reference	Objective/s	Methodology	Result/s
Finch (2004)	The objective is to determine if large companies increase their exposure to risk by having SMEs as partners in business critical positions in the supply chain and to make recommendations regarding best practices.	Secondary analysis of published and grey literature and case studies. IS environment and risk identification framework is used to structure the review.	Large companies' exposure to risk increase by inter-organizational networking. Furthermore, the risk increase having SMEs as partners. In addition, SMEs increased their own exposure to risk becoming partners in a supply chain. Consequently, business continuity planning is very important for companies that are exposed to inter-organizational networking.
Šimonová & Šprync (2011)	Modeling of monitor overview for the category System, including CPU activity, disc activity, file system usage, system memory usage, and virtual memory usage.	The created model was verified on SW tools OpenEdge.	Paper is focused on usage of SW tools which monitor chosen sources and automatically inform while defined limits exceed.
Arduini & Morabito (2010)	Review of the Business Continuity concept.	Conceptual paper.	Authors presented the basics of Business Continuity concept highlighting the importance of it. At the very beginning, they indicated two main reasons for developing the BC approach in the finance sector: regulations and business specificities. However, at the end, they conclude that that organizations need to adopt the BC approach for strategic reasons because it is increasingly viewed as a driver to generate competitive advantage in the form of resilient information systems and as an important marketing characteristic to attract and maintain customers
Baskerville & Sainsbury (2005)	To explain how decision-making in information security becomes tied to inappropriate assumptions, and how to correctly anchor certain decisions.	Conceptual paper.	The logical basis for decisions about normal compromises shifts from foundations in probability theory to foundations in possibility theory.
Bell & Gomez (2011)	To provide an evaluation of the applicability of PS-Prep (nation's preparedness and resilience) to small businesses, and to provide the needs assessment for parallel research of leveraging the capabilities of a Business Emergency Operations Center (BEOC) in the development of a Virtual Small Business Emergency Operations Center (VSBEOC).	Review paper.	PS-Prep coupled with the capabilities of the BEOC can be leveraged to create a virtual organization that can realize the benefits afforded large organizations, mainly better sense making capabilities and increased shared awareness during emergency response activities.

continued on following page

Table 3. Continued

Reference	Objective/s	Methodology	Result/s
Botha & Von Solms (2004)	Presentation of Business Continuity Planning (BCP) concept	Conceptual paper.	Seven phase BCP methodology is discussed, as well as an implementation method for this BCP methodology. This implementation method simplifies the BCP process for organizations and authors suggest it to be applicable to any continuity planning methodology.
Braun & Martz (2007)	To explore why firms in the financial services industry make varying decisions for business continuity planning.	Mindfulness / mindlessness cognitive processes and decision making theories. Exploratory interviews with management and executives from the financial services industry.	Organizational state of mind and inhibited decision making, coupled with the perceived value and dependency on information technology have a direct relationship with the level of BCP preparedness, in financial institutions.
Dynes, Pixley, & Madory (2009)	Identifying critical applications and formulating plans for organizational and departmental responses in cases of IT and communication failures.	Semi-structured interviews.	Description of the development and use of a process designed to manage the risk to patient safety and clinical operations due to IT and communications failures.
Fang, Zhang, & Ma (2005)	To present a concept of business continuity security management and to give a management module of EDCA in business continuity security.	-	Basing on EDCA module, this paper gives implementation which has good performance and finally discusses the merits and scope of the implementation.
Hiete & Merz (2009)	Development of a conceptual methodology for the assessment of the indirect disaster vulnerability (the susceptibility of production losses due to disasters) of different industrial sectors.	A conceptual indicator framework with empirical testing.	The indicator framework focuses on the industrial vulnerability to primary indirect losses (production losses as a result of the unavailability of necessary input factors due to (i) direct disaster losses, (ii) supply chain disruptions, and (iii) critical infrastructure disruptions.
Iwatsuki (2016)	To describe the propose structure of Cyber Physical Systems CPS in order to realize resilient society.	Conceptual paper.	Conceptual framework of BCP engine to support the resilient society. The configuration of resilient CPS consisting of ICT and physical system is discussed to introduce "autonomous, distributed, and cooperative" structure, where subsystems of ICT and physical system are simultaneously coordinated and cooperated with Business Continuity Planning (BCP) engine, respectively. They proposed the structure and key technology of resilient ICT.
Iyer & Bandyopadhyay (2000)	To describe how health organizations (HCOs) have justifiably become dependent on health management information systems (HMIS) and how these organizations may proactively plan for disasters which can impact on HMIS.	Conceptual paper.	A phased approach, referred to as the disaster recovery and business continuity (DRBC) planning model, is presented as an approach to develop and implement business continuity plans in HCOs.

continued on following page

Table 3. Continued

Reference	Objective/s	Methodology	Result/s
Jamieson, Smith, & Jamieson (2005)	To investigate the key drivers and key inhibitors from an Information System (IS) Security and Business Continuity Management (BCM) perspective.	Qualitative methodology with the Delphi rating technique (forum, focus group, roundtable discussion)	The summary of the main issues across the four focus questions of the forum and follow-up interviews includes the majority of the four following issues: 1. Training; 2. Management Support; 3. Budget / Cost / Resources; and 4. Awareness.
Kwok & Longley (1999)	To develop model to manage organizational information security data and facilitate risk analysis studies.	-	The risk data repository (RDR) computer model is was developed and it provides a form of computer documentation that can assist the security officer to maintain a continuous record of the organisational information security scenario and facilitate system security development, business continuity planning and standards conformance audits.
Lawler & Szygenda (2007)	To review the financial significance of IT systems and business process downtime and observes data that indicates a general lack of business priority and investment in DR and BCP in US businesses.	-	This paper reviews the effects that disasters have on business investment in DR and BCP and provides an analysis of evidence indicating inadequate traditional DR and BCP practices.
Mcmanus, Carr, & Adams (2011)	To analyze solar activity in order to evaluate risk and threats.	Conceptual paper.	3 types of risk strategies and possible responses: i) dependence on single-source wireless communications; ii) dependence on single source electrical power: and iii) failure to prepare globally.
Naqvi, Dallons, & Ponsard (2010)	To highlights the role of digital forensics in the corporate ICT infrastructure.	Conceptual paper.	Framework for embedding digital forensics analysis techniques at various stages of corporate ICT lifecycle is proposed as well as a set of best practices for the corporate ICT security policy.
Nicolle (1999)	To present Y2K and need for BCP.	-	Brief presentation of Y2K.
Noguchi, Ohtaki, & Kamada (2015)	To present a file backup system designed for a university on the basis of its experiences with the 2011 east Japan earthquake.	Paper based on the case study.	They have redesigned the information system for Ibaraki university and implemented a file storage system that keeps the original copy on premise in a campus and its backup copy in one of the other two campuses
Okuda, Ohashi, & Hori (2011)	To present how the fishing industry should be restored and rebuilt after Great East Japan Earthquake on March 2011.	-	Damage of earthquake is reported as well as disaster outlines, the movements toward restoration, reconstruction and how to do the Business Continuity.
Paton (1999)	To present business continuity planning concept.	-	Adopting a human resource perspective, this paper discusses the implications of staff vulnerability, hazard and risk assessment, organizational systems, training and recovery management for disaster business continuity.
Peterson (2009)	To explore information systems security management topic of Business Continuity Management.	Literature review.	Recommended guidelines and trends to consider when developing a business continuity plan strategy.

continued on following page

Table 3. Continued

Reference	Objective/s	Methodology	Result/s
Šimundić & Boban (2008)	To present Business Continuity Planning concept.	Conceptual paper.	Presentation of BCP model as a combination of main processes which are as following: the model analysis, solution design, implementation of the model, testing and organizational acceptance and the maintenance of the mode
Wester (2006)	To present Business Continuity Planning concept.	Conceptual paper.	Presentation of the development and implementation of a concept of operations that can be applied not only to emergency preparedness planning for nuclear facilities, but also to business continuity planning for the organizational entity as a whole.
Yao, Turoff, & Hiltz (2010)	To design, implement, evaluate, and evolve a Web-based group support system to collaboratively design scenarios, particularly those that might be used for planning and training for emergency management.	Qualitative/ quantitative methodology. Scenarios and simulations.	The system is useful to support creation and discussion of emergency scenarios in virtual teams and to share knowledge and experiences among geographically distributed emergency professionals and researchers. It was also found that the system is not hard to learn and use.
Zambon, Bolzoni, Etalle, & Salvato (2007)	Presentation of Business Continuity Planning model.	Conceptual paper.	Model and a tool (can be integrated in COBIT-based risk assessment applications) supporting BCP auditing by allowing IT personnel to estimate and validate the Recovery Time Objectives set on the various processes of the organization is presented.
(Bajgoric & Moon, 2009)	To present a framework for developing an integrated operating environment within an enterprise information system by incorporating business continuity drivers.	Conceptual paper: holistic and top-down approach.	Key disconnection points are identified, where systems integration technologies can be used to integrate platforms, protocols, data and application formats, etc. Downtime points are also identified and explained. A thorough list of main business continuity drivers (continuous computing (CC) technologies) for enhancing business continuity is identified and presented. The
Beranek (2011)	To present risk analysis procedures which have been successfully applied by Czech small and medium enterprises (SMEs).	Conceptual paper (At the end, they indicate that they also conducted a brief survey among the nine SMEs to obtain feedback about the performed analysis.).	Besides using the CRAMM methodology, the authors have created a new method based on combining the BITS and FRAP method and they briefly explained the method steps.
Blos, Quaddus, Wee, & Watanabe (2009)	To identify the supply chain risks in the automotive and electronic industries in Brazil, and to highlight the urgency of supply chain risk management (SCRM) implementation.	Exploratory study methodology (questionnaire - descriptive analysis).	Conclusions such as: there are significant practices to implement SCRM: better supply chain communication, SCRM and business continuity planning training program, and the creation of a chief risk officer position to manage the supply chain risks.
Chander, Jain, & Shankar (2013)	To identify various information security management parameters and develop a conceptual framework for it.	Interpretive Structural Modeling (ISM) and MICMAC Approaches.	A classification of key parameters according to their driving power and dependence which enable information security management in an organization as well as parameters on which management should pay more attention.

continued on following page

Table 3. Continued

Reference	Objective/s	Methodology	Result/s
Chen (2009)	To explore how ERP implementation can facilitate the organization development of new ventures. RQs: What are the appropriate ERP implementation considerations for a newly established firm's growth? How can ERP implementation and organizational development activities be aligned over time?	In-depth case study method.	To leverage the value of ERP system, the implementation should consider the firm's growth stages, the unique industrial characteristics, the influences from the business group, and the alignment of the internal control and audit function, corporate governance, and information technology governance
Choudhuri, Maguire, & Ojiako (2009)	To explore various constructs in ICT outsourcing.	Qualitative: exploratory, descriptive methods of case study approach.	Two themes emerged: i) the critical success parameters associated with ICT outsourcing are a little different from those which are applicable from other ICT-based implementation projects; ii) in some cases, there appears to be major differences between presented theory and actual industry practice as relates to ICT outsourcing.
Cigolini, Pero, & Sianesi (2016)	To study the application of organizational and cultural tools within the intermodal rail and road transport industry. RQs: What organizational and cultural tools do companies use within the intermodal rail and road industry? How do organizational and cultural tools influence security performance? How do environmental factors affect the use of organizational and cultural tools?	Qualitative: Case study and semi-structured interviews	Organizational and cultural tools positively affect SC security performance, by reducing the collusion and operative and planning mistakes which are the cause of manipulation and theft. In addition, such tools mitigate the problems connected to the lack of cooperation and communication between partners and to inadequate partners, which are the cause of delays in the delivery of goods to the final customers.
Dinnie (1999)	Presentation of the results of the second annual Ernst & Young Global Information Security Survey.	Survey, Descriptive analysis	Conclusion consists of several key findings related to the increase security risks and security options.
Doomun (2008)	To evaluate the potential risks and information system security needs when outsourcing takes place and analyze the different security level in outsourcing agreements.	Literature review.	IS security risks can be effectively identified, monitored and evaluated by the concept of a layered security model that fits best in the complex outsourcing domain. There are three levels of security, first guidelines of technical security, second risk analysis and, third compliance and evaluation criteria, including managing information security.

continued on following page

Table 3. Continued

Reference	Objective/s	Methodology	Result/s
Foster & Dye (2005)	To present a framework that will enable managers of corporate real estate to take a more active leadership role in managing business continuity and to move to a strategy and continuity model for managing corporate real estate.	Conceptual paper.	The framework is presented including pre-event, during event and post-event phases, together with prevention, preparedness, response and recovery and restoration roles of managers of corporate real estate.
Halliday, Badenhorst, & von Solms (1996)	To propose IT risk management approach together with the review of current methodologies.	Conceptual paper.	Formalized methodologies were developed to provide a structured approach to IT risk analysis and management.
Hesson & Al-Ameed (2007)	To contribute to making the use of the Dubai e-government services more secure and facilitating the process of introducing new services, while maintaining the integrity and security of the whole system.	Case study, based on the ISO 17799 standard.	The system has achieved its objectives in terms of performance, cost, reliability and flexibility.
Järveläinen (2012)	To understand how managers of IT and information security aim to enhance information security and business continuity management in interorganizational IT relationships, such as outsourcing, cloud computing and interorganizational systems.	Qualitative: explorative study, semi-structured interviews.	Several methods such as contracts, audits and standards were applied to balance power relationships between organizations or transfer responsibilities to other parties. The objectives of these methods are different within organizations.
Ma, Johnston, & Pearson (2008)	To propose a framework for information security management (ISM).	Literature review, conceptual.	The framework is presented including four factors: information integrity, confidentiality, accountability, and availability.
Martin (2007)	To provide a timely consideration of how regional governments in Asia and other national governments around the world collect, manage, and share critical geo-technical information in what is becoming an increasingly global community.	-	Potential research agenda for government warning information systems and management.
McGovern & Samuels (1998)	To explain the problems associated with the continuing reliability of electronic systems at universities.	-	Institutions must develop and exercise appropriate risk management strategies that can respond adroitly to all communities and constituencies served.
Mitchell, Marcella, & Baxter (1999)	To describe an MSc project that aimed to investigate the issues surrounding corporate information security management.	Interview and questionnaire: descriptive analysis.	Firms are not proactively tackling information security management and thus are not prepared for security incidents when they occur. Reasons for this lack of action

continued on following page

Table 3. Continued

Reference	Objective/s	Methodology	Result/s
Singh, Gupta, & Ojha (2014)	To identify management factors that address organizational information security challenges.	Qualitative (keyword analysis and experts' opinion) and quantitative (questionnaire survey) research routes + EFA.	The paper categorizes various organizational ISM functions into ten factors.
Bajgoric (2012)	To define a systemic framework for the implementation of business continuity management.	Conceptual paper: systems approach.	A conceptual framework has been proposed to develop a framework for a systemic implementation of several continuous computing technologies that enhance business continuity (BC) in the form of an "always-on" enterprise information system.
Wan & Chan (2008)	To provide an overview of disaster recovery and contingency planning for digital library systems.	Best practice.	Develops a context for developing business continuity and disaster recovery plans.
Pinta (2011)	To present emergency and recovery plans and setting recovery objectives significantly affecting their efficiency.	-	Emergency and recovery plans presentation.
Wan & Chan (2008)	To present the benefits from implementing IT service management in an organization for managing campus-wide IT operations	Quantitative analysis using real operational data.	This paper highlights the value of effective IT service management, placing particular emphasis on service outsourcing consideration and the mechanism in service-event correlation.
Whitworth (2006)	To present continuity of operations plans.	-	Components of continuity of operations plans include identification of essential functions, establishment of plans and procedures, access to information systems and vital data, provisions for delegation of authority and orders of succession, dispersal of operations across geographical locations with alternate sites, multiple critical personnel to conduct essential functions and redundancy of communications.

[1] BS25999-1 British Standards Institution's Code of Practice for Business Continuity Management

Chapter 5
Always-On Sport Content Multimedia Delivery Over Internet in Croatia

Ivan Kovačević
Hrvatski Telekom d.d., Croatia

Mirjana Pejić Bach
University of Zagreb, Croatia

Božidar Jaković
University of Zagreb, Croatia

ABSTRACT

Multimedia allows and encourages different ways and methods of human sense manipulation using the highest achievement of technological development with the aim of communication, education, or entertainment. The most frequent contents that are transmitted in real time are contents based on voice services, the so-called VoIP services. In order to shed some light to the opportunity of the media delivery of sports content in always-on mode in Croatia the following goals are fulfilled. First, the possibilities of transfer services of multimedia content live via Internet are analyzed. Second, the competitive advantages over the same or similar services and check its influence on the development of society and the general economic activity are examined. Third, habits of potential customers using multimedia services as well as their expectations are analyzed based on the survey research results. Finally, based on this information, the canvas model of providing a service of sport content multimedia delivery in always-on mode in Croatia is developed.

DOI: 10.4018/978-1-5225-3704-5.ch005

INTRODUCTION

Hardly any industry has undergone through so many changes like multimedia, particularly in the last 20-30 years, mainly due to significant development of the Internet and its availability. Technological development and technological innovations provides an availability of multimedia to all users through the Internet regardless of their geographical location.

Multimedia and its content experience adjust daily to the user expectations (Cecchinato, et. al., 2017). Changes and technological advances have been recognized by the advertisers themselves so that the EU Member States recorded growth in Internet advertising 20% per year in the last decade. The cause of such increase is the growth in the number of Internet users, the variety of technological achievements which enables different models of Internet advertising and the increase in number of electronic services, all of which are followed by the progress in the electronic business domain. The subject of this research is the analysis of multimedia content live streaming through the Internet, and analysis of the business model that would be applicable in the Republic of Croatia.

The goals of this chapter are: (1) to analyze the possibilities of multimedia content live broadcasting via Internet, its technological characteristics and customer orientation; (2) to explore the competitive advantages over the same or similar services and check its influence on the development of society and the general economic activity; (3) by using survey research, data of interviewees was collected about their habits of using multimedia services as well as their expectations.

BACKGROUND

In the digital age the mobile phones are the devices that everyone has and use regularly on daily basis. Furthermore, many people are always-on either they are working, communicating, browsing Internet or playing games. These trends are increasing (Baron, 2010, Williams, 2017). Many authors examine mobile phones as mobile TV devices. Chipschase et al. (2004) point out that we could consider mobile phone as tool for sharing. Mobile TV service offer personal experiences and user have choice of selecting the content that they wanted to watch (Koroleva, 2016). According to Kaasinenet. al (2009), the mobile TV broadcasting content already seems to be exciting and attractive to the consumers. Mobile phones are personal gadgets equipped with positioning devices providing location data to services and consumers are also used to interacting with the device (Crnkovic, 2013). Finally, mobile devices provide the consumers with more topical, more local and more personal content than on other media.

Mobile TV services are not yet accepted to the higher extent. There are many of reasons why the launch of different services related to mobile TV around the world has been delayed. Orgad (2009) indicated that the various issues are surrounding technology progress, ranging from the unsustainable business models, and urgent need for relevant regulatory frameworks. Various subjects such as manufacturers and marketing companies, as well as broadcasters, aim to related the new and unknown with the already established, in order to advance the understating of the always-on emerging technologies, as the ascendants of the current familiar and safe social worlds (Orgad, 2009).

According to Fontaine et. al (2010) the circumstances related to the TV industry transfer to the Internet are occurring, with numerous effects to the entire sector. Authors indicate that the typical model will no longer be the exclusive rights model, some of the clients will move on from the traditional networks, and globalization will aims towards the benefit of the major rights holders. However, the TV industry will become of the major players on the Internet.

Raats et al. (2016) discuss the importance of public funding for the development of the infrastructure needed to support the market of multimedia streaming, since the financing of multimedia production is changing rapidly, especially at the smaller markets. In order to increase the financial viability of multimedia business model, Du et. al (2015) propose a prefetching scheme. Katusic, et. al (2013) in their paper examine machine to machine systems and their importance on mobile networks. They stress out that main aids of machine to machine communication are automated services and data management, remote diagnostics and real-time statistics.

Rarely did something have such an influence like the Internet had on the transfer of information and multimedia in general. So called ‘millennials’ have different expectations and learning styles, that will become predominant in the “always on” world of massive communication over the Internet. Baird & Fisher (2005) stress that these group of users take into account the opportunity to use the content in a self-paced manner, and including different forms of social media. Through the 20th century, domination of multimedia, which for many years held the television, slowly but surely is endangered by the Internet that is taking over more and more users. Young people want to have a freedom of choice which refers to choosing content and terms of watching different from the one that the television offers.. All the traditional forms of transferring multimedia’s content, television, radio and newspapers have one characteristic which is common for all of them and it is a one-way transfer from sender to user. Using new technologies, especially Web 2.0 technology, the two-way communication between the sender and the user became available (Roblek et al., 2013). Interactivity, which in some cases gives the ability of creating content, participation and impact on final appearance of the product, is provided to the user.

Frequency extent is a limiting factor for distribution of multimedia's content via terrestrial TV systems by limiting the number of channels which can be distributed. However, the Internet has been released of such limiting factors which, on the other hand, have a large number of unnecessary, unwanted, monotonous and poor quality multimedia content as a consequence.

Appearance of the Internet has negatively reflected on a traditional media and a traditional way of communication. Internet had caused reduced usage of the traditional media, but on the other hand it had opened new domain of activity and provided a new channel of distribution for the traditional media, which they had eagerly accepted. On the Internet we can find electronic editions of various newspapers, magazines and electronic books. Publishing news and contents on the Internet increases the number of visitors, users and readers, therefore the publishers mostly publish their materials parallel in a written and electronic form. Some of them, such as New York Times have completely passed on publishing content on the Internet, while the written edition has been abandoned.

Internet has given multimedia the new value by providing transfer of multimedia on different physical places (Houliez et al., 2012). As availability grows via mobile or fixed networks, so the difference of available places for using multimedia via Internet grows too. In everyday life we can use multimedia in our houses, shopping centers, public transport, schools. In more developed countries, Internet is available on the almost entire territory, and thus the multimedia in all of its forms.

The telecommunications market in the Republic of Croatia began to separate from the social sector to the private by the end of the last century when the Croatian telecommunications enterprise was transformed into a joint stock company and when a part of the stocks was bought by a German giant Deutsche Telekom. However, for many years the real opening of the market has not happened nor the appearance of competition or significant investments into a telecommunications market. One of the main reasons is the legal uncertainty which was usual in all areas of national economy. In the telecommunications sector, in addition to the general level of risk that was present, more significant restrictions were set up by various unclear and risky regulatory provisions and their application. To remove the obstacles and to start with a significant recovery of that part of economy the strong political will was needed which during the middle of the last century opened the door to revitalization of Croatian telecommunications market.

European commission, as a crucial normative institution, is in charge of even development of telecommunications market and has set up two goals with the aim to lower the price of equipment and service: (1) Standardization- creating a single common market in Europe and (2) Competition- creating an encouraging environment for development of competition.

It is as hard to come to a new market as it is hard to keep a leading position in a company which has a monopoly, respectively the one that showed up before everyone. Companies that had monopoly were in advantage due to couple of reasons: it is easier to gain and keep deficit goods, they aim to the most profitable parts of the market, migration of expenses, loyalty of the users, but also distrust of the users in the new suppliers.

In the Republic of Croatia, the dominant technology in a broadband access is DSL (Digital Subscriber Loop) technology of transfer, relatively immobile is more dominant than the mobile, however in the last few years that relationship is significantly changing thanks to, especially appearance of smart phones, tablets and their expansion. At the moment, the most present is ADSL (Asymmetric Digital Subscriber Line) technology which is not in ability to provide more important transfer speeds and capacities. Just shifting to VDSL (Very-high-bit-rate Digital Subscriber Line) or one of the FTTX technologies comes a more significant increase in capacity of broadband connections. FFTX is a collective term for various optical fiber delivery topologies that are categorized according to where the fiber terminates.

Lagging behind of Republic of Croatia is noticeable in relation to the rest of the European countries. It is illustrative that 76.7% of the Croatian households had the access to Internet in 2015, while EU's average is 82.6%. The furthest advanced in this area is Luxembourg, which has reached a figure of 96.8% of households with Internet connection. The situation is similar if we look at the availability of next generation access (NGA) that enables higher data rates. Also, the lack of it is noticeable comparing to other EU members. Croatia is located at the very bottom rankings by the availability of NGA networks households with 52% availability, while the EU average in 2015 was 70.9%. Malta has the most developed NGA network in its area which provided an access to NGA network for 100% of the households. According to one American study, 35% of the children lived in a home where the television is on "always" or "most of the time," even if no one is watching (Vandewater et. al., 2005).

eSport is the fastest growing entertainment industry and because of its growing popularity it has the same potential in terms of live streaming via Internet, as other multimedia content. e-Sport is a name including individuals or teams which compete in strategic, card-playing, martial or sport games. It is about competitions whose popularity is growing with incredible speed by parrying total numbers in traditional sports events, rarely do they incomparably outstrip them. On first sight, it seems like anyone could be engaged in e-Sport, however it is about professional players who train around 16 hours every day, who make money out of their profession, and who have a hundred thousands of their fans, setting trends and have sponsor contracts. Number of such events is growing rapidly, and the smaller ones have become too small for maintenance in sports hall, even the bigger ones, a long ago. Bigger competitions are being held on stadiums with around ten thousand visitors and prizes of several million dollars. The biggest and the most numerous tournament in 2015 ''Worlds'' was watched by over 20,000,000 people. Just to compare, NBA finals was watched by 19,500,000 people. According to the survey by portal Superdataresearch, total value of eSport market in 2016 was worth around 900,000,000 dollars, and the greatest potential is seen in North America, Europe and Asia.

The most known service for live streaming of eSport via Internet is Twitch. Every user can register on web sites, install all the necessary programming tools on his computer and live stream the games he is playing via Internet, and, of course, overall competition or organized competitions can be streamed. In December 2016, the largest provider of Internet service in Croatia ''Hrvatski Telekom'' organized a competition in playing sports video game FIFA 2017 with live stream via Internet, and the number of over half a million Internet visitors was recorded, which is more than a good indicator of interest for service of streaming and watching multimedia events live via Internet that grows in Croatia.

MAIN FOCUS OF THE CHAPTER

Methodology

To get a clearer picture of the habits of Croatian citizens, their expectations and way of thinking regarding multimedia streaming, the survey was conducted. The main objective of the research is to acquire the information that is used for the basic assumptions about potential services of transfer of multimedia content in Croatia. The goal is to get the information about the type of content which is interesting to the potential customers, as well as information about the costs that the abovementioned customers would be willing to take.

To acquire that kind of information it is necessary to know the current habits of the Internet users, and get the information about the level of usage and knowledge about multimedia technologies. It is required to find out the habits and expectations of the younger population, the millennials who are one of the most demanding age groups, growing up with alongside high-tech and who will be the bearers and initiators of development in the near future, not only of multimedia services but also of high-tech in general.

The poll was conducted using Google Docs application and the system of questionnaires. No authorization was needed for the access to the web page as well as filling out the questionnaire. Web polls enable questioning a large number of people in a short period of time, require small costs, but at the same time enable a relatively simple processing and analysis of collected data. The questionnaire was accessible by anyone, anytime. The examinees were not targeted, as there was no target group of examinees, but were chose in a way that a request for participation in a survey, as well a plea to freely invite acquaintances to participate, was sent to various age groups no matter of their gender and whose information could be accessed. The period of collecting data was not strictly defined or limited. It lasted approximately 2-3 weeks, as long as the participants showed interest in participation.

The questions asked in the questionnaire were clearly stated without using professional terminology which could have confused the examinees and lead them to a wrong answer. Therefore, the terminology is adjusted to the wider population. When a professional term would be used, a brief explanation of it would be provided. The way and simplicity of filling out the questionnaire was minded, as well as the total number of questions which was optimal to keep the participants interested and lead them to the right answers. The time necessary to fill out the questionnaire was relatively short to avoid losing the participants' attention.

The questions were structured into two categories: Questions of qualification and Main part of the questionnaire (General questions and Individual questions). Through the Questions of qualification the examinees were classified into specific categories; age and gender. The Main part of the questionnaire is divided into two parts; the General questions which provided the information about the general habits of the Internet users and Individual questions which provided the information about expectations of the multimedia content transfer services.

The notification and the request for participation was sent to 250 e-mail addresses chosen at random from the list of the persons that volunteered to participate in market research surveys, and 150 of them responded, which is a 60% participation rate. The participation in the survey was anonymous, and required no registration and providing the personal information that could reveal the identity of the respondent. The survey lasted for a month, during June 2015. The highest participation was recorded in the first 10 days since launching the survey, but the interest declined gradually and completely disappeared by the end of June.

From the age classification point of view, the structure looks as follows: 18-24 (6 participants) – 4%, 25-30 years of age (45 participants) – 30%, 31-40 years of age (47 participants) – 31%, ˃ 40 years of age (52 participants) – 35%. It can be noted that number of participants is pretty evenly divided across the age groups, which is certainly positive and enables relatively good and accurate comparisons of habits among these categories which are also the largest potential users of multimedia content transfer services via the Internet in real time. They are literate enough, have encountered various advanced technologies and services offered by these technologies, therefore they know their preferences and are mostly independent and can afford specific services. Referring to the gender classification of the participants, we can notice that the number of male participants is larger. Out of 150 participants, 97 of them are men, respectively 65%.

The Opinions of the Potential Customers of Multimedia Content Transfer Service via the Internet in Real Time in Croatia

To understand the expectations from the multimedia content transfer service via the Internet we shall provide the indicators of current habits of following general multimedia contents that were collected over the survey:

- **Daily TV Watching:** Somewhat more than 60% of examined participants said to watch TV for less than 2 hours a day, while 32% of them spend between 2 and 4 hours, watching multimedia content on the TV and TV channels. Generally, consumption of multimedia content on the TV is still dominant, but constantly declining.
- **Daily Multimedia Content Watching:** Habits of the multimedia content users via the Internet are somewhat different. More than 72% of examinees spend less than 2 hours consuming the multimedia content on the Internet using computers, smart phones or tablets, while 20% of them spend 2-4 hours.
- **The Choice of Multimedia Content:** Over 90% examinees said to follow the multimedia content on the Interned based on their own preferences, while only 10% of them said to follow the content based on popularity. Those are consumers with clear expectations, changing their traditional ways of following the multimedia content and are not subject to the influence of the masses.
- **The Most Preferred Events to Watch:** We asked the participants to choose one or more of the provided events which they would like to follow. They were given the option to state an event of their own choice which may not be specific, but is interesting for them to follow. Most of examinees, 51% of them, stated their wish to follow a concert of their favorite band. On the second place is the broadcast of the children shows. More than 90% of the examinees who are also parents expressed their wish to follow the shows of their kids, which is for sure a big potential knowing how many kids take part in various activities, and the number of organizations, groups and clubs involving children. Thirdly, there are wishes to follow the games of local sports clubs. A considerable interest shown by examinees was for the broadcast of either sports, cultural or some other kinds of programs in which they take part themselves. A circle of 5 most desired contents is completed by social or cultural events.

Results of the survey of the global research organizations about consuming multimedia contents in 2014 are also indicative for this research (Austin et al., 2015). In comparison to the 2010, the consummation of the multimedia content over Internet in 2014 increased for 5.1. In the same period the time of consuming the media content via the Internet has almost doubled from 59.6 minutes to 109.5 minutes. The time of consuming the media content via traditional media (TV, newspapers, magazines, radio, and cinema) has decreased by 7%. It is forecasted that globally the consumption of the media content in 2017 in comparison to 2014 will increase by on average 1.4% annually, while the consumption of media content via the Internet is expected to rise on average 9.8% annually. The result of our survey as well as the global ones state that consumption of the multimedia content via the Internet is becoming dominant. The main reason behind that is the freedom of Internet users who can consume multimedia contents where - and whenever they want, in comparison to the consumers of the classical media.

Projection of the Market Development Based on the Results of Survey Research

Globally conducted researches show that a share of multimedia content transfers via the Internet is increasing annually, and the citizens of Croatia are also a part of that statistics. They also follow the trends of technological development and spend an increased amount of time on their computers, tablets and smart phones, following multimedia contents on the Internet.

Broadcast of multimedia content via the Internet in real time has a significant advantage in comparison to the classical TV broadcast because the user is not physically tied to a specific location, their home being the usual locatin. Via the Internet users can follow contents anywhere, at work, while travelling, in a restaurant, etc. The only restriction is the coverage of the area by the Internet capacities which have recently been increasing rapidly. The market has to be adjusted to the wants of the customers and must provide the broadcast of those contents in real time which satisfy the specific tastes of the viewers.

According to the survey and the answers of the examinees, we identified three different categories of events that are interesting for potential viewers, which in turn provide the guidelines for further market development.

1. Events including children, acquaintances or the customers themselves
2. Concerts of beloved musical bands
3. Social events

Sports and Cultural Events of Local or International Character Presenting Children, Acquaintances or the Very Participants of the Event

This group of events is the largest and has the most potential. On a daily basis, various local and international sports or cultural events are organized, which are not interesting for a live broadcast by larger TV stations, but hold the interest of specific viewers. Examinees have expressed a wish to follow live the events in which their children, acquaintances of they themselves are taking part. That is a good indicator for the organizers of all kinds of events, in terms of what they can expect in the future. The participants of smaller events, mostly on amateur or volunteer basis, or less followed sports activities have an interest to connect with their professional colleagues. Therefore, the organizers will have to change the philosophy of organizing events. In will not be enough only to organize a specific activity or to provide the consumers with the pleasure of engaging in an activity. It will be necessary to provide the customers with an experience. A fact that over 90% of parents stated that they want to follow their children's activities is very important. Reports of the Croatian Bureau of Statistics from 2009 show that in Croatia there were 4165 sports organizations, which is a 17,6% increase in comparison to 2006. A total number of members in sports organizations was 284 365, which is more than a sufficient indicator of a potential market for multimedia content broadcasting in real time via the Internet.

Concerts of Beloved Musical Bands

It was to be expected that the broadcast of concerts of beloved musical bands would be a choice of mostly younger age groups, but the result of the survey show different parameters. All age groups want to follow the concerts of their beloved musical bands evenly, which makes this type of contents attractive and interesting. However, the examinees that have chosen this kind of broadcast have different expectations than those who have left out concert broadcasts. Through their comments they have shown a different way of thinking, a different wish list which greatly exceeds a mere broadcast of multimedia content and music. They want to be active participants of the concerts, for their experience to be multimedia, not just musical. The specific expectations of these customers create big challenges, obstacles and demands for the concert and broadcast organizers. They are not easy to satisfy, but that is the thing that gives additional value to the overall experience of the concert and increases the amount of the interested audience.

SOLUTIONS AND RECOMMENDATIONS

Business Model of Multimedia Content Broadcast in Real Time in Croatia

A business model is a way in which a company is conducting business, using its resources, dealing with the competition, positions itself on the market with a goal of creating new value for the customers. A business model cannot be exactly defines. Its application and appearance are a choice of each specific company. Each company sets foundations and ways of doing business, while trying to create the best possible business model. The companies which copy their competitors' models, ignoring the specific environment in which they operate might be in danger. Sports events are often unpredictable in terms of duration and beginning and ending times, therefore it is necessary to have a beforehand recorded content which could be broadcasted in event of an interruption of prolonging of the event (Ašenbrener et. al., 2012). Referring to the service of multimedia content broadcasting in real time via the Internet, the function of business models would be to determine the ways and conditions of making revenues, to determine a segment of the target market, to estimate the cost structure, to position the business in the market and to form a strategy based on innovation with a goal of securing the long-term advantage over their competition (Spremić, 2004).

Strategy Based on Innovation

Multimedia streaming live service is an ideal opportunity for interactive communication with audience and better connection between event planner and their fans or clients. Therefore, business model should provide certain advantages over the competition, must have additional services that will distinguish it from a simple transmission and must be recognizable. Calero (2015) presents the following:

To Broadcast Events Live

The idea is to approach more closely event with the audience and to create a greater sense of connection between the audience and the players on the field, and represented club. It is necessary to allow a spectator to be part of the event in order to increase interest in multimedia content. Transfer becomes monotonous and uninteresting, if event is transferred without imaginative ideas. It is indispensable to show what happens on the field and around it, to create story, answer users to their inquiries, ask them what they want to see and who they want to meet. It is necessary to be a user's "eyes and ears" and to show them some special moments of event.

Interview With the Players and the Audience on the Playing Field

If the interviews with certain players are record in advance or during the event, interest of the audience will increase. Not only that club is showing their „human“ side, but also some new ideas would occur. Regular communication with the audience and respond to their inquiries must not be ignored and public must be able to communicate with players. It is essential to enter new ideas, news and events before devote too much attention to the club and its players.

Introduction to Live Streaming

The audience is usually not able to see what is happening behind neither the cameras nor the creation of multimedia content. This is a good opportunity to present themselves and their ideas to the public, to introduce its brand and obtain new potential clients and partners and thus increase the interest for them.

Show Events off the Playing Field

Allow viewers access to some areas and scenes where they usually do not have insight. Show what is happening on the bench and how players prepare for the game, some unusual events, video report while traveling to the match, allow the audience to question and comment. All of these are possibilities how to increase public interest for your product.

Camera on Players or Sports Judges

One major innovation that has emerged recently is a small wireless camera that can be placed on a judge's chest or head. It is a miniature transmission system which is remotely controllable and which is able to give viewers an insight into the tiniest parts of the game and include them maximally in the game. They can view players from very short distance, hear how they communicate and how they move. The system was first used in football and hockey in the US, but later began to use in almost all sports.

Questions and Answers

Organize a short conference for its viewers after the game where the audience will ask questions. That way you will show the audience that their opinion is valuable which will result in increased interest in multimedia content, but be careful to show only interesting questions.

The key to a successful recognition and live broadcast of multimedia content is good understanding of the factors that raise the viewership, which are: curiosity, the need for originality, a sense of group belonging, control, exclusivity.

Ways and Conditions of Providing the Revenue

Ways of providing the revenue, as in other service industries within business informatics, would be multiple (Spremić, 2004): (i) Revenue from charging the services of transferring the media content live online; (ii) Revenue from sponsors; (iii) revenue from marketing and promotions; and (iv) revenue from fees or prepayment.

Revenue from charging the services makes a majority of all revenues that is why it's necessary to devote attention to it. Croatian market is not fully developed yet, like for example American market where the ratio of revenue is different and where the base of potential viewers who are ready to spare a specific amount for a specific content is bigger. In Croatia, dominant way of making profit is by selling services or making profit by organizing sports events if one wants to popularize a specific sport, sport organization or a sport event. Revenue from charging the services makes 60% of total revenue.

Revenue from sponsors can be categorized in the same category with revenue from marketing and promotions. Sports events are an ideal opportunity for promoting two subjects, both business and social. Sports events, especially the big ones which are held on a international level are a great opportunity for promoting tourist attractions. In that kind of competitions there are a lot of competitors and staff from countries all around the world, which makes a great opportunity for advertising the city, local history and culture. It is well known that sport fans are world travelers. Besides towns and communities, different manufacturers, sports equipment distributers, informatics equipment distributers, car industries, can find benefits in advertising their products.

Prepayment has the smallest percentage in the total revenue. That is because Croatian users do not have the habit of paying for sport events. There is a significant amount of users who pay subscriptions to sports channels to different operators, because there they can watch international sports events. However, when it comes to subscriptions to online contents, Croatian viewers prefer that content to be free to watch.

Detailed Description of the Business Model-Service of Broadcasting Sporting Events in Real Time

While defining the business model, it is required to define: phases of development, contentment we need to process, target audience and funding models. Dr. Robert G. Cooper created the 8 rules that greatly assist in products market entry (Brands,

2013). The process flow is the result of research why some companies succeed, and some may not: (1) Creating a product/service- when you create a product or a service or a new innovative product, it is required to conduct a external and internal analysis of the environment and marketing trends (2) Analysis of the ideas – to define clear criteria on the basis of which we decide whether there will be a product or service launch or not; (3) Testing of the concept; (4) The business analytics-analyze in detail all of the elements in the business process, monitor productivity, track the effectiveness and progress of each individual phase of the project: (5) A market tests-Create private groups of tests and test user who will give the value of the product before it is put into production; (6) Product development and (7) The commercialization of the product.

Osterwald and Pigneur (2010) defined Canvas business model as a tool for designing of new or documenting an already existing business model. Canvas business model consists of nine mutually connected blocks that describe how a business creates, distributes and documents new values: key partners, key activities, core values, and key resources, relations with consumers, user segmentation, channels, and cost structure and revenue sources.

Key Partners

There are different categories of partners who are necessary to the business model of broadcasting of multimedia content live for it to function properly. It is necessary to create strong relationships with platforms for the broadcasting of multimedia content such as Youtube or Twich. Furthermore, content distribution can be and preferably will take place via social networks and services with the most activities,an ideal network for it is Facebook Live. Potential major clients in need for these services are sports clubs, sports organizations, tourist boards, municipalities and cities. Suppliers of equipment needed for the recording and distribution of content, such as: Livestram one of the leading manufacturers and distributors of equipment, technical and software solutions for media streaming live, but also a platform for content distribution. To transfer content we require a quality Internet connection at the minimum speed of 1Mb/s that offers various access technologies: mobile, optical or copper. As a leading provider of telecommunications services in Croatia, Croatian Telecom would be a quality choice.

Key Activities

It is necessary to define all the activities that are necessary for the functioning of the business model, and for the service of transmission of multimedia content key activity is the process of recording and distribution of multimedia content in real time, during which we seek to enrich the multimedia content, give additional users interesting ideas and content and enrich the broadcasting to make it interesting for the end user

Key Values

The most important value of a project which deals with the broadcasting of multimedia content live is interactivity and innovation as key factors of differentiation which results in greater user experience. The idea is to involve users in the heart of the event and allow him to turn from a passive observer to active participant. Also, offer a new form of product promotion using interactive technologies that enable better and more direct communication between the provider and the customer

Key Resources

Each project must have its key resources that allow it to create additional value and create new products. Those key resources are intuitive software tools that allow interaction, ability of e-business, starting capital and creative employees that are also resources for starting a business model and for his sustainable functioning.

Customer Relations

Through this block it is needed to create ways of communicating with users of multimedia content. With the tool of interactivity with users to establish direct communication and direct contact and through the automatic service to recognize the user's habits and need by analyzing its behavior and data within the profile and according to the conclusions of users offer custom marketing campaign. They can also create a certain community of users with the same habits and interests which are later offered customized multimedia content. Through certain software tools that users can install on their smartphones it is possible to enter into contact with the customers and turn devices into a sort of video sources that will give you a new perspective on the event and turn viewers into co-creators.

Consumer Segmentation

Every business model is oriented towards customers and to profitable customers, without them the company cannot survive. Multimedia content can be designed for the mass number of users as well as individual users and even users who are not intended to monitor content, but still for some reason decide to do so. Customers of the service are organizers of various social and sporting events.

Channels

The only channel of distribution of multimedia content is the Internet, looking from the standpoint of distribution channels. If we look to the smart receiving party, content can be traced to smartphones, PCs, smart TVs or game consoles.

Cost Structure

The objective of the business model is to minimize operating costs wherever possible using the maximum level of automation and activities that are not essential to operations. The Most important expenses are personnel costs, equipment and services.

Sources of Revenue

Each company must answer the question which segment of customers is willing to give money for the service. The answer to this question brings one way of revenue sources. Sources of revenue would be predominantly one/off and that by the organizers of the event, but can also be by end users. Also, a regular monthly fee or subscription for specific content may be the answer.

Similarities and Differences with other Models of Content Transmission on the Croatian Market

Services of providing Multimedia content over the Internet, without regard to the technology are different. Each has its advantages and disadvantages for end users, different business models, offering different levels of service and different levels of user experience. Service transmission of multimedia content live over the Internet is unique because no similar service distributes content in real time. There are different services transmission of multimedia, but not live content, it is pre-recorded content. These are mostly services of recorded that is somewhere on the servers and is available on demand. All large Croatian TV stations (HRT, Nova TV and RTL) have their own service through which they broadcast their own channels on the Internet, but these are mainly facilities which are pre-recorded and for which a specific TV house has distribution rights and ownership. The service of HRT is called HRTi, RTL has RTL now and Nova TV has a service called OYO TV. HRTi is the only one free of charge, while the others require a monthly fee.

The above services have significant shortcomings, and that is to provide access only to the content that they produced themselves or who are in their ownership or contents that are broadcast on their TV channels or will be broadcast. In contrast Pickbox service offers the ability to view famous domestic and foreign TV shows on

Table 1. Canvas business model of live broadcast of multimedia content via the Internet

<table>
<tr>
<td rowspan="2">Key Partners
Croatian Telecom
Facebook Live
Youtube
Twitch
Livestream
Blackmagic
Sports clubs
ports organizations
Tourist boards
Cities and counties
Companies
Religious organizations</td>
<td>Key Activities
Recording and distribution of multimedia content
Marketing services
Internet as a distribution channel
Interactive functionalities</td>
<td rowspan="2">Value Proposition
Allow the potential business partners the promotion of their ideas and products over the social media and new Internet platforms in interesting and interactive manner, in order to increase the quality of customer relationships</td>
<td>Customer Relationships
Direct communication
Automatic services
Communication for the community
Co-creation of events</td>
<td rowspan="2">Customer Segments
Individual users
Random users
Marketing companies
Event organizers</td>
</tr>
<tr>
<td>Key Resources
Initial funding for launching the business project
Softver for broadcasting
E-business functions
Equipment for the satellite access
Creative employees with the programming, web design and business skills</td>
<td>Channels
Internet
Personal computers
Smart phones
Smart TVs
Play consoles</td>
</tr>
<tr>
<td colspan="2">Cost Structure
Personnel costs
Hardware and sotware costs
Distribution costs
Internet access</td>
<td colspan="3">Revenue Streams
Subscription
One time revenue
Renting equipment
Revenue from the organization of events
Advertising
Content reselling</td>
</tr>
</table>

Source: Author's work

Table 2. Canvas business model of live broadcast of multimedia content via the Internet

Service Name	Description	Price
OYO TV	Series, movies and shows broadcast by NOVA TV as well as content transfer live via the Internet	4,74 €/per month
HRTi	Multimedia service for monitoring HRT radio and TV live channel, series and shows on demand	0 €/per month
RTL sada	Series, movies and shows broadcast by RTL as well as content transfer live via the Internet	2,03 €/per month

Source: Author's work

Table 3. Multimedia services for the live transmission of TV channels in Croatia

Service Name	Description	Price
Pickbox	Best known international and domestic series on request	6,63 €/per month
HBO GO	Series made in the production house HBO. It is related to the providers of telecommunications services.	7,98 €/per month

Source: Author's work

demand, regardless of their production or ownership. A similar service is HBO Go, but it offers TV shows which are produced by HBO so again it has a limiting factor.

In Croatia, there are several Internet TVs that are owned by telecommunications operators and the best know are MaxTV owned by THT with over 300,000 users, VIP TV owned by VIP and H1 telecom. It's IPTV services deliver Internet users with different world and domestic TV channels embedded in certain TV packages.

In addition to these services there are also services of Bnet, Croatian Post Office, Optima Telekom, Terrakom, Amis Telekom, and others. What distinguishes them from the services of transmission of multimedia content to live is that this is a commercial service that can end the viewer charged and for which ultimately own the service provider guarantees the quality and delivery, as opposed to the services that are in the paper processing and for which there is no guaranteed deliveries.

The main difference between the service distribution of multimedia content live over the Internet and all the above services is in their purpose. The original service

Table 4. The most popular Internet televisions in Croatia

Service Name	Description	Price
MaxTV	Internet television from Croatian Telecom	20,30 €/per month
Vip TV	Internet television from VIP	24,36 €/per month
Iskont TV	Internet television from Iskon telecom	32,34 €/per month

Source: Author's work

Table 5. The best-known Internet television in Croatia for viewing on computers or smartpohones

Service Name	Description	Price
MaxTv to GO	MaxTVInternet television available to everyone in Croatia	6,77 €/per month
VIP tv to go	Internet television only for users of VIP landline	6,77 €/per month
ISKON tv to go	Internet television only for users of Iskon	4,81 €/per month

Source: Author's work

was aimed at a small number of spectators, viewers who know exactly what they want viewers with a keen sense of quality, while all other services and services intended for commercial distribution, and a larger number of viewers.

In addition, the services of distribution of multimedia content to live the free services where service providers do not own Internet connections and therefore cannot guarantee the quality of services nor content delivery, and such services for users is mostly free, all the other services the distribution of multimedia content are guaranteed deliveries.

The Expenditures of Starting a New Business Model

Caution and prudence are needed when creating a budget for starting a business model of live broadcast of multimedia content by Internet. The equipment on the market can be extremely expensive, so if a budget isn't carefully planned, a collapse of balance can easily occur. The resources which can be invested in such a project are virtually unlimited, but there must be a dose of caution which will coordinate the possibilities with the needs on the market so that the output of the invested resources is constant and in a reasonable deadline.

The expenditures in the table refer on the initial phase of starting a business model, while additional resources will be needed to be invested in the later phases in order to acquire additional equipment with more possibilities. The biggest the process of budgeting and financing is the acquirement of hardware and software. In order to reduce the initial price of financing, instead of acquiring equipment via CAPEX, the equipment can simply be rented, i.e., we can acquire it via OPEX.

Table 6. The main differences between the service of live broadcast of multimedia content and other similar services

Service	Internet TVs and maintenance	Live broadcast of multimedia content by Internet
Purpose	To a larger number of viewers	To a smaller number of viewers
Adjustment to the user	Smaller	Focus on the user
Guarantee of shipment	Yes	No
Innovations	No	Yes
User experience	No	Yes
Interaction	No	Yes
Price for the ultimate user	With a fee	Usually for free

Source: Author's work

Table 7. The expenditures of starting a business model

Description of Expenditures	Sum (€)
Camera, stand, additional battery…	1342,68
Equipment for satellite Internet	469,94
Hardware for video signal processing	671,34
Internet platform for distribution of multimedia content	805,61
Software for video content processing and production	268,54
Service for Internet access (annual)	1342,68
Equipment for mobile access to the Internet	268,54
Other equipment, computers, printers, microphones…	1342,68
Website design	402,80
In total	6914,79

Source: Author's work

FUTURE RESEARCH DIRECTIONS

Future research directions should be oriented towards the viable models of the liver distribution over the Internet. Here, we can specify two classifications depending on the demanding of the audience, and the complexity of the transfer organization. There is a need for a smaller amount of equipment, a smaller number of sound and image sources, most often only one source, and there is no need for additional content, marketing actions neither interactivity. Typically, this type of content is:

- Distribution of various religious events and celebrations (widely popular in the United States)
- Distribution of small sports events (sports competitions of younger age groups)
- Distribution of rare natural phenomena
- Conferences with smaller audience
- Fashion and music events
- Weddings
- Social, cultural and political events

Conducting of more complex events requires more equipment, a higher level of competence and experience in dealing with complex live distribution. These kinds of distributions are organizationally complex and the target audience of those complex events typically has high expectations.

- Distribution of video games events (e-sports competitions)
- Significant Concerts
- Significant sport events
- Interactive business and educational conferences with interaction between participants and instructors
- Drone race (recently such a competition in Dubai was live distributed by a Croatian company)
- Pay Per View for different kind of content and events. Mostly these are educational conferences, concerts and sports events
- Distribution of social and tourist events that need to pass a strong marketing campaign

CONCLUSION

A certain progress in transfer of multimedia events live via Internet was noted in Croatia in 2016. To home public has been offered several multimedia events recorded with the latest systems which allow the view of 360 degrees, and the events that attract the most users by transferring live via Internet have begun to be organized, such as competitions in playing video games or so called eSport competitions that attracted over half a million visitors in December, 2016.This chapter investigated the always-on sport content multimedia delivery over internet in Croatia, and fulfilled three goals.

First, we have analyzed the possibilities of multimedia content live broadcasting via Internet, its technological characteristics and customer orientation, and we can conclude that the Republic of Croatia is following global trends, but with a certain distance. There are few reasons for that, from insufficient economic development which causes less demand for updated technological innovations at which the transfer of multimedia content live via Internet rests, to worse Internet access, especially higher speed Internet to poor organization of multimedia events which demand engaging more complicated systems for providing service of transferring multimedia content live via Internet.

Second, we explored the competitive advantages over the same or similar services and checked their influence on the development of society and the general economic activity. We found out that the most limiting factor is currently the capacity of the network. Competitiveness can be attained only by building a network infrastructure through European funds and other forms of financing Internet technology of high speeds will be available to the greater number of users in Croatia, and the existing users will get an increase of capacity which will lead to an increase of number of potential users of multimedia's content service live via Internet.

Third, by using survey research we have collected information about the usage multimedia services as and expectations of users in Croatia. A survey showed that there is a great interest for watching multimedia content live via Internet in the Republic of Croatia. Users want to keep up with certain contents they have no chance to keep up on classic media such as concerts of their favorite bands, and they also want Internet to watch their kids performing in sports fields or on social events.

REFERENCES

Ašenbrener, M., Šimunović, D., & Dovedan Han, Z. (2013). Model informacijskogsustavaplaniranja TV emisija. *Culture and Public Relations*, *4*(1), 61–69.

Austin, A., Barnard, J., Hutcheon, N., & Parry, D. (2015). *Media Consumption Forecast*. London: ZenithOptimedia.

Baird, D. E., & Fisher, M. (2005). Neomillennial user experience design strategies: Utilizing social networking media to support always on learning styles. *Journal of Educational Technology Systems*, *34*(1), 5–32. doi:10.2190/6WMW-47L0-M81Q-12G1

Baron, N. S. (2010). *Always On: Language in an Online and Mobile World*. New York: Oxford University Press.

Brands. (2013). *8 Step Process Perfects New Product Development*. Retrieved March 01, 2017, from http://innovationexcellence.com/blog/2013/05/27/8-step-process-perfects-new-product-development/

Calero, A. (2015). *6 Ways to Use Live Streaming Video for Business*. Retrieved March 01, 2017, from http://www.socialmediaexaminer.com/live-streaming-video-for-business

Cecchinato, M. E., Cox, A. L., & Bird, J. (2017, May). Always On (line)?: User Experience of Smartwatches and their Role within Multi-Device Ecologies. *Proceedings of the 2017 CHI Conference on Human Factors in Computing Systems*, 3557-3568. doi:10.1145/3025453.3025538

Crnkovic, J. Y. (2013). The Future of CRM is UX. *Business Systems Research*, *4*(1), 4–13.

Cui, Y., Chipchase, J., & Jung, Y. (2007). Personal TV: A Qualitative Study of Mobile TV Users. In P. Cesar, K. Chorianopoulos, & J. F. Jensen (Eds.), Lecture Notes in Computer Science: Vol. 4471. *Interactive TV: a Shared Experience. EuroITV 2007*. Berlin: Springer. doi:10.1007/978-3-540-72559-6_21

Du, M., Kihl, M., Arvidsson, Å., Zhang, H., Lagerstedt, C., & Gavler, A. (2015). Prefetching Schemes and Performance Analysis for TV on Demand Services. *International Journal on Advances in Telecommunications*, *8*(3&4), 162–172.

Dvornik, D. (2000). An investment view on mobile telecommunications market in the Europe with special review of Croatia. *Ekonomski Pregled*, *51*(9-10), 1033–1052.

Fontaine, G., Le Borgne-Bachschmidt, F., & Leiba, M. (2010). Scenarios for the Internet Migration of the Television Industry. *Communications & Stratégies*, *77*(1), 21–34.

Heikkinen, M. V., Casey, T., & Hecht, F. (2010). Value analysis of centralized and distributed communications and video streaming. *Info*, *12*(5), 42-58.

Houliez, C., & Gamble, E. (2012). Augmented focus groups: On leveraging the peculiarities of online virtual worlds when conducting in-world focus groups. *Journal of Theoretical and Applied Electronic Commerce Research*, *7*(2), 31–51.

Kaasinen, E., Kulju, M., Kivinen, T., & Oksman, V. (2009). User Acceptance of Mobile TV Services. *MobileHCI '09 Proceedings of the 11th International Conference on Human-Computer Interaction with Mobile Devices and Services*, 34-43.

Kanellopoulos, D. N. (2014). Multimedia networking issues for digital video libraries. *The Electronic Library*, *32*(6), 898–922. doi:10.1108/EL-01-2013-0009

Katusic, D., Marcev, A., Vulas, R., & Jezic, G. (2013). Machine-to-Machine: Emerging market and consequences on existing regulatory framework. *Proceedings of the 12th International Conference on Telecommunications*. Zagreb: University of Zagreb.

Koroleva, D. (2016). Always Online: Mobile Technology and Social Media Usage by Modern Teenagers at Home and at School. Retrieved March 10, 2017 from: https://cyberleninka.ru/article/n/always-online-mobile-technology-and-social-media-usage-by-modern-teenagers-at-home-and-at-school

Nicholson, J., & Nicholson, D. B. (2010). A stream runs through IT: Using streaming video to teach information technology. *Campus-Wide Information Systems*, *27*(1), 17–24. doi:10.1108/10650741011011255

Orgad, S. (2009). Mobile TV. *Convergence (London)*, *15*(2), 197–214. doi:10.1177/1354856508101583

Pejić Bach, M., Zoroja, J., & Jirouš, Ž. (2013). Croatian Telecommunication Market: Concentration Trends in the Period from 2003 to 2008. *Interdisciplinary Description of Complex Systems, 11*(1), 131–142. doi:10.7906/indecs.11.1.11

Raats, T., Evens, T., & Ruelens, S. (2016). Sustaining local audiovisual ecosystems. Analysis of financing and production of domestic TV fiction in small media markets. *Journal of Popular Television, 4*(1), 129–147. doi:10.1386/jptv.4.1.129_1

Roblek, V., Pejić Bach, M., Meško, M., & Bertoncelj, A. (2013). The impact of social media to value added in knowledge-based industries. *Kybernetes, 42*(4), 554–568.

Sabolić, D. (2009). Telecommunications reforms in Croatia. *Technology in Society, 31*(1), 11–110. doi:10.1016/j.techsoc.2008.10.005

Spremić, M. (2004). *Menadžment i elektroničko poslovanje*. Zagreb: Narodne novine.

Vandewater, E. A., Bickham, D. S., Lee, J. H., Cummings, H. M., Wartella, E. A., & Rideout, V. J. (2005). When the television is always on heavy television exposure and young childrens development. *The American Behavioral Scientist, 48*(5), 562–577. doi:10.1177/0002764204271496

Wankel, L. A., & Blessinger, P. (2013). Inventive Approaches in Higher Education: An Introduction to Using Multimedia Technologies. In In Increasing Student Engagement and Retention using Multimedia Technologies: Video Annotation, Multimedia Applications, Videoconferencing and Transmedia Storytelling (Cutting-edge Technologies in Higher Education, Volume 6 Part F) Emerald Group Publishing Limited, pp.3 – 16.

Williams, S. (2017). Always On: Managing Online Communities in a 24/7 Society. In Promotional Strategies and New Service Opportunities in Emerging Economies (pp. 314-328). IGI Global.

Chapter 6
The Risk Management Profession in Australia:
Business Continuity Plan Practices

Adela McMurray
RMIT University, Australia

Jean Cross
University of New South Wales, Australia

Carlo Caponecchia
University of New South Wales, Australia

ABSTRACT

This study aimed to identify to what extent Australian organizations have any plans to manage business continuity threats, and the nature and content of these plans. Sixty-four respondents who were risk management professionals were surveyed to explore the Business Continuity Practices within their organizations. The ANOVA analysis showed 39 per cent of the organizations had developed an enterprise-wide plan of which just over half stated that the plan was tested. However, 36 per cent of respondents had no plan, an "informal plan," were developing a plan, or did not know whether they had a plan. Standardized guidelines for a process to manage risks have been developed across many spheres and countries and are brought together in the international risk management standard ISO31000 (ISO, 2009), which presents a process applicable to all organizations and all risks. Human resource practices that promote consistent communication and an organizational culture that allows business continuity plan values, attitudes and beliefs to become embedded and to move across traditional organizational boundaries are therefore important for gaining the cooperation needed to implement plans in an organization's operational areas pertaining to business continuity.

DOI: 10.4018/978-1-5225-3704-5.ch006

INTRODUCTION

The growing importance of risk management is recognized by government and industry with regulation increasingly requiringorganizations to have a formal risk management policy and processes. Disaster response and emergency plans are integral to an organization's survival (Kahn, 2012). Safety and environmental regulations in most countries have required risk management processes for many years but following the Enron collapse in the United States, the Sarbanes Oxley Act was introduced requiring listed companies to have an enterprise risk management system such as outlined in the COSO Enterprise Risk Management – Framework (2004).Risk management has moved from the periphery to the centre of business planning.The US September11 terrorist attackremindedbusinesses globally of the need toincorporate adequate disaster recovery and business continuity planninginto theirpolicies and practices (Savage 2002). US President George W Bush issued an executive order within hours of the terror attacks to facilitate continuity of government, later making Executive Directive 51 (Presidential Directive NSPD 51, 2007). It required executive departments and agencies and provided guidance for other levels of government and the private sector to have a continuity program in case of catastrophic emergency, which is described as "any incident, regardless of location, that results in extraordinary levels of mass casualties, damage, or disruption severely affecting the U.S. population, infrastructure, environment, economy, or government functions" (NSPD 2007).Standardizedguidelines for a process to manage risks have been developed across many spheres and countries and are brought together in theinternational risk management standard ISO31000(ISO, 2009) which presents a process applicable to all organizations and all risks. Writing on the impact of this and new standards on the preparedness of business to recover from disaster Tucker (2014) reported that many emergency and business continuity managers believed that lessons were learned from September, but contrasts this with: "A simple study of the unclassified literature shows that the method of attack was entirely predictable and the only lesson learned was that we did not learn our lessons." (Tucker 2014, p.10). In light of the development of Business Continuity Planning, especially after major disasters such as the US 9/11 attacks, the UK Manchester and Westminster attacks, the Sydney Lindt Café seizure, Avian flu and Ebola, this study aimed to identify to what extent organizations in Australia have any plans to manage business continuity threats, and the nature and content of these plans. This is of interest and has relevance to other global organizations based in various countries as Australian organizations increasingly engage in global business practices.

BACKGROUND

A new twist on disruptive threats to continuity of government emerged in late 2016 with allegations of a State-sponsored information warfare by Russia against the Democratic party and, in turn, the US electoral process. Writing in Survival magazine (Inkster, 2016) former British Secret Intelligence Service operations director, Nigel Inksterstated:"It should hardly be surprising that the intelligence services of a foreign power in a confrontational relationship with the United States should take an interest in the latter's presidential election and seek to gather intelligence on the process and candidates, including through computer-network exploitation" (p. 23).

Risk management involves managing threats and opportunities, and includes communication, accountability in decision-making, rigorous, forward and balanced thinking and is viewed as a vital part of good business practice (ISO, 2009). In the context of disasters, areas of risk include telephone communications, computer processing, vital facilities and critical operations (Myers, 2006), and human resource control systems(Verano-Tacoronte, Santiago &Melián-González, 2008; Duncan. Yeager, Rucks & Ginter, 2011) are an important part of managing risks is Business Continuity Management (BCM). The concept of BCM is broadly defined as the uninterrupted provision of operations and services to customers (Pink, 2004). Specifically, the Business Continuity Institute defines BCM as "a holistic management process that identifies potential impacts that threaten an organization and provides a framework for building resilience and the capability for an effective response that safeguards the interest of its key stakeholders, reputation, brand and value creating activities" (BCI, 2005).

Business Continuity Management refers to all activities to manage risks that may affect the long-term sustainability of the business. In some organizations, this is seen to include both risks that arise from disaster events or disruptions, and risks that arise gradually such as those associated with obsolescence or long-term staff shortages. In many casesmanaging such risks requires staff that is competent in soft skill sets (Carvalho & Rabechini Junior, 2015). BCM enables the organization to move from disruption to "business as usual" and embeds appropriate practices into its cultural fabric to ensure that business continuity capabilities consistently reflect the needs, technology and structure of the business. BCM is a long-term, proactive and responsible approach to ensuring that the business is operationally resilient to disaster and can make the most of opportunities during recovery. To reduce disaster recovery time, business managers and employees can implement flexible and dynamic approaches through an organizational culture that has embedded BCP and in turn BCM values (Sax & Torp, 2015) thereby facilitating minimal disruption to daily operations.

Herbane, Elliott and Swartz (2004) draw parallels between BCM and strategic planning. In both cases, there must be effective plans, combined with flexibility, creativity and adaptation (Herbane et al.2004).To achieve this end, processes must be embedded in the organization with strategic thinking and participation occurring throughout the organization, rather than only within the senior management team, or a specific BCM team. Organizations that are proactive in their preparedness, using Business Continuity Planning (BCP) are likely to be more resilient to disaster by defining a minimum continuity level (Sahebjamnia, Torabia & Mansouri, 2015).According to Herbane *et al.* (2004), it is the embeddedness that transforms Business Continuity Planning (BCP) into Business Continuity Management (BCM). Traditional BCP can be seen as one step in the risk management process, a treatment to reduce the consequences of disaster when prevention has failed. The aspect of BCP is that part of BCM that involves producing formal plans that are accepted and activated. As part of BCM, the business continuity planning process is comprised of the process for producing formal plans which are activated if certain thresholds of disruption are exceeded. In this way, BCP can be viewed as similar to having insurance, where organizations hope they will not have to use it but reap rewards when they do (Lam, 2002).

The philosophy of BCP has evolved over the years. Ellott *et al.* (2002) perceive the 1970s as an era when continuity activities were directed only to technology (IT continuity plans are often referred to as Disaster Recovery Plans (DRP)). In the 1980s, disaster planning extended to facilities in general and the new DRP was called Business Continuity Planning. This was followed in the 1990s, with continuity management which extended to the entire organization including human and social values (Elliott *et al.* 2002). The rise and growth of online e-commerce has meant the need for business to be 'always-on' which illustrates the increasing importance and emphasis of strong business continuity and risk mitigation. Industries including telecommunications, energy, banking and healthcare depend on successful BCP which precedes, and is an antecedent, to BCM (Ibrahimović&Bajgorić, 2016). Cloud computing has, in recent years, enabled an improved high business availability rate (Bajgorić, 2014). In February 2017, research published by the Business Continuity Institute(Alcantara & Riglietti, 2017) with the British Standards Institute, revealed digital threats as the top concern for business continuity professionals with 88 per cent fearing cyber attack, data breach (81 per cent) and telecommunications outage (80 per cent). Furthermore, physical threats were cited by 55 per cent of respondents following major weather incidents across the globe in 2016 – Japan's earthquake, floods in China, Hurricane Matthew in the Americas, storms and flash floods in France and Germany, plus wildfires in Canada (Alcantara & Riglietti, 2017).

In addition to these changes, globalization and the wider impact of disasters have alerted business to the importance of the supply chain to business continuity (Ho,

Zheng, Yildiz & Talluric, 2015). Christopher and Peck (2004) maintain that the biggest risk to business continuity may well come from the wider supply chain rather than from within the organization. To minimize effect, supply chain partners can improve business continuity by collaborating to share and equally understand risks in the chain (Li, Fan, Lee & Cheng, 2015) or supply chain integrations (Wiengarten, Humphreys, Gimenez & McIvor, 2016). Recognition of the importance of the supply chain to business continuity plans has led to a much closer link between concepts of supply chain risk management, BCP and BCM. Modern BCM applies all steps of the risk management process to risks that affect the continuity of the business whether they concern internal or external stakeholders and whether they are initiated by a disaster event or not.

In practice, many organizations in the 21st century are still at the early stages of this evolution. The relatively recent nature of changes in practice is illustrated by the annual surveys of the Chartered Management Institute carried out since 1999. The loss of supply chain appeared on the list of threats perceived by managers only in the 2002 survey, and the loss of people appeared in 2003 and telecommunications in 2004.From 2004 onwards, instead of being asked about their perception of potential threats, managers were asked what disruptive events had occurred in the previous 12 months.In most years, the loss of IT and telecommunications was the common disruptive event and the loss of people ranked second. In 2010 and 2011 there were severe weather events in the UK and in these years weather became the highest cause of disruption.

In the latest 2017 Business Continuity Incident report, malicious attacks via the internet (nominated by 80 per cent of respondents) topped “emerging trends and uncertainties”(Alcantara & Riglietti, 2017). The authors noted the social media’s rise as a perceived threat (53 per cent) when disruptions and subsequent online reaction could impact on corporate reputation. And the growing use of cloud services were perceived as a potential risk by 46 per cent. Political change (40 per cent) “coincides with a wave of populism sweeping across democracies worldwide, culminating in Brexit, the rise of the populist far-right in countries such as France and Austria…as well as the election of Donald Trump in the United States” (Alcantara & Riglietti, 2017, p.11).

In 1995, Sanchez, Korbin and Viscara recognized that effects of disasters on employees need to be incorporated into BCP to minimize factors such as employee absenteeism, resignation, worker’s compensation costs, and to encourage ongoing employee commitment to the organization. Commitment correlates with an organization’s climate which is inter-subjective with the organizational culture (McMurray, Scott & Pace 2004). Ten years later Zsidisin, Melnyk and Ragatz(2005) were still urging businesses to be prepared not only for the increased mobility of populations, but for the unavailability of staff through a disease pandemic and the possibility of terrorist attack. In practice, very few large organizations require their critical supply chain to have business continuity plans. Yet given the low take-up of BCP in small organizations, such gaps in planning and readiness could influence a large organization's ability to recover from widespread disaster (Deloitte, 2005).

In general, changes in practice appear to be precipitated by particular events. Thus the evolution from Disaster Recovery Planning to Business Continuity Planning occurred in many organizations with the passage of Y2K. The September 11, 2001 attacks, and Avian Flu fears demonstrated the essential role of people in an organization and these issues appeared in the Chartered Management Institute (CMI) surveys shortly afterwards. Ferguson (2002) noted that failure to plan for disasters that extend over a wide area with removal of much of the infrastructure on which a traditional BCP relies on was a problem following the 9/11 attacks. The unavailability of staff and the widespread telecommunications outages through both failure and overloading at the time were specifically mentioned.

Business Continuity Planning and Disaster Recovery Planning are emerging as the latest issue to address in corporate IT circles (Snedaker, 2013). Organizations focus on retaining high availability, reliability and scalability (Bajgorić& Moon, 2009), creating "safe sets" of operating procedures (Parise G., Hesla, Parise L & Pennacchia, 2016). Surveys of the current state of BCP in organizations are regularly carried out internationally by large providers of business continuity services and by interested professional institutions. They may ask questions about BCP in general, or about the presence of BC plans, though it is not always clear that the terminology is consistent. For example, a survey of 158 security officers in the United States (Hanson, 2005) found that 60 per cent of their organizations had BCPs prior to September 11, 2001 and 93 per cent by 2005. The operational definitions or descriptions of BCP were not stated. Larger organizations are more likely to have a BCP than smaller ones, both within the larger business sector (CMI, 2005; Deloitte, 2005; Hanson, 2005) and the smaller business sector (Yoshida & Deyle, 2005). The survey of members of the Chartered Management Institute in the United Kingdom showed that a more or less constant ratio of 50 per cent of the organizations represented had a BCP between 2002 and 2010 but that there was a rise over the final two years of the survey. This rise was mostly attributable to the not-for-profit sector (CMI, 2012).Deloitte (2005) found 80 per cent of organizations on their US database had a BCP. However, for nearly half of the sample, the plans applied to only select parts of the business. An organization's perceived exposure to disaster events and in-house risk management or BCP expertise were important indicators for the likelihood of having a formal BCP program.

Small business contributes significantly to local economies in the United States, United Kingdom and Australia. A quantitative study addressing BCP in 230 US small businesses with less than 100 employees situated in Florida found that although these businesses were highly vulnerable to natural disasters, they were ill-prepared for recovery (Yoshida & Deyle, 2005). Forty-eight per cent reported that they had some form of BCP (or were developing one) but the percentage fell with the size of the company. Businesses which had access to risk management expertise were generally better prepared, demonstrating the importance of some form of mentoring to help organizations that do not have in-house specialists. Their study concluded that educational programs, technical assistance and government efforts were essential in enhancing small business resilience to disaster recovery. Florida is likely to provide an atypical sample as it is prone to hurricanes. Other literature indicates small business is generally very poorly prepared (Webb, Tierney & Dahlhamer, 2000).

The disaster plan is a key training and policy document in any organization and commitment from management towards disaster awareness and prevention is essential within an organization's culture(Muir & Shenton, 2002; Sax & Torp, 2015). It should be noted that organizational culture, national culture and intra-national subculture differences should be taken into account when developing any safety programs (Perez-Floriano &Gonzalez, 2007). The literature shows that human factors are neglected in the majority of BCP studies, yet people are a critical capital resource without which the organization cannot function. An appropriate organizational culture and strategy are also essential to provide the resilience that allows business continuity plans to adapt to the variety of scenarios that emerge in a disaster (Sax & Torp, 2015). An organization's employees are critical to an organization's culture -- embracing the values, attitudes and beliefs integral to BCP implementation and ultimately leading to BCM effectiveness. One explanation for the lack of inclusion of human and cultural aspects in these plans could be the issue of measurement and hence concept definition in a newly emerging discipline. For example, the BCP discipline and literature are relatively recent and it is understandable that measurement and definitions do not result in immediate tangible and quantifiable outcomes. Hence the literature is scant when addressing human capital, which is qualitative in nature and more complex in terms of measurement and definition. In a 2006 report, the IBM Corporation concurs that studies neglect the human side of BCP and proposes that BCP be the responsibility of every individual in an organization. Their work shows only 34 per cent of companies address the human aspect of crisis preparedness that embraces human capital risks. Examples of these risks relate to health and safety conditions, transportation, trauma, employee tracking, succession and training, payroll, communications, ability to attend work, ability to deliver critical internal services, and to maintain business operations (IBM, 2006). Organizations that embrace human resource management strategies in their processes enhance their performance and innovation through organizational learning and knowledge management capability (Kuo, 2011). Therefore, in addition to appropriate insurance coverage, and the installation of physical suppression systems to circumvent disasters, careful consideration needs to be taken into account when selecting personnel who are responsible for disaster management in their organizations (Eden & Mathews, 1996).

Managers' perceptions of organizational risk were identified as a factor impacting on a company's ability to generate comprehensive contingency plans in both manufacturing and service industries. Managers' reluctance to consider external risks other than competitive risks, a tendency toward rigid systems of control (to maintain equilibrium), and avoidance of planning based on uncertainty may contribute to a climate in which response plans that produce resilience (i.e. a return to equilibrium after a disaster) are not developed (Smallman & Smith, 2003; Smith 2005; Smith & Fischbacher, 2009). The misperceptions that a well-managed organization is immune to crisis, or that responsibility for risk lies with upper management, impacts on the amount ofresources an organization spends on crisis prevention (Smallman & Smith, 2003; Smith 2005).

In a case study of Jardine, Matheson and Company, a Hong Kong trading firm responsible for developing a network of shipping trading partnerships with China, Connell (2002) found network building, embedded in a culture of trust, cooperation and learning were central in addressing business operations and external organizational risk reduction. In a similar vein, Castillo (2004) utilized Boeing (US) as a case study for establishing a culture embracing an integrated and organizational collaborative BCP model. The model embedded BCP processes across a number of departments and served employees, customers, stakeholders and the community through education (including role definition) as well as professional development. The execution of a BCP to ensure Boeing's business continuance, saw the changing of processes, systems, people or location to remain operational through an unforeseen event. Castillo (2004) implies that BCP is specific to Boeing's product or service (i.e. identified critical suppliers, contract commitments and logistics in terms of delivery to external customers). This highlights the complexity of BCP and its context specific elements within an organization's culture.

The literature shows there appears to be no equivalent surveys of Australian organizations and details of the implementation of BCP in Australia and its state of evolution is largely unknown. Accordingly, the current study aimed to discover to what extent organizations in Australia have any plans to manage business continuity threats, and the nature and content of these plans. In light of the development of BCP,especially after major disasters such as the 9/11 attacks, Ebola, Sydney Lindt Café siege attack, Zika virus and Avian Flu, this study aimed to identify to what extent organizations in Australia have any plans to manage business continuity threats, and the nature and content of these plans. This is of interest and has relevance to other global organizations based in various countries as Australian organizations increasingly engage in global business practices.

MAIN FOCUS OF THE CHAPTER

Sample

The convenience sample was comprised of respondents who were recruited at the Risk Management Institution of Australasia conference and a large workplace safety conference and trade show in Queensland, Australia. The sample consisted of 64 respondents who wererisk management professionals and randomly drawn from the attendees at the risk management profession conference. Of those, 57 gave a valid response to industry type and of these 48 per cent represented government (including local government). The remainder of the sample comprised finance/IT/administration (14 per cent); infrastructure including transport, health and education (24 per cent); and private industry including manufacturing, mining and construction (10 per cent). As with the overseas studies, the nature of the sample was such that organizations did have in-house expertise, and hence are likely to have more advanced BCP systems than organizations without that expertise. It was intended that this preliminary study provide the groundwork for future extensive BCP studies.

Measures

A 13-item questionnaire was developed and consisted of closed questions addressing demographic, business continuity planning and management items. A typical sample question and format included, "Which best describes your organization's Business Continuity Plan?" and was followed by a selection of seven alternatives including "other." The questionnaire was pre-tested on a sample of 18 industry professionals prior to conducting the main study.

Analysis

Anova was used to analyze the 13-item questionnaire. This method of analysis is viewed as being suitable for an exploratory study (McMurray, Pace& Scott, 2004). Analysis showed that 39 per cent of the organizations had developed an enterprise-wide plan of which just over half stated that the plan was tested.

RESULTS

Forty per cent of respondents had no plan, an "informal plan", were developing a plan, or did not know whether they had a plan. None of those in this category felt they had a completed BCP plan for any organizational functions. The organizations

Figure 1. Business Continuity Plans in organizations with the Australian Risk Management Professionals

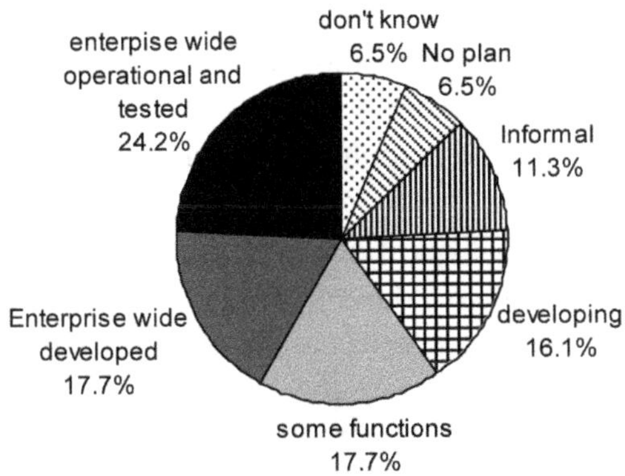

reporting no plan were all represented by Occupational Health and Safety professionals rather than by general risk management professionals. The most common reason for having no plan was a belief that the organization's exposure was limited. Five respondents gave this as a reason for lack of having a BCP although only four said they had no plan.

Figure 1. summarises the results and shows that the respondents indicated that an enterprise-wide operational (developed and tested) BCP existed in 15 organizations or 24 per cent of the study's respondents. Another 18 per cent had developed an enterprise-wide BCP, which had not been tested. A further 16 per cent had a BCP for some functions.

Eight respondents reported that they had experienced a significant business interruption in the last three years but a one-way ANOVA showed that there were no differences in the extent to which organizations had a plan between organizations that had experienced a disruption ($M = 4.25$, $SD = 1.28$) and those that had not ($M = 4.43$, $SD = 1.38$), ($F(1,30) = .111$, $p = .742$). Previous studies have shown that large organizations are more likely to have well-developed business continuity plans than small organizations. Yet in this study there were no significant differences in the level of preparation of the plan between large (>100 employees; $M = 4.09$, $SD = 1.69$) and smaller (<100 employees; $M = 3.12$, $SD = 2.09$) organizations ($F(1, 61) = 3.574$, $p = .064$). Of the 48 responses to the question addressing where the plan was located, 35 (73 per cent, including all those with well-developed plans) responded that there were multiple copies. Ten organizations had a single copy, seven of which were located at head office, and three respondents did not know of the location of the plan(s).

Forty-eight respondents answered the question about how the plan was developed. Most (31) used spreadsheets, Microsoft Word documents, or a combination of the two. Only five used a software package (in one case an in-house package). Overwhelmingly (36 responses), the most common reason given for developing a plan was "good risk management practice", but 18 responses cited legislative or audit requirements (multiple responses were allowed to this question, and 57 respondents gave 91 reasons).

The questionnaire included questions addressing the types of hazard and the critical resources that were included in their organization's BCP. It was hoped that these questions might indicate whether a hazard approach or a business impact approach had been followed. However, there was little difference in the way these questions were answered and it was not possible to tell which approach had been formally considered in preparing the plan. The results are shown in Table 1.

A large number of respondents either did not answer this question at all, or left some fields blank, or stated they did not know what the plan covered. The noteworthy result is therefore where respondents knew their plan was lacking. No one reported that their plan did not cover fire, but 11 of 32 (36 per cent) responses where the

Table 1. Content of Business Continuity Plans a) Hazards

Hazard	Yes	No	Don't Know or Blank
Fire	44	0	18
Flood	33	3	26
Sabotage	32	2	28
Pandemic	19	11	32
Terrorism	31	5	26

Source: Authors

Table 2. b) Critical Resources

Resource	Yes	No	Don't Know or Blank
IT	41	3	18
facilities	42	1	19
Equipment	36	2	24
Data	39	2	21
People	32	5	25
Telecommunications	38	1	23

Source: Authors

content was known, reported that the plan did not cover a pandemic, and five out of 36 (14 per cent) reported that terrorism was not covered.

With respect to critical resources, facilities and IT had received the most attention. This is the traditional focus of BCP. People were the critical resource most likely to be omitted (13.5 per cent of responses) but the number of responses was low. Six of the 15 companies with fully developed plans were among those reporting gaps. One only covered fire as a hazard and IT facilities and equipment as a critical resource. Four others reported no coverage for a pandemic. Gaps were more likely to have been noted by respondents with more fully developed plans. For the organizations without a plan, the main reason stated was that the organization had other priorities (10 respondents), with the perception of "no need" (5 respondents) being the second most common response.

SOLUTIONS AND RECOMMENDATIONS

This study showed that a slightly lower percentage of organizations with a risk management professional had some form of BCP than in studies outside of Australia. That is, 58 per cent of Australian organizations sampled reported plans of some type, compared with between 66 per cent and 93 per cent of organizations in the United States. Several companies reporting fully developed plans also noted gaps in coverage of hazards or critical resources, leaving only nine of the 62 respondents (15 per cent) with fully tested plans covering all major hazard types and critical resources. In contrast to other studies, experience of a significant interruption was not more likely to be associated with a higher level of development of plans. Larger organizations were not more likely to have more developed BCPs, though an increased sample size may change this result.

It was not possible to identify from this study what the specific form of the business continuity plans were or how the plans had been developed. However, the reported BCP approaches ranged from using spreadsheets (31 responses), Microsoft Word documents, or a combination of the two, with only five using a software package designed to lead them through a formal BCP process.

The lack of response to questions relating to the coverage of the plans where all other questions were answered suggests a possible lack of detailed knowledge of content of the BCPs by the risk-management professionals surveyed. Consistent with previous studies, the likely absence of people through a pandemic, and considering people as a critical resource, were least likely to be covered in the plans. This common finding is inconsistent with general human resource management practices.

Regardless of the specific resource emphasis in an industry, the human resource factor is viewed as a fundamental element in an organization's success (Nankervis, Compton & Baird, 2005). Proactive organizations take a people-focused approach to BCP and build resilience through the coordination and succession planning of key human capital. This approach not only assists the organization's ability to adapt to threats posed to its workforce, but also responds to changes in workforce demographics and customer buying patterns.

Rapid, unpredictable workplace change brings risks in the form of opportunities and threats to today's organization. Embedding BCP as a core principle into an organization's culture through actively managing and tracking the BCP in the management of the business and systems design processes would promote acceptance of BCP in workplace processes and everyday practices. Furthermore workshops, review meetings, and embracing the human component with formal training for both technical staff and management would educate staff and raise BCP including management awareness and proactivity. Continual integrated change management lies at the heart of BCP and management, organizational dynamism and resilience. These qualities address both risk minimization and opportunity exploration and are hallmarks of proactive, innovative organizations that utilize integrated frameworks and methodologies specific to their organization's culture. With business forming the backbone of a nation's social and economic fabric, it is essential that government and business work collaboratively to develop a transferable BCP structure that informs the development of a BCM framework that enlightens policy, practice and procedure.

FUTURE RESEARCH DIRECTIONS

A limitation of this study is that the respondents were drawn from a convenience sample of employees working in roles associated with risk management in their organizations. However, convenience samples are consistent with the majority of the BCM studies found in the literature. A further limitation is that the respondents were risk-management professionals attending a trade show or conference and thus they may not be representative of the status of business continuity planning in Australian organizations. In addition, the study uses self-reports on the state of the business continuity planning and thus the respondents may overestimate how good the plans actually are. Therefore, further research on the communication of business continuity plans in all business contexts (small business, large business, not-for-profit, and government) is required.

CONCLUSION

This preliminary study shows there is scope for a more consistent approach to BCP studies in Australian organizations. Aspects of BCP, which relate to availability of human resources, are least likely to be adequately covered even in organizations with well-developed plans. The study has shown a similar pattern of business continuity plan development in Australia as has been reported in studies in the United States. This study shows there is scope for a more consistent approach to BCP in Australian organizations. Aspects of BCP which relate to the availability of human resources are least likely to be adequately covered even in organizations with well-developed plans and future studies may consider going one step further and uncovering BCP in various organizational contexts and countries. The coordination of resources including staff availability in the event of a business disruption is central to maintaining the capacity, effectiveness, growth and wealth creation of the business. In many instances, when addressing BCP in today's organizations, the importance of the human resource function is overlooked and this poses a concern to the organization's sustainability in today's highly competitive environment.

Finally, human resource practices that support and promote consistent communication and an organizational culture that allows BCP values, attitudes and beliefs to become embedded and to move across traditional organizational boundaries are therefore important to gain the cooperation needed to implement plans in an organization's operational area. The capacity to implement such plans would assist the organization to recover quickly from relatively small incidents and to prevent them from escalating to a major disruption, which would enable an organization to survive a rare and serious disaster.

REFERENCES

Alcantara, P., & Riglietti, G. (2017). *Business Continuity Institute Horizon Scan Report 2017*. Caversham: BCI.

Bajgoric, N. (2014). Business continuity management: A systemic framework for implementation. *Kybernetes*, *43*(2), 156–177. doi:10.1108/K-11-2013-0252

Bajgoric, N., & Moon, Y. B. (2009). Enhancing systems integration by incorporating business continuity drivers. *Industrial Management & Data Systems*, *109*(1), 74–97. doi:10.1108/02635570910926609

BCI. (2005). Retrieved from http://www.thebci.org/Glossary.pdf

Bush, G. W. (2007). *National Security and Homeland Security Presidential Directive*. Retrieved from https://georgewbush-whitehouse.archives.gov/news/releases/2007/05/20070509-12.html

Carvalho, M. M. D., & Rabechini Junior, R. (2015). Impact of risk management on project performance: The importance of soft skills. *International Journal of Production Research*, *53*(2), 321–340. doi:10.1080/00207543.2014.919423

Castillo, C. (2004). Disaster preparedness and business continuity planning at Boeing: an integrated model. *Journal of Facilities Management, 3*(1), 8-26.

Christopher, M., & Peck, H. (2004). Building the resilient supply chain. *International Journal of Logistics Management*, *15*(2), 1–13. doi:10.1108/09574090410700275

CMI. (2005). *Chartered Management Institute: Business Continuity Management*. Available at: www.managers.org.uk/docs_docs/BCM_20052865.pdf

Connell, C. M. (2002). Jardine, Matheson, & Company: The role of the external organization in risk reduction and learning. Academy of Management Proceedings, 2002(1), B1-B6.

Deloitte. (2005). *CPM Global Assurance and Deloitte and Touche LLP 5th annual survey of BCM professionals entering the mainstream business continuity planning*. Available at: http://www.deloitte.com/dtt/cda/doc/content/us_ers_Final_DeloitteCPM_BCMSurvey.pdf

Duncan, W. J., Yeager, V. A., Rucks, A. C., & Ginter, P. M. (2011). Surviving organisational disasters. *Business Horizons*, *54*(2), 135–142. doi:10.1016/j.bushor.2010.10.005

Eden, P., & Matthews, W. (1996). Disaster management in libraries. *Library Management*, *17*(3), 5–12. doi:10.1108/01435129610112743

Elliott, D., Swartz, E., & Herbane, B. (2002). *Business Continuity Management: A Crisis Management Approach*. London: Routledge.

Ferguson, W. R. (2002). *Remarks by vice chairman of Federal Reserve to Institute of International Bankers.* Available at: www.federalreserve.gov

Herbane, B., Elliott, D., & Swartz, E. M. (2004). Business continuity management: Time for a strategicrole? *Long Range Planning*, *37*(5), 435–457. doi:10.1016/j.lrp.2004.07.011

Ho, W., Zheng, T., Yildiz, H., & Talluri, S. (2015). Supply chain risk management: A literature review. *International Journal of Production Research*, *53*(16), 5031–5069. doi:10.1080/00207543.2015.1030467

IBM Global Services. (2006). *In the Spotlight: The Human Side of Business Continuity Planning*. New York, NY: Somers.

Ibrahimović, S., & Bajgorić, N. (2016). Modeling information system availability by using bayesian belief network approach. *Interdisciplinary Description of Complex Systems*, *14*(2), 125–138. doi:10.7906/indecs.14.2.2

Inkster, N. (2016). Information Warfare and the US Presidential Election. *Survival: Global Politics and Strategy*, *58*(5), 23-32. Retrieved from https://www.iiss.org/en/politics%20and%20strategy/blogsections/2016-d1f9/november-b3f2/information-warfare-and-the-us-presidential-election-e9ad

International Standards Organisation (ISO). (2009). *ISO31000 Risk Management: Principles and Guidelines*. Geneva: ISO.

Kahn, M. B. (2012). *Disaster Response and Planning for Libraries*. Chicago, IL: American Library Association.

Kuo, T.-H. (2011). How to improve organizational performance through learning and knowledge? *International Journal of Manpower*, *32*(5/6), 581–603. doi:10.1108/01437721111158215

Lam, W. (2002, May). Ensuring business continuity. *IT Pro*, 19-25.

Li, G., Fan, H., Lee, P. K., & Cheng, T. C. E. (2015). Joint supply chain risk management: An agency and collaboration perspective. *International Journal of Production Economics*, *164*, 83–94. doi:10.1016/j.ijpe.2015.02.021

McMurray, A. J., Pace, R. W., & Scott, D. (2004). *Research: A commonsense approach*. Melbourne: Thomson Learning Social Science Press.

McMurray, A. J., Scott, D., & Pace, R. W. (2004). The relationship between organizational commitment and organizational climate in manufacturing. *Human Resource Development Quarterly*, *15*(4), 365–377. doi:10.1002/hrdq.1116

Muir, A., & Shenton, S. (2002). If the worst happens: The use and effectiveness of disaster plans in libraries and archives. *Library Management*, *23*(3), 115–123. doi:10.1108/01435120210697216

Myers, K. N. (2006). *Business Continuity Strategies* (3rd ed.). Hoboken, NJ: John Wiley & Sons.

Nankervis, A., Compton, R., & Baird, M. (2005). *Human Resource Management*. Melbourne: Thomson.

Parise, G., Hesla, E., Parise, L., & Pennacchia, R. (2016). Switching Procedures and Business Continuity Management: The Flock Logic of Multiple Source Systems. *IEEE Transactions on Industry Applications*, *52*(1), 60–66. doi:10.1109/TIA.2015.2463791

Perez-Floriano, L. R., & Gonzalez, J. A. (2007). Risk, safety and culture in Brazil and Argentina: The case of TransInc Corporation. *International Journal of Manpower*, *28*(5), 403–417. doi:10.1108/01437720710778394

Pink, R. (2004). Looking for continuity. *Corporate Finance*, *135*, 32–35.

Sahebjamnia, N., Torabi, S. A., & Mansouri, S. A. (2015). Integrated business continuity and disaster recovery planning: Towards organizational resilience. *European Journal of Operational Research*, *242*(1), 261–273. doi:10.1016/j.ejor.2014.09.055

Sanchez, J., Korbin, W., & Viscara, D. (1995). Corporate support in the aftermath of a natural disaster: Effects on employee strains. *Academy of Management Journal*, *38*(2), 504–521. doi:10.2307/256690

Savage, M. (2002). Business continuity planning. *Work Study*, *51*(5), 254–261. doi:10.1108/00438020210437277

Sax, J., & Torp, S. S. (2015). Speak up! Enhancing risk performance with enterprise risk management, leadership style and employee voice. *Management Decision*, *53*(7), 1452–1468. doi:10.1108/MD-10-2014-0625

Smallman, C., & Smith, D. (2003). Managerial risk perceptions: Exploring the dimensions of managers accepted risks. *Risk Management*, *5*(1), 7–32. doi:10.1057/palgrave.rm.8240137

Smith, D. (2005). Business (not) as usual: Crisis management, service recovery and the vulnerability of organisations. *Journal of Services Marketing*, *19*(5), 309–320. doi:10.1108/08876040510609925

Smith, D., & Fischbacher, M. (2009). The changing nature of risk and risk management: The challenge of borders, uncertainty and resilience. *Risk Management*, *11*(1), 1–12. doi:10.1057/rm.2009.1

Snedaker, S. (2013). *Business Continuity and Disaster Recovery Planning for IT Professionals*. Maryland Heights, MO: Elsevier.

Tucker, E. (2014). *Business Continuity from Preparedness to Recovery: A Standards-Based Approach*. Butterworth-Heinemann.

Verano-Tacoronte, D., & Melián-González, S. (2008). Human resources control systems and performance: The role of uncertainty and risk propensity. *International Journal of Manpower*, *29*(2), 161–187. doi:10.1108/01437720810872712

Webb, G. R., Tierney, K. J., & Dahlhamer, J. M. (2000). Business and disasters: Empirical patterns and unanswered questions. *Natural Hazards Review*, *1*(2), 83–90. doi:10.1061/(ASCE)1527-6988(2000)1:2(83)

Wiengarten, F., Humphreys, P., Gimenez, C., & McIvor, R. (2016). Risk, risk management practices, and the success of supply chain integration. *International Journal of Production Economics*, *171*, 361–370. doi:10.1016/j.ijpe.2015.03.020

Yoshida, K., & Deyle, R. E. (2005). Determinants of small business hazard mitigation. *Natural Hazards Review*, *6*(1), 1–12. doi:10.1061/(ASCE)1527-6988(2005)6:1(1)

Zsidisin, G. A., Melnyk, S. A., & Ragatz, G. L. (2005). An institutional theory perspective of BCP Planning for purchasing and supply management. *International Journal of Production Research*, *43*(16), 3401–3421. doi:10.1080/00207540500095613

Chapter 7
Enterprise Risk Management Software:
User Requirements

Dražena Gašpar
University of Mostar, Bosnia and Herzegovina

Mirela Mabić
University of Mostar, Bosnia and Herzegovina

ABSTRACT

This chapter presents research results on user requirements related to enterprise risk management software. The authors developed a questionnaire to investigate the standpoints of risk managers, quality managers, and others in charge of risk management regarding the functionality they expect risk management software to support. In today's globalized and volatile world, the recognition, understanding, and management of risks is critical for an organization's survival. Adequate software support enables organizations to take an innovative, risk-based approach to governance and compliance and to gain a holistic, enterprise-wide view of risk exposure and near-real-time risk management and monitoring. Research results show the main attributes that risk management software should have in order to fulfill user expectations. The chapter also provides some important guidelines and suggestions for risk management software development and improvement.

DOI: 10.4018/978-1-5225-3704-5.ch007

INTRODUCTION

This chapter presents research results on user requirements related to enterprise risk management (ERM) software. This research was based on a survey of companies in Bosnia and Herzegovina and it is a continuation of the preliminary research conducted by authors in 2015. The preliminary research was based on a limited number of respondents (41)—namely, participants of a risk management seminar organized by Oskar, a center for development and quality in Zagreb, Croatia. This preliminary research was used to test the questionnaire developed by the authors in order to investigate the standpoints of risk managers, quality managers, and others in charge of risk management regarding the functionality they expect ERM software to support. The results of the preliminary research showed that most respondents did not use ERM software. However, they were aware of the importance of ERM software for efficient risk management, and they declaratively supported the purchase and implementation of that software. According to the preliminary research results, there was no need to change the questionnaire for the new research substantially.

Today, organizations face global challenges regarding competition, resources (human and physical), business safety (especially digital data protection), exposure to terrorist attacks, and so forth. Generally, the world is becoming less benign, with more discontinuity and volatility. Organizations' viability and success in this increasingly volatile world heavily depend on the extent to which their managers are aware of the environment in which they operate, keep up with the changes, and how fast and how successfully they can respond to them. This means that managers must think in multiple time frames—that is, work on immediate tactics to counteract new threats (competition, market changes, etc.), and in the long term, work on selection and development of new long-lived capabilities. Managers and risk managers across all lines of business have become accountable for a sustainable risk framework.

Although heads of successful companies have always given a certain degree of priority to risk management when handling daily business, they usually deal with individual risks one by one as they occur instead of having an integrated and proactive approach with the entire organization in mind. This is called the *silo approach*. A silo approach is when individuals or departments within an organization deal with a risk facing their own unit without considering that the entire organization (and, in particular, its overall reputation) is exposed to the same risk. A silo approach can be very dangerous in a globalized, complex, and volatile business environment. Such an environment needs a team of various people with different risk knowledge and experience working together in continuous interaction and coordination. Providing an efficient integrated and overall risk management approach is extremely demanding, and even an impossible task, without adequate software support.

Many ERM software solutions are available in today's market, but they differ in features and maturity. Most organizations are faced with the problem of how to choose the appropriate software solution for their risk management processes. Finding the right software that will suit the organization's needs is not always easy, but it is even more demanding to adjust the organization to the software's requirements. Therefore, the software solutions that offer adaptability to user requirements can significantly shorten the implementation time. A major challenge in selecting and implementing risk management software is that there are many variations in the practical implementation of risk management, especially at the detailed level.

In order to ensure a structural approach to risk management, risk management frameworks like COSO Enterprise Risk Management and ISO 31000:2009 were developed. Risk management frameworks define activities that are required to manage risk effectively. Activities for managing issues and opportunities are not explicitly specified in the risk management framework. Although risk management can be integrated with the issue and opportunity management, the details for achieving an integrated approach to managing risks, issues, and opportunities is beyond the framework's scope. The framework is implementation independent—it defines key risk management activities but does not specify how to perform those activities. In particular, the framework helps to provide a foundation for a comprehensive risk management methodology basis for evaluating and improving a program's risk management.

Regardless of the framework, the heart of the risk management process is concerned with preparing for and then conducting a risk assessment, leading, as necessary, to risk treatment. The process starts by defining what the organization wants to achieve and the external and internal factors that may influence success in achieving those objectives. In order to ensure that the risk management process flows smoothly and is efficient and effective, organizations must apply information technology (IT).

From the very beginning, COSO ERM recognized the critical role of IT support in the risk management process, and that recognition has continued in updated versions of the COSO ERM framework, which also reflects the increased relevance of technology.

Adequate software support enables organizations to take an innovative, risk-based approach to governance and compliance and to gain a holistic, enterprise-wide view of risk exposure and near-real-time risk management and monitoring. Software support for the risk management process should provide organizations with efficient risk evaluation and assessment, continuous monitoring, reporting, and easier improvement of the process.

The research results show the main features that ERM software should have in order to fulfill user expectations. The chapter also provides some important guidelines and suggestions for ERM software development and improvement.

BACKGROUND

The origin of modern risk management dates to 1955 when Wayne Snider, professor of insurance at Temple University, proposed that insurance managers should be called *risk managers* because they were, at that time, more focused on risk and risk control than on purchasing insurance (Douglas, 1993). The following year, Gallagher (1956) used the term *risk management* in a business context. The first books related to risk management were published by Mehr and Hedges (1963) and Williams and Heins (1964). The first definitions of the term *risk management* reflected a close identification with insurance management. Mehr and Hedges defined risk management as "the management of those risks for which the organization, principles, and techniques appropriate to insurance management are useful" (p.23). Over the next two decades, some authors (Bannister & Bawcutt, 1981; Crockford, 1982; Giarini, 1976; Hamilton,1988) proposed broader definitions of risk management, outlining it as linking functions inside organizations. For example, Bannister and Bawcutt defined risk management as "the identification, measurement and economic control of risks that threaten the assets and earnings of a business or other enterprise" (p.19). Despite intensive theoretical development, in practice, risk management continued to be closely related to insurance management until the late 1990s, when it became an integral part of business decision making and the position of chief risk officer (CRO) emerged (Dionne, 2013). The result of this evolution was the emergence of a new term: *enterprise risk management*. Lam (2003) defined enterprise risk management as "an integrated framework for managing credit risk, market risk, operational risk, economic capital, and risk transfer in order to maximize firm value" (p.2). The Committee of Sponsoring Organizations of the Treadway Commission ([COSO], 2004a, p. 13) defined ERM as:

A process, effected by an entity's board of directors, management, and other personnel, applied in strategy setting and across the enterprise, designed to identify potential events that may affect the entity, and manage risk to be within its risk appetite, to provide reasonable assurance regarding the achievement of entity objectives.

The International Organization for Standardization (ISO), in standard ISO 31000:2009, defined risk as the "effect of uncertainty on objectives" and risk management as "coordinated activities to direct and control an organization with regard to risk" (AIRMIC, 2010, p. 5).

However, it is important to emphasize that ERM is not a new form of risk management but rather a holistic view of risks in organizations. Namely, some authors (Dickinson, 2001; Razali &Tahir, 2011; Wolf, 2008) stated that the main difference between risk management and ERM is that risk management is a silo approach where risks are managed individually, while ERM represents an integrated approach to risk management.

Globalization and increasing business complexity are the main driving forces that have influenced ERM development and implementation (Grose, 2015).

In order to ensure a structural approach to risk management, risk management frameworks were developed. There are two widely recognized and implemented risk management frameworks:

- COSO Enterprise Risk Management
- ISO 31000:2009

COSO ERM does not state risk processes explicitly but instead highlights eight interrelated components. These are derived from the way management runs an enterprise and are integrated with the management process (see Figure 1). These components are as follows (COSO, 2004a):

- **Internal Environment:** This encompasses the tone of an organization and sets the basis for how risk is viewed and addressed by an entity's people, including risk management philosophy and risk appetite, integrity and ethical values, and the environment in which they operate.
- **Objective Setting:** Objectives must exist before management can identify potential events affecting their achievement.
- **Event Identification:** Internal and external events affecting achievement of an entity's objectives must be identified, distinguishing between risks and opportunities. Opportunities are channeled back to management's strategy or objective-setting processes.
- **Risk Assessment:** Risks are analyzed, considering likelihood and impact, as a basis for determining how they should be managed. Risks are assessed on an inherent and a residual basis.
- **Risk Response:** Management selects risk responses—avoiding, accepting, reducing, or sharing risk—developing a set of actions to align risks with the entity's risk tolerances and risk appetite.
- **Control Activities:** Policies and procedures are established and implemented to help ensure the risk responses are effectively carried out.

- **Information and Communication:** Relevant information is identified, captured, and communicated in a form and timeframe that enable people to carry out their responsibilities.
- **Monitoring:** The entirety of ERM is monitored, and modifications are made as necessary.

ISO 31000:2009 adopted abroad process for managing risk, consisting of the following steps:

- Establishing context is the first step in the risk management process. It includes defining what the organization wants to achieve and the external and internal factors that may influence success in achieving those objectives (AIRMIC, 2010).
- Risk assessment comprises the three steps of risk identification, risk analysis, and risk evaluation. Risk identification requires the application of a systematic process to understand what could happen, how, when, and why. Risk analysis is concerned with developing an understanding of each risk, its consequences, and the likelihood of those consequences. Risk evaluation involves making a decision about the level of risk and the priority for attention through the application of the criteria developed when the context was established (Purdy, 2010).
- Communication and consultation with internal and external stakeholders.
- Monitoring and review involve environmental scanning by risk owners, control assurance, taking on board new information that becomes available, and learning lessons about risks and controls from the analysis of successes and failures (AIRMIC, 2010).
- Risk treatment is the process by which existing controls are improved or new controls are developed and implemented (Purdy, 2010).

From the very beginning, the evolution of risk management has been supported by IT. The first risk management information system (RMIS) was developed in 1967. Because risk management was related to insurance processingat that time, the first RMIS was designed to computerize and consolidate all of a company's claims reports so that the information could be viewed in one place. Guyon Saunders is widely recognized as the founder of the RMIS industry. He was the first to realize that computer technology could be used to consolidate and report claim and risk data to help organizations better understand and more effectively manage their total cost of risk (Marsh ClearSight, 2016). COSO ERM also recognized from the very beginning that "technology plays a critical role in enabling the flow of information in an organization, including information directly relevant to enterprise risk management" (COSO, 2004b, p. 70).

Since 1967, software support for risk management has evolved from the mainframe's batch mode of processing to the cloud era. As software support has become more powerful, ERM software vendors constantly innovate and empower their solutions to meet changing business needs in the ever-expanding discipline of ERM that now extends to terrorism, cyberattacks, and political unrest (Marsh ClearSight, 2016).

The key risks facing decisionmakers in implementing their objectives in 2017 is indicated by research conducted in the fall of 2016 by the company Protiviti and North Carolina State University's ERM Initiative. Participants in their survey were 735 board members and executives across several industries, of which 407 respondents were from the United States, and 328 were from other parts of the world. Respondents were asked to give their opinions on the possible effects of 30 selected risks on their organizations in 2017. These risks were observed through the following three dimensions (Protiviti, 2017):

- **Macroeconomic:** Specifically those that are highly likely to influence the organization's growth.
- **Strategic:** Those facing the organization and that may affect the validity of the strategy and achievement of the organization's growth.
- **Operational:** Those that may affect performance of the key operations essential for implementing the organization's strategy.

Table 1. shows the top 10 risks with the percentage responses for the three risk classifications (significant impact, potential impact, and less significant impact) and the type of risk (macroeconomic, strategic, and operational).

In 2016, the Federation of European Risk Management Associations (FERMA) conducted a risk management benchmarking survey. It was the eighth edition of the FERMA European Risk and Insurance Report, and it has been published every two years since 2002. The study population was composed of all FERMA members (22 national associations in 21 countries) and was conducted from April to June 2016. In total, 4,407 invitations were sent.

The survey (39 questions) received 634 responses (FERMA, 2016). Table 2 shows the top 10 risks, according to the FERMA survey, currently seen as the highest threats to the successful achievement of an organization's strategic goals regarding likelihood and trend versus the last survey conducted in 2014 (FERMA, 2016).

The results of both surveys are very similar, with economic conditions as the number one threat in each case. This proves that economic globalization and related risks are our new reality.

Table 1. Top 10 risks for 2017 (Protiviti, 2017)

Risk Description	% of Significant Impact Responses	Type of Risk
Economic conditions	72%	Macroeconomic
Regulatory changes and scrutiny	66%	Strategic
Rapid speed of disruptive innovations and new technologies	63%	Strategic
Cyberthreats	60%	Operational
Privacy/identity management and information security	57%	Operational
Sustaining customer loyalty and retention	57%	Strategic
Succession challenges and the ability to attract and retain top talent	55%	Operational
Organization's culture may not encourage timely identification and escalation of risk issues	55%	Operational
Resistance to change operations	54%	Operational
Volatility in global financial markets and currencies	53%	Macroeconomic

Table 2. Top 10 risks in 2016 according to FERMA survey (FERMA, 2016)

Top 10 Risks in 2016	Trend Versus 2014	Likelihood
Economic conditions	↑↑↑	High
Business continuity disruption	NEW	High
Political, country instability	↓↓↓	High
Noncompliance with regulation and legislation	↓↓↓	High
Competition	↓↓↓	High
Reputation and brand	↓↓↓	Medium
Cyberattack/data privacy	↑↑↑	High
Market strategy, clients	↓↓↓	High
IT systems and data centers	↑↑↑	Medium
Interest rate and foreign exchange	↑↑↑	Medium

In addition, these surveys showed that managers' perceptions of risks are changing from one year/period to another. The consequence is that ERM software must provide adequate solutions for those changes. Management expectations have constantly increased related to high-quality risk data and sophisticated ERM. This resulted in a great need for adequate software support, leading to the development of different ERM software that varies in maturity and capability. In fact, most organizations today are struggling to identify the best way to acquire adequate software solutions for the risk management process.

Vendor solutions purchased to support ERM are more difficult to categorize because the market is in rapid transition, with little consensus among leading analysts on market segmentation. Several systems based on insurance risk management (RMIS) now offer ERM features, while others approach the ERM market from an operational risk management or compliance background. Some niche players offer stand-alone ERM systems. However, the key question is what users expect to get from ERM software. Thirty years ago, Brooks (1987) wrote, "The hardest single part of building a software system is deciding precisely what to build"(p.11), meaning that users should be more intensively included in all phases of software development, not just at the beginning and the end. Research conducted by Bano and Zowghi (2013) from 1980 to2012 showed the positive relationship between involving users in the process of software development and software success.

Recently, research was conducted on software vendors and the main characteristics of their solutions and user expectations (Ambrose, Spencer,& Weinstein, 2016; Aon Risk Solutions, 2014; Capterra, n.d.; Chambers, 2016; Gartner, 2017; Tweedy, 2013). The results of this research were used for forming the list of main features that ERM software solutions should have, and this list is used in research related to user requirements toward ERM software conducted by the authors.

WHAT USERS EXPECT FROM ERM SOFTWARE

Issues, Controversies, and Problems

As organizations have continued to use ERM software, their expectations, especially related to the fulfillment of ERM vendors' promises, have increased. Namely, ERM vendors promised organizations an integrated, holistic view and management of organizational risks and easier linking between risks with the achievement of organizational strategic goals. Moreover, a high growth of different ERM software created the illusion that if organizations choose the appropriate ERM software, then everything related to risk management will go smoothly. Unfortunately, that is not the case. The open issues and problems related to users' expectations of ERM software can be categorized into two main groups, as follows:

- Technical challenges
- Organizational challenges

The technical challenges related to user expectations of ERM software includethe following (Patterson, 2015):

- The inability of ERM software to address all of an organization's current or future ERM information needs. The reason for this lies in the fact that most organizations, especially large ones, need to manage very complex risk portfolios (strategic, business, financial, operating, legal, supply chain, regulatory, and reputation risks), which require data collection from very diverse sources inside, and sometimes outside, the organization. The task of connecting all these diverse data can be challenging if not fully built with a clear, concise project plan, one that captures all the requirements regarding technologies, resources, architectures, data flows, and data management.
- The inability to ensure effective support for management's appetite for risk and mitigation of enterprise risk results from the challenges related to the integration of currently available enterprise IT systems and ERM tools.

Organizational challenges related to user expectations from ERM software includethe following (PricewaterhouseCoopers, 2015):

- **Changing of the Guard:** Constant changes inuser requirements can dramatically slow the process of ERM software implementation.
- **Organizational Culture:** An integrated ERM software approach can be in conflict with a decentralizedorganization and its culture. Moreover, decision-making culture may not support ERM integration with organizational strategic goals.
- **Communication:** There is often a lack of communication amongenterprise risk assessment expectations, current risk management activities and responsibilities, ERM information, and future ERM software plans.
- **Skills Gap:** ERM software implementation can require additional staffing and the defining of different user roles. ERM activities need managers with strong political skills to navigate organizational issues and strong technical skills to identify, prioritize, and analyze risks. It is difficultto find all theseskills in one person, so teamwork is necessary.
- **Lack of Value Proposition:** ERM software needs a value proposition, but enterprise risk managers sometimes cannot articulate the value beyond the compliance requirements that drive the ERM software implementation.
- **Lack of Risk Program Discipline:** ERM software usually expects continuous user involvement in the process of risk assessment, monitoring, and further development of ERM capabilities. However, reality has its own challenges, so after the initial enterprise risk assessment, management might become distracted by other business issues and therefore may be unwilling or unable to invest time in further developing ERM software.

SOLUTIONS AND RECOMMENDATIONS

In order to explore which technical and functional characteristics risk management software must have, an empirical research study was carried out.

The questionnaire was used for the research that was prepared by the authors and based on theoretical knowledge and practical experience in software development. The questionnaire was divided into two main sections. The first part of the questionnaire related to the fundamental characteristics of the companies to which the questionnaire was sent: industry, size, the number of employees, income, property, and so on. The second part of the questionnaire related to ERM software and was made up of two sets of allegations. The first related to technical characteristics (see Table 3) and the second to the functional properties of ERM software (see Table 4).

Table 3. A set of technical software characteristics

Code	Software for Risk Management Should...
tz1	enable data acquisition from different external sources
tz2	be installed on the local user's equipment
tz3	be Web oriented
tz4	be offered as "Software as a service" (SaaS)
tz5	have a context for help (help)
tz6	enable exporting reports in MS Word
tz7	enable exporting reports in PDF
tz8	enable exporting reports in MS Excel
tz9	enable working with multiple currencies
tz10	be multilingual
tz11	enable users with screen adjustments (colors, fonts, etc.)
tz12	enable usage on mobile devices (smartphones)
tz13	enable usage on tablets (iPad, Android)
tz14	have technical support or help desks 24/7/365
tz15	enable sending automated e-mails
tz16	enable displaying risks on the map
tz17	enable automatic warnings (alerts)
tz18	contain dashboards
tz19	enable the adjustment of dashboards
tz20	enable working with multiple organizations

Table 4. Set of functional software characteristics

Code	Software for Risk Management Should...
fz1	enable integration of standard key performance indicators and risk indicators
fz2	contain standard risk definitions and process taxonomy
fz3	be in compliance with the ISO 31000 standard
fz4	be in compliance with the COSO ERM framework
fz5	enable working with multiple organizations
fz6	enable customization of the organization's hierarchy
fz7	enable users to define rights for data access
fz8	contain a register of risk management system users
fz9	enable categorization, establishing threat hierarchy
fz10	enable definition of criteria for risk assessment
fz11	enable definition of the risk matrix
fz12	enable definition of a structure for all activities in process or project
fz13	enable definition of the structure of all threats and threat sources that could arise in the structure of activities in project or process
fz14	enable identification of threats and threat sources
fz15	enable risk identification
fz16	enable binding documents with risk
fz17	enable connection of loss with risk
fz18	enable risk analysis
fz19	enable follow up of the history of events connected with activities and the risk being assessed
fz20	enable automatic evaluation and risk ranking
fz21	enable definition of a risk treatment plan
fz22	enable definition of reporting and responsibilities
fz23	enable definition of risk treatment rules on the basis of a defined level of risk tolerance
fz24	support the process of risk approval (i.e., risk acceptance)
fz25	enable risk quantification
fz26	enable qualitative risk assessment
fz27	enable quantitative risk assessment
fz28	enable definition of threat indicators
fz29	enable connection (treatment) of risk (control and action) that is a definition of measures to be taken in the process of risk treatment

Questions about the company were created in the form of closed questions, and allegations about ERM software were evaluated on a scale from 1 to 5 (1 = no need at all; 2 = not necessary; 3 = doesn't matter; 4 = preferable; 5 = a must have).

The online questionnaire was sent to 215 companies during one month in 2017 (the pattern included companies of all sizes, i.e. small, medium and big). Completing the questionnaire took about 7–8 minutes. The empirical research results were based on 83 valid questionnaires (they have passed control activities prior to statistical analysis). The response rate was 38.6%. The online questionnaire was used. The pattern was formed by random choice of companies in BiH. The precondition for participation in research was that workplace of participant includes risk management activities. According to this precondition, the risk managers, managers and employees of risk departments fulfilled the questionnaire. A descriptive statistical analysis was performed on the collected data (the shares and average scores were calculated), and factor analysis was used to test characteristics of ERM software in order to aggregate the individual properties. The results are presented in tables and graphs.

The characteristics of the companies that completed the survey are presented in Table 5.

ANALYSIS AND DISCUSSION OF RESULTS

Fewer than a quarter of respondents (18, or 21.7%) stated that they have a special department or section in their companies whose primary task is risk management. The remaining respondents gave a negative answer. According to the respondents, risk management is also performed in these companies, but administration or owners and top managers usually perform these activities.

As for the questions about which software is used in companies as a support for risk management, only 15 respondents (18.1%) stated that their companies have software for risk management, while other respondents gave a negative answer (81.9%).

Respondents whose companies have software for risk management report that it has used for a maximum of 5years. However, only six respondents from companies that are not using the mentioned software stated that they plan to acquire it in the next 12 months.

Figure 1. shows the average score of the importance of certain technical characteristics of software for risk management.

Looking at all assessments of the technical characteristics in a given range of evaluations but omitting the two previously mentioned attributes that have the lowest average scores, it could be concluded for all other attributes that it should, almost necessarily, be the property of ERM software according to the respondents'

Table 5. Characteristics of the companies in which the respondents work

Characteristics		f	%
Your company's/ organization's foundation date	Before 1990	45	54.2
	Between 1990 and 2000	21	25.3
	After 2000	17	20.5
	Total	83	100.0
Primary activity is	Production and sale of products	10	12.0
	Provision of services	69	83.1
	Equally production and service	4	4.8
	Total	83	100.0
Annual income of your organization in the previous year	Up to 200,000 €	18	21.7
	200,000 € to 500,000 €	10	12.0
	500,000 € to 1,000,000 €	14	16.9
	1,000,000 € to 5,000,000 €	14	16.9
	5,000,000 € to 20,000,000 €	6	7.2
	over 20,000,000 €	21	25.3
	Total	83	100.0
How is your company/organization organized?	Public company	10	12.0
	Limited liability company (Ltd)	32	38.6
	Holding company	14	16.9
	State/public institution	17	20.5
	Other form of organization	10	12.0
	Total	83	100.0
What is the ownership form of your company/organization?	State	28	33.7
	Private	34	41.0
	Joint	14	16.9
	Other	7	8.4
	Total	83	100.0
What is the ownership structure of your company/organization?	Domestic owners	74	89.2
	Foreign owners	9	10.8
	Total	83	100.0
You consider yourself to belong to the group of	Micro company	12	14.5
	Small company	27	32.5
	Medium company	26	31.3
	Large company	18	21.7
	Total	83	100.0

opinions. This is confirmed by the distribution of scores. With certain characteristics, scores 4 and 5, and respectively, responses like "desirable to have" and "must have," predominate. The greatest diversity of responses was noticed in the properties of multilingualism and the ability to customize the display feature - user interface (colors, fonts, etc.) - thus confirming the lowest average scores.

As shown in Figure 1, the most important technical software characteristic for risk management is the automatic risk alert (tz17). The second most important characteristic is the ability to export reports to PDF files, followed by the possibility to export reports to MS Word. This was noted by more than 27% of respondents, who, in addition to these properties, also pointed out the importance of a Web-oriented property, the possibility to be installed on users' local machines, the need for context-sensitive help functionality, the ability to enable risk display on the map, the ability to enable automatic alerts, and the ability to contain the control panel as important technical characteristics the software should have.

Figure 2. shows the average score of the importance of certain functional properties of software for risk management.

As expected, functional properties have relatively higher average scores than technical features because the software is an "assistant" whose "interface" is important but cannot take precedence over functionality.

The lowest ratings were given to properties relating to compliance with the ISO 31000 standard, compliance with the COSO ERM framework, and providing work with more organizations, but average scores of even these properties are above 3.5.

Figure 1. Mean ratings of the importance of certain technical characteristics of ERM software

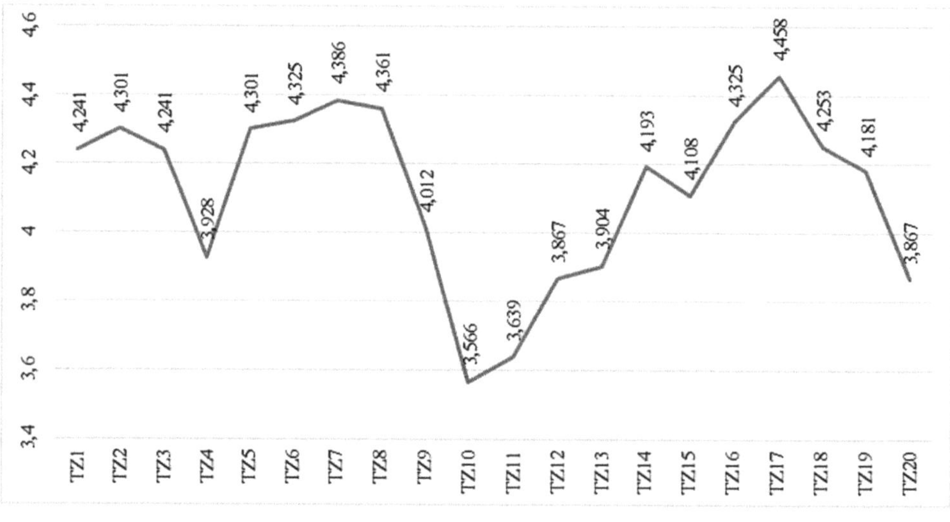

Observed through the representation of individual scores in these properties, the proportion of scores 4 and 5 ("desirable to have" and "must have") ranges from 65% to 82%. Despite the lowest scores, those ratings show that it is important to adjust the software to the standards because it is the only way it can offer assistance, which satisfies practical needs. In addition to these functional properties, a slightly lower share of 90% is determined for properties to "allow adjustment of the hierarchy of the organization" and to "contain a register of users of the risk management system."However, these results also suggest that these two properties are important components of the overall functionality of ERM software. In all other characteristics, the share of 4s and 5s is higher than 90%. The results presented in Figure 2 note that the average scores mostly range between 4.4 and 4.6, confirming the previously mentioned results.

Although the uneven representation of companies already using ERM software (SW(yes)) and those who do not use it (SW(no)) is in the sample, the comparison between the importance of both technical (see Figure 3) and functional software features was performed (see Figure 4).

Regarding the analysis of differences in opinions about the importance of the technical characteristics of ERM software, the biggest consensus of opinions shows at feature tz2, the possibility of installing the software on a user's local equipment. If the average score of these characteristics is perceived in terms of set scale ratings and their importance, then it is evident that both parties consider it desirable for

Figure 2. Mean ratings of the importance of certain functional characteristics of ERM software

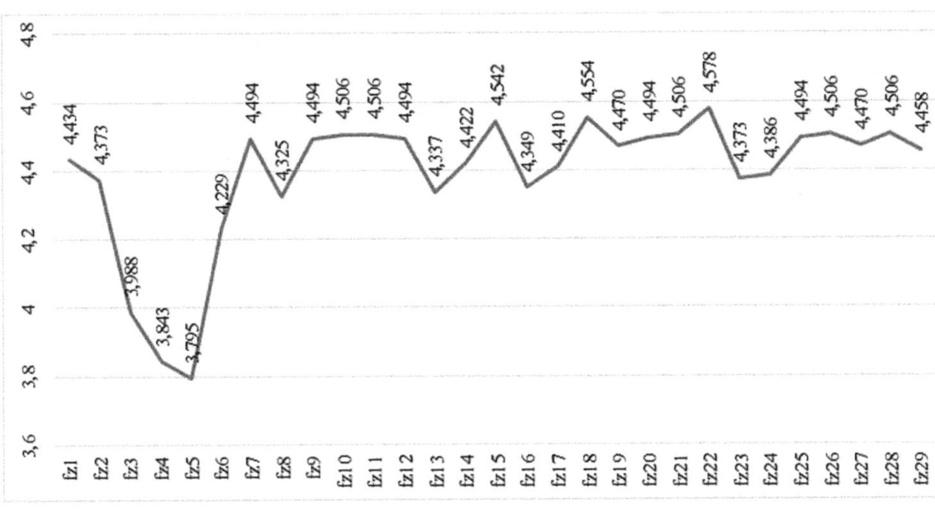

Figure 3. Mean ratings of the importance of certain technical characteristics of ERM software according to their previous practice of using ERP software

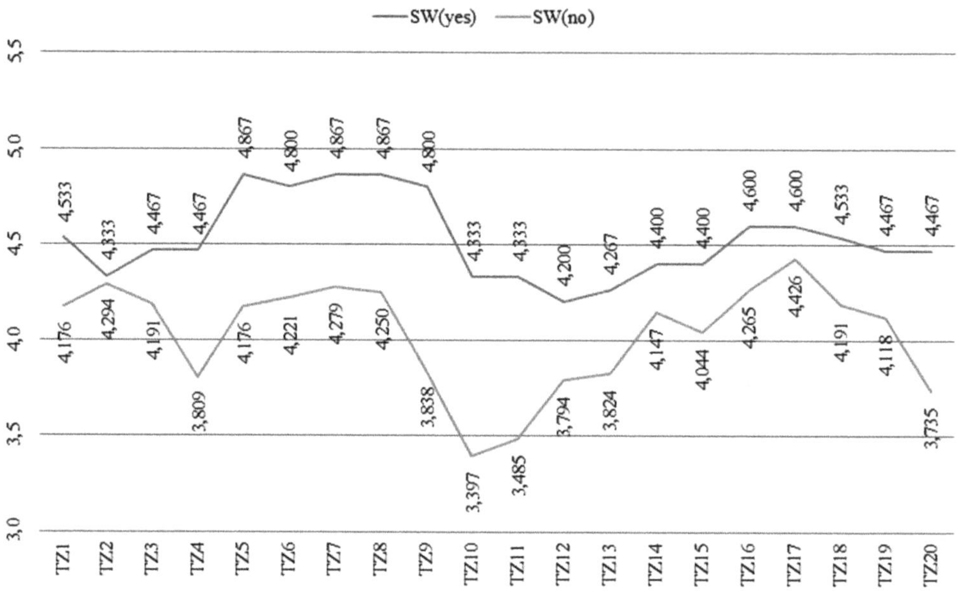

ERM software to be installed on a user's local equipment. This means that users do not have any or have minor costs related to hardware.

On the other hand, the largest discrepancy was observed regarding the result that ERM software should be multilingual. For respondents who currently do not use the software, this characteristic is not important, but respondents using ERM software in their businesses find it advisable that ERM software has the option of multilingualism.

Related to functional characteristics of ERM software, the biggest difference between respondents who already use ERM software and those who do not use it were observed regarding the characteristics "be in compliance with the ISO 31000 standard," "be in compliance with the COSO ERM framework," and "enable working with multiple organizations." The respondents who already use ERM software gave higher importance to these characteristics. The smallest differences in average ratings were observed with the characteristics "enable customization of the organization's hierarchy," "enable integration of standard key performance indicators and risk indicators," and "contain standard risk definitions and process taxonomy."

Generally, in line with the results presented in Figure 2 (the ratings for the whole sample), both groups of respondents present ratings greater than 3.5, which shows that respondents recognized the importance of the aforementioned characteristics for the reporting part of ERM software.

Figure 4. Mean ratings of the importance of certain functional characteristics of ERM software according to their previous practice of using ERP software

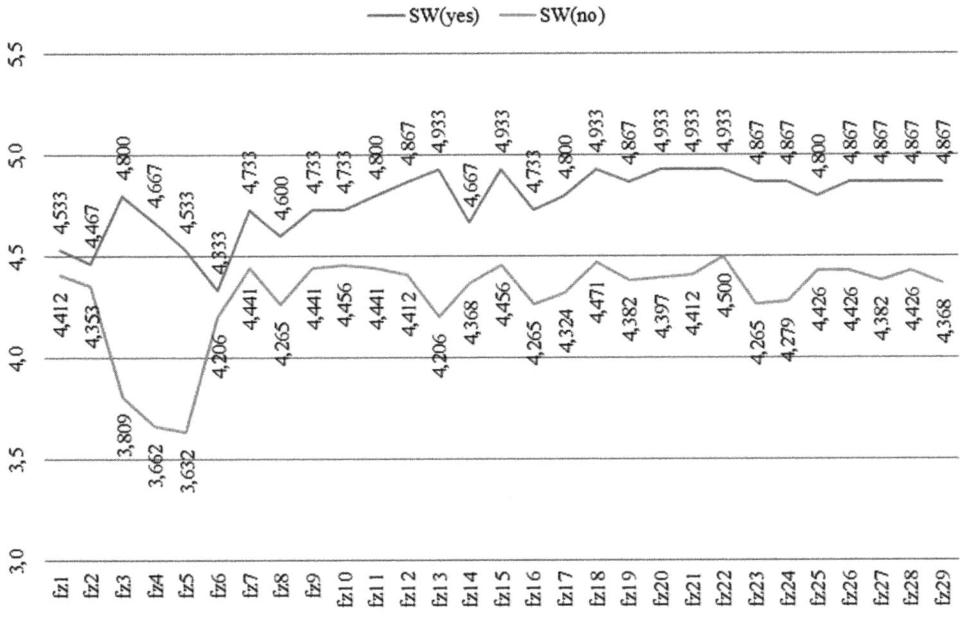

Figures 1, 2, 3, and 4 show the results for particular technical and functional characteristics. However, to facilitate easier analysis of technical and functional characteristics of ERM software, factor analysis was conducted separately on the set of technical and functional characteristics.

Before factor analysis, it was tested if data were suitable for this type of analysis (Kaiser-Meyer-Olkin and Bartlett's test). The testing deduced the following:

- **Set of Technical Characteristics:** Middling adequacy of data for dimension reduction. Kaiser-Meyer-Olkin value is 0.712, and Bartlett's test of sphericity is significant ($p<0.001$).
- **Set of Functional Characteristics:** Meritorious adequacy of data for dimension reduction. Kaiser-Meyer-Olkin value is 0.900, and Bartlett's test of sphericity is significant ($p<0.001$).

In accordance with satisfied conditions for conducting factor analysis, the analysis was conducted on the collected data (Varimax rotation with Kaiser normalization).After analysis, the factors with Initial Eigenvalues >1 (Kaiser rule: "Keep the components with eigenvalues above 1") were kept. As additional criteria, the breakpoint on scree plot was analyzed. The analysis showed that, in the set of technical characteristics of ERM software, identified factors explained 79.815% of the variance, and in the set of functional characteristics, 81.386%.

Both results are in compliance with the recommendations of Hair, Black, Babin, and Anderson (2010), who suggested that the recommended share for social sciences is 60%.

Identified technical factors and characteristics are shown in Table 6. Identified functional factors and characteristics are shown in Table 7. These tables also present the value of Cronbach's Alpha coefficient in order to analyze the internal consistency of the identified factors.

In the set of technical characteristics of ERM software, seven factors were identified, where just one statement (statement tz20) made one factor, while

Table 6. Identified factors and their Cronbach's alpha coefficients in a set of technical characteristics

Factor	Code	Software for Risk Management Should . . .	Cronbach's Alpha
tf1	tz6	enable exporting reports in MS Word	0.907
	tz7	enable exporting reports in PDF	
	tz8	enable exporting reports in MS Excel	
	tz9	enable working with multiple currencies	
	tz10	be multilingual	
tf2	tz16	enable displaying the risks on the map	0.853
	tz17	enable automatic warnings (alerts)	
	tz18	contain dashboards	
	tz19	enable the adjustment of dashboards	
tf3	tz12	enable usage on mobile devices (smartphones)	0.938
	tz13	enable usage on tablets (iPad, Android)	
tf4	tz5	have a context for help (help)	0.748
	tz14	have technical support or help desks 24/7/365	
	tz15	enable sending automated e-mails	
	tz3	be Web-oriented	0.529
	tz4	be offered as "Software as a service" (SaaS)	
	tz1	enable data acquisition from different external sources	0.580
	tz2	be installed on the local user's equipment	
	tz11	enable users with screen adjustments (colors, fonts, etc.)	
	tz20	enable working with multiple organizations	

Table 7. Identified factors and their Cronbach's alpha coefficients in a set of functional characteristics

Factor	Code	Software for Risk Management Should . . .	Cronbach's Alpha
ff1	fz10	enable definition of criteria for risk assessment	0.986
	fz11	enable definition of the risk matrix	
	fz12	enable definition of a structure for all activities in process or project	
	fz13	enable definition of the structure of all threats and threat sources that could arise in the structure of activities in project or process	
	fz14	enable identification of threats and threat sources	
	fz15	enable risk identification	
	fz16	enable binding documents with risk	
	fz17	enable connection of loss with risk	
	fz18	enable risk analysis	
	fz19	enable follow up of the history of events connected with the activities and risk being assessed	
	fz20	enable automatic evaluation and risk ranking	
	fz21	enable definition of a risk treatment plan	
	fz22	enable definition of reporting and responsibilities	
	fz23	enable definition of risk treatment rules on the basis of a defined level of risk tolerance	
	fz24	support the process of risk approval (i.e., risk acceptance)	
	fz25	enable risk quantification	
	fz26	enable qualitative risk assessment	
	fz27	enable quantitative risk assessment	
	fz28	enable definition of threat indicators	
	fz29	enable connection (treatment) of risk (control and action) that defines measures to be taken in the process of risk treatment	

continued on following page

Table 7. Continued

Factor	Code	Software for Risk Management Should . . .	Cronbach's Alpha
ff2	fz6	enable customization of the organization's hierarchy	0.922
	fz7	enable users to define rights for data access	
	fz8	contain a register of risk management system users	
	fz9	enable categorization, establishing threat hierarchy	
ff3	fz3	be in compliance with the ISO 31000 standard	0.945
	fz4	be in compliance with the COSO ERM framework	
ff4	fz1	enable integration of standard key performance indicators and risk indicators	0.807
	fz2	contain standard risk definitions and process taxonomy	
	fz5	enable working with multiple organizations	

statement tz11 was not part of any factor. In the set of functional characteristics of ERM software, four factors were identified.

The final decision about the number of factors that should be kept and named was based on the analysis of confidence - that is, on the internal consistency of factors. Related to both technical and functional factors, it was determined that, in both groups, there are four factors with satisfied confidence (Cronbach's Alpha coefficient >0.7). Those factors were kept for further analysis, while the other factors were removed. The other statements can be analyzed regardless of the factors.

Identified technical and functional factors were named as shown in Table 8. Table 8also presents average ratings for each factor and their range of importance.

Table 8. shows that the second factor, visualization, has the most important role among the technical characteristics. Next is user support, and the third factor is data import/export. The factor of portability comes in last. In the group of functional characteristics, the most important factor is a risk assessment, followed by the strategic framework and then customization; the compliance with standards factor is in the last place. According to the average ratings for factors, three technical and three functional factors are very important for ERM software (means >4). Portability and compliance with standards have ratings slightly below 4, which means they

Table 8. Names of factors, average values, and rank relevance

Code	Name of Factor	Mean	Relevance (rank)
Technical Characteristics of ERM Software			
tf1	Data import/export	4,13012	**3**
tf2	Visualization	4,30422	**1**
tf3	Portability	3,88554	**4**
tf4	User support	4,20080	**2**
Functional Characteristics of ERM Software			
ff1	Risk assessment	4,46807	**1**
ff2	Customization	4,38554	**3**
ff3	Compliance with standards	3,91566	**4**
ff4	Strategic framework	4,40361	**2**

are slightly less important. Analysis of the statements for these factors shows that in the case of technical characteristics of ERM software, portability should not be necessarily applied for the software to work properly. It could be said that portability is a desirable, but not obligatory, characteristic of ERM software. In the case of functional characteristics, despite the fact that the compliance with standards factor had a slightly lower rating, the compliance of ERM software with the most important standards and frameworks (ISO 31000, COSO ERM) should be treated as obligatory characteristics because they guarantee the quality, standardization, and ease of applicability of ERM software.

Figure 5. shows the comparison of average ratings for identified factors among respondents who use ERM software (SW(yes)) and those who do not use it (SW(no)). Table 9 presents the ranges of importance by individual factors.

Discrepancies in the importance of individual identified factors for respondents whose organizations use ERM software (SW(yes)) and for those who do not use it (SW(no)) are expected. All factors (technical and functional), according to average ratings, are more important for respondents from organizations that already use ERM software. Separated analysis of ratings for respondents who use ERM software and those who do not use it show that the variations in average ratings for individual factors are significantly higher for respondents who do not use ERM software.

Table 9. and Figure 5 show that there are differences in respondents' opinions related to the importance of individual factors. When technical characteristics are in question, the factor of data import/export is most important for the respondents who use ERM software, while that same factor is listed as third in importance for respondents who do not use ERM software. The opposite is true for the factor of

Figure 5. Mean ratings of the importance of identified technical and functional factor characteristics of ERM software according to their previous practice of using ERP software

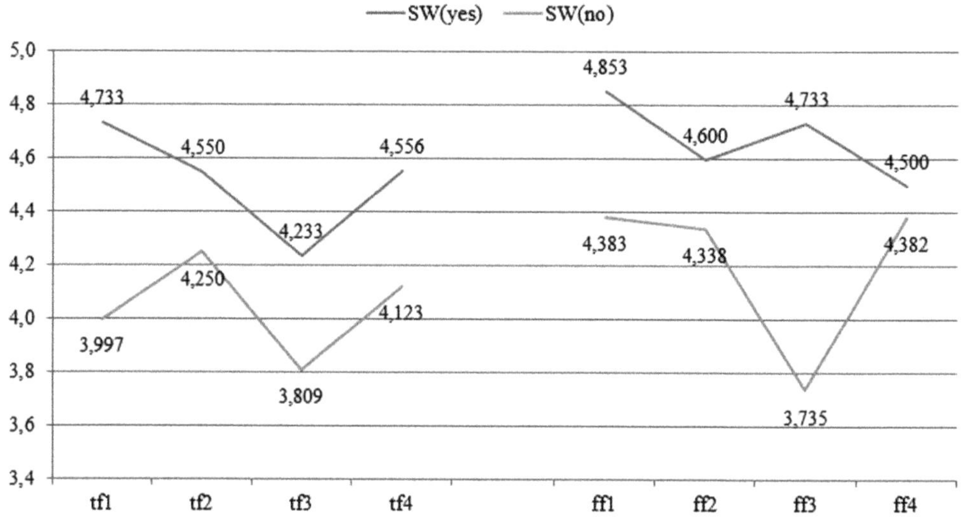

Table 9. Factors' rank relevance according to their previous practice of using ERP software

Code	Name of Factor	Relevance of Factor (rank)	
		SW(yes)	SW(no)
Technical Characteristics of ERM Software			
tf1	Data import/export	1	3
tf2	Visualization	3	1
tf3	Portability	4	4
tf4	User support	2	2
Functional Characteristics of ERM Software			
ff1	Risk assessment	1	1
ff2	Customization	3	3
ff3	Compliance with standards	2	4
ff4	Strategic framework	4	2

SW(yes) = respondents whose companies use ERM software
SW(no) = respondents whose companies do not use ERM software

visualization, which is listed as third in importance for respondents who use ERM software and first for respondents who do not use it.

In the group of functional characteristics, the difference is visible for the factors compliance with standards and strategic framework. Compliance with standards is more important for respondents who use ERM software than for those who do not use it, while the situation with the factor of strategic framework is inverse.

FUTURE RESEARCH DIRECTIONS

The ERM software market is rapidly changing, and the number of vendors and solutions is constantly increasing, which offers many opportunities for further research exploration. To reach the full potential of ERM software, fundamental and revolutionary change is necessary—change that causes the management world, whether private or public, to take note and to acknowledge that managing risk is the key to survival in a turbulent and uncertain milieu (Grose, 2015). Future research directions related to ERM software use requirements can be discussed from the following two perspectives:

- User requirements related to ERM software capabilities in the near future.
- What users (organizations) must change on their ends to reach the full potential of ERM software.

User requirements related to ERM software capabilities in the near future include the following:

- Holistic view and management of all organizational risks.
- Standardization and consistency of ERM software.
- Application of predictive analytics, which can unlock the strategic intelligence of risk data to help organizations understand not only what happened but also why it happened and what is likely to happen next (Marsh ClearSight, 2016).
- Integration of different functional tools, like agent software, that will "crawl" across the Internet, social media sites, or an organization's internal big data warehouses and collect emerging risk event data for analysis. Future ERM software should enhance the automation of traditional manual control activities, forming the basis for effective information and communication, monitoring, and related processes critical to a future organization's enterprise risk framework (Patterson, 2015).

The user (organization) changes necessary for successful implementation of ERM software include the following:

- Continuous work on raising risk awareness across the organization.
- Alignment of objective setting, risk management, and organizational control capabilities (Patterson, 2015).
- Systematic approach to enterprise risk management based on a standard framework (COSO, ISO).
- Raising the awareness that enterprise risk management is more than a simple risk assessment and that it involves comprehensive risk identification, judicious prioritization and analysis, careful action planning, close monitoring, and transparent reporting (PricewaterhouseCoopers, 2015).
- Proactive approach to risk management based on a development plan created by ERM software and on an analysis of which actions were working and which were not.
- Implement enterprise risk management training programs to improve the capabilities of all key stakeholders (PricewaterhouseCoopers, 2015).
- Train or recruit risk leaders with the hard and soft skills needed to efficiently use ERM software.

CONCLUSION

Recognizing, understanding, and managing risks are strategic imperatives for organizations to survive in a globalized and turbulent world. IT is a key ally of the organization in the process of risk management. Without software support, it is almost impossible to identify, analyze, and evaluate the huge number of risks that organizations face on a daily basis. Adequate software support enables organizations to take an innovative, risk-based approach to governance and compliance and to gain a holistic, enterprise-wide view of risk exposure and near-real-time risk management and monitoring. However, technology (i.e., software support) is not enough. For efficient risk management, the human factor is critical. Organizations must establish adequate environments for risk management; implement risk frameworks; establish procedures and discipline in the process of risk identification, analysis, and evaluation; define risk responses; develop policies and procedures for ensuring risk responses are effectively carried out; and continuously monitor and communicate all activities related to risk management. Moreover, continuous work on raising risk awareness across the organization and aligning objective setting, risk management, and organizational control capabilities are fundamental for the effective adoption of ERM software.

ERM software vendors should more carefully listen to user requirements in order to provide powerful and user-friendly solutions for risk management. Well-defined user requirements can significantly ease ERM software development and implementation. However, for standardized software products, not enough requirements have been received from users. That is why authors conducted research related to ERM software user requirements on a greater number of users, targeting respondents who use ERM software and those who still do not use it. In the present research, user requirements related to ERM software were grouped into factors. As a result, the main technical and functional characteristics of ERM software were defined. In addition, the research showed differences between users who already use ERM software and those who still do not use it. The opinions of respondents who already use ERM software can be especially valuable for ERM software vendors because they are based on practical experiences. The research results showed that user requirements related to risk management software reach one level of standardization, which could be important for ERM software vendors because, if requirements are known, then they do not have to "waste" a lot of time investigating what to do and can focus instead on how to best to suit user needs. Namely, software companies that develop or plan to develop ERM software could use the results of this and similar research to confirm whether their software has the attributes that users expect.

REFERENCES

AIRMIC. (2010). *A structured approach to enterprise risk management (ERM) and the requirements of ISO 31000*. Retrieved February 23, 2015, from https://www.theirm.org/media/886062/ISO3100_doc.pdf

Ambrose, C., Spencer, J., & Weinstein, E. (2016). Magic quadrant for IT vendor risk management. *Gartner*. Retrieved January 22, 2017, from https://www.gartner.com/doc/reprints?id=1-2ZVRYZA&ct=160229&st=sb

Aon Risk Solutions. (2014). *2014 software survey*. Retrieved February, 27, 2015, from https://www.theirm.org/media/1163669/software_survey.pdf

Bannister, J. E., & Bawcutt, P. A. (1981). *Practical risk management*. London: Witherby & Co.

Bano, M., & Zowghi, D. (2013). User involvement in software development and system success: A systematic literature review. In *Proceedings of the 17th International Conference on Evaluation and Assessment in Software Engineering* (pp. 125–130). doi:10.1145/2460999.2461017

Brooks, F. (1987). No silver bullet: Essence and accidents of software engineering. *IEEE Computer*, *20*(4), 10–19. doi:10.1109/MC.1987.1663532

Chambers, M. (2016). Risk software survey 2015: Speed, compliance and valuation. Risk. Retrieved March 02, 2017, from http://www.risk.net/risk-management/2440870/risk-software-survey-2015-speed-compliance-and-valuation

Committee of Sponsoring Organizations of the Treadway Commission. (2004a). Enterprise risk management—Integrated framework: Executive summary. Retrieved September 15, 2016, from http://www.theiia.org/media/files/virtual-seminars/COSO_ERM_Integrated_Framework.pdf

Committee of Sponsoring Organizations of the Treadway Commission. (2004b). Enterprise risk management—Integrated framework: Application techniques. Retrieved September 15, 2016, from http://www.macs.hw.ac.uk/~andrewc/erm2/reading/ERM%20-%20COSO%20Application%20Techniques.pdf

Crockford, N. (1982). The bibliography and history of risk management: Some preliminary observations. The Geneva Papers on Risk and Insurance, 7(23), 169–179. doi:10.1057/gpp.1982.10

Dickinson, G. (2001). Enterprise Risk Management: Its Origins and Conceptual Foundation. *The Geneva Papers on Risk and Insurance*, *26*(3), 360–366. doi:10.1111/1468-0440.00121

Dionne, G. (2013). Risk Management: History, Definition, and Critique. *Risk Management & Insurance Review*, *16*(2), 147–166. doi:10.1111/rmir.12016

Douglas, B. (1993). The Evolution of Risk Management. *Risk Management*, *40*(4), 38.

FERMA. (2016). *FERMA Risk Management Benchmarking Survey 2016* (8th ed.). Retrieved March 29, 2017, from http://www.ferma.eu/app/uploads/2016/09/FERMA-European-Risk-and-Insurance-Report-Full-set-of-results.pdf

Gallagher, R. B. (1956). Risk management: New phase of cost control. *Harvard Business Review*, *34*(5), 75–86.

Gartner. (2017). *Reviews for operational risk management*. Retrieved from March 18, 2017,https://www.gartner.com/reviews/market/operational-risk-management

Giarini, O. (1976). A macro-economicapproach to risk management. *The Geneva Papers on Risk and Insurance*, *1*(2), 5–9. doi:10.1007/BF02420933

Grose, V. L. (2015). *Five weaknesses of enterprise risk management.* Retrieved January 19, 2017, from http://www.omegainc.com/hs-fs/hub/142206/file-23577569-pdf/docs/5_weaknesses_of_enterprise_risk_management.pdf

Hair, J. F., Black, W. C., Babin, B. J., & Anderson, R. E. (2010). *Multivariate data analysis* (7th ed.). Upper Saddle River, NJ: Prentice Hall.

Hamilton, G. (1988). This is risk management. Stockholm, Sweden: Lund.

Lam, J. C. (2000). *Enterprise-Wide Risk Management and the role of the Chief Risk Officer.* Retrieved June 22, 2013, from http://www.erisk.com/learning/research/011_lamriskoff.pdf

Marsh ClearSight. (2016). *Revolutionizing the way risk is viewed and managed: The evolution of risk management information systems.* Chicago, IL: Author.

Mehr, R. I., & Hedges, B. A. (1963). *Risk management in the business enterprise.* Homewood, IL: Irwin.

Patterson, T. (2015). *The use of information technology in risk management.* Retrieved March 09, 2017, from http://www.aicpa.org/InterestAreas/FRC/AssuranceAdvisoryServices/DownloadableDocuments/ASEC_Whitepapers/Risk_Technology.pdf

PricewaterhouseCoopers. (2015). *How ERM programs evolve.* Retrieved March 09, 2017, from https://www.pwc.com/us/en/risk-assurance-services/publications/assets/pwc-how-erm-programs-evolve.pdf

Protiviti. (2017). *Executive perspectives on top risks for 2017.* Retrieved March 22, 2017, fromhttps://www.protiviti.com/US-en/insights/protiviti-top-risks-survey

Purdy, G. (2010). ISO 31000:2009—Setting a new standard for risk management. *Risk Analysis, 30*(6), 881–886. doi:10.1111/j.1539-6924.2010.01442.x PMID:20636915

Razali, A.R., Tahir, I.M. (2011). Review of the Literature on Enterprise Risk Management. *Business Management Dynamics, 1*(5), 8-16.

Tweedy, D. (2013). *2013 RMIS review.* Retrieved June12, 2016,from http://pdf32.keenbooks.org/pdf/for-now-7_5p6pp.pdf

Williams, A., & Heins, M. H. (1964). *Risk management and insurance.* New York, NY: McGraw-Hill.

Wolf, R. (2008). The Evolution of Enterprise Risk Management. *The Actuary.* Retrieved January 12, 2017, from https://www.soa.org/Library/Newsletters/The-Actuary-Magazine/2008/June/act-2008-vol5-iss3-wolf.aspx

KEY TERMS AND DEFINITIONS

Enterprise Risk Management: The process of planning, organizing, and controlling the activities that an organization takes in order to minimize the effects of risk on the achievement of organizational goals.

Functional Software Characteristics: Description what software should do.

Risk: Effect of uncertainty on the achievement of organizational goals.

Risk Management: The process of identification, assessment, control, and monitoring of risks that can endanger the achievement of organizational goals.

Risk Management Framework: A disciplined and structured approach to risk management.

Technical Software Characteristics: Description how software will accomplish required functionality.

User Requirements: Description about what users want or expect from the software.

Chapter 8
Two Approaches in Assessing Business Continuity Management Attitudes in the Organizational Context

M. Spremic
University of Zagreb, Croatia

L. Turulja
University of Sarajevo, Bosnia and Herzegovina

N. Bajgoric
University of Sarajevo, Bosnia and Herzegovina

ABSTRACT

The paper presents two approaches in assessing the business continuity management (BCM) attitudes in the organizational context: qualitative and quantitative. The first approach - case study analysis is based on a series of in-depth interviews with the key people involved in the BCM processes in Croatia (Chief Information Officers – CIOs, Chief Executive Officers – CEOs and BC managers). The second approach is an empirical research that was conducted among companies in Bosnia and Herzegovina based on Confirmative Factor Analysis (CFA) which is used for psychometrically validation of the measurement scale of BCP and Structural Equation Modeling (SEM) and t-test for the hypotheses testing. The empirical research has shown that there is a statistically significant difference in terms of attitudes of respondents regarding business continuity depending of companies' size and sector that company

DOI: 10.4018/978-1-5225-3704-5.ch008

belongs to. Specifically, financial sector is in all of BCM segments more coherent than other sectors.In addition, qualitative research revealed the results showing that business continuity plan (BCP) and disaster recovery plan (DRP) were the only IT governance areas that were implemented in business practice. The reason for that may be found in the fact that BCP and DRP are very expensive to implement especially for small companies.

INTRODUCTION

Today's businesses are increasingly concerned about the risks that threaten the "continuity of business" as they are operating in an e-business environment. They are under continuous pressure to "keep their business in business". Data/information availability is of particular importance because continuous data access and availability is expected by employees, customers, suppliers and other stakeholders. Most businesses today seek for an information system infrastructure that is running 24/7/365 ensuring that data and applications are continuously available. Therefore, every business needs an effective business continuity management (BCM) focusing on several issues of ensuring continuity of business operations with a particular focus on business critical processes. However, BCM is a very complex process that must be integrated throughout the entire organization.

Recently, with advances in Internet/Web technologies and e-business, the need for achieving continuous or "a near 100%" level of data/application availability was brought up yet again. Consequently, the term of business continuity management was coined up and became a significant part of organizational information management. Business continuity strategy has become critical item for both CEO's and CIO's priority lists. According to the Forrester Report (2011), almost 80% of respondents reported that their firms have had to provide proof of BC readiness. Business continuity relies on so-called continuous computing technologies that are aimed at providing an efficient operating environment for an "always-on" computing in terms of an "always-on information system" which is a technological prerequisite for "always-on" business (Bajgoric, 2006). Simply put, implementation of continuous computing technologies provides a platform for continuity of business-critical applications, in other words, for "keeping business in business".

The main objectives of this chapter are twofold. First, an analysis of the state of the BCP in transition economies and defining the influencing factors of BCP. Second, the validation of the measurement model of business continuity planning using as a framework model presented by Oyha and Gokhale (2009) for the logistical business continuity planning (LBCP) operations. In order to meet these objectives,

Croatia and Bosnia and Herzegovina were selected as transition economies of South-Eastern Europe.

The first –a qualitative approach, was based on a case analysis employed to identify circumstances and factors that influence BCM activities in real business environment. Case study analysis was based on a series of comprehensive and in-depth interviews with the key people involved in the BCM processes in Croatia (Chief Information Officers – CIOs, Chief Executive Officers – CEOs and BC managers).

The second approach was based on an empirical research that was conducted among companies in Bosnia and Herzegovina. A BCP questionnaire for the logistic operations suggested by Oyha and Gokhale (2009)was adapted and used in order to apply it for all organizational functions. Confirmative Factor Analysis (CFA) which is employed for the psychometrically validation of the measurement scale of BCP and Structural Equation Modeling (SEM) and independent t-tests for the hypotheses testing were used within the quantitative approach.

It is important to highlight that business continuity is the management segment which is in particular relevant issue for banks and other financial institutions. Therefore, Basel Committee issued regulative that addresses the management of operational risk and provides specific guidelines for business continuity. Even if these regulations are designed for the banks and financial institutions, the principles regarding operational risk management and business continuity planning can be applied to most industries and to organizations of all sizes. In addition, business continuity is the issue which is regulated by many national laws related to financial institutions. Furthermore, since discontinuity in business processes can lead to the organization brand name weakening, many large and respectable organizations tend to implement BCP in their planning processes. Thus, it is expected that larger and more respectable firms in addition to financial organizations implement BCP. When it comes to transition economies, it is expected that firms with foreign capital, especially if capital comes from the developed countries will have more aware management regarding BCP. In accordance with the discussion, after the validation of the measurement model for the BCP, following hypotheses will be tested:

H1: Size of the organization positively influence the awareness and level of BCP implementation.

H2: The level of application and implementation of the business continuity concept is higher in companies with foreign shares compared to those that are fully owned by domestic stakeholders (private or state owned).

H3: Banks and other financial institutions are on the higher level of BCP implementation.

BUSINESS CONTINUITY: DOWNTIME AND ITS IMPACT ON BUSINESS; LITERATURE REVIEW

Herbane (2010) noted that BCM has evolved since 1970s in response to the technical and operational risks that threaten an organization's recovery from hazards and interruptions.

Business continuity has been treated as both IT and managerial issue particularly after the e-business boom and the "9/11" event. However, in most cases, senior executives are not aware of such a kind of "IT-business" dependency and lack understanding of business continuity. The nature and characteristics of IT-associated risks have dramatically changed over two recent decades. While some 20-30 years ago an IT-related problem on a computer center's mainframe was viewed only as a 'technical' problem causing a delay in payday, similar problem on today's application servers may affect company's finance, competitive position or even "shut down" the whole business.

In short, business continuity is achieved by implementing continuous computing IT platforms having high availability ratios. According to IDC (2009), high availability systems are defined as having 99% or more uptime. IDC defined a set of different availability scenarios according to availability ratio, annual downtime, user tolerance to downtime with regard to several continuous computing technologies that are available today:

Business Continuity Institute (www.thebci.org) defined business continuity management as a:

Holistic management process that identifies potential impacts that threaten an organization and provides a framework for building resilience with the capability for an effective response that safeguards the interests of its key stakeholders, reputation and value creating activities. Its primary objective is to allow the executives to

Table 1. IDC classification of availability scenarios (IDC, 2009)

	Availability	Average Annual Downtime	User Tolerance to Downtime
Fault Tolerant Continuous Availability	99.999%	5 minutes	None
Cluster High Availability	99.9%	8 Hours45 Minutes	Business Interruption Lost Transaction
Stand-alone GP or Blade Server w/ RAID	99.5%	43 Hours 23 Minutes	Tomorrow is Okay

continue to manage their business under adverse conditions, by the introduction of appropriate resilience strategies, recovery objectives, business continuity and crisis management plans in collaboration with, or as a key component of, an integrated risk management initiative.

Symantec's SMB (Small and Medium Business) Disaster Preparedness Survey (2011) revealed that disasters can have a significant financial impact on SMBs. At the time of this survey, the median cost of downtime for an SMB was $12,500 per day. Aberdeen Group found (Csaplar, 2012) that between June 2010 and February 2012, the cost per hour of downtime increased on average by 65%. In February 2010, the average cost per hour of downtime was reported to be about $100,000. Martin (2011) quoted the results of the study by Emerson Network Power and the Ponemom Institute which revealed that the average data center downtime event costs $505,500 with the average incident lasting 90 minutes.

The importance of the availability issue is reflected in reports of how incidents affect business. According to the Aberdeen Report (2014) the average hourly costs of downtime are $686,250, $215,638 and $8,581 for large, medium, and small companies, respectively. The Veeam Data Availability Report (2014) revealed that "*...there are clear demands for 24/7 access to IT services and applications, with over 90 percent of enterprises increasing their requirements for minimizing downtime and guaranteeing access to data.*" Ponemon Institute and Emerson Network Power (Ponemon Institute Report, 2016) reported that the average cost of a data center outage has steadily increased from $505,502 in 2010 to $740,357 today (or a 38 percent net change). As IDC stated recently (IDC, 2016), business cannot tolerate the same levels of planned and unplanned downtime that they could before they started on their digital transformation journey.

Research papers on BCM focus either on frameworks or separate technologies that are used in order to improve the availability levels. Broder and Tucker (2012) underlined that business continuity planning is defined in many different ways reflecting the author's particular slant, background, or experience with the process. Brenes et al. (2011) focused on assessing the impact of business continuity-related governance structures on family business performances, while Nollau (2009) introduced the term of "enterprise business continuity". Lindstrom, Samuelson, and Hagerfors (2010) noted that organizations rely too much on the checklists provided in existing BC standards. They proposed a multi-usable BC planning methodology based on using a staircase or capability maturity model. Avery Gomez (2011) underscored the fact that resilience and the continuity of business are factors that rely on sustainable ICT infrastructures. The author presented a model for alignment of business continuity and sustainable business processes with regard to ICT usage behavior and response readiness. Zobel (2011) defined an analytic approach in representing the relationship between two primary measures of disaster resilience: the initial impact of a disaster and the subsequent time to recovery. Blackhurst et al. (2011) provided a framework that can be used to assess the level of resiliency and a supply resiliency matrix that can be utilized to classify supply chains according to the level of resiliency realized. Sapateiro et al. (2011) presented a model of a mobile collaborative tool that may help teams in managing critical computing infrastructures in organizations with regard to Business Continuity Management. Kim and Cha (2012) presented the improved scenario-based Security Risk Analysis (SRA) method which can create SRA reports using threat scenario templates and manage security risk directly in information systems. Greening and Rutherford (2011) proposed a conceptual framework based on network theories to ensure BC in the context of a supply network disruption. Winkler et al. (2010) focused on the relationships between BCM and business process modeling. They proposed a model-driven framework for BCM which integrates business process modeling and IT management. Williamson (2007) found that in BC, financial organizations are ahead of other types of businesses. King (2003) introduced a term of "Business Continuity Culture" and underscored the fact that "*If you fail to plan, you will be planning to fail*". Gerber and Solms (2005) emphasized the need for a holistic approach that should include a carefully planned security policy, the use of technology and well-trained staff. Finch (2004) revealed that large companies' exposure to risk increased by inter-organisational networking and that having small and medium enterprises (SMEs) as partners in the supply chain management (SCM) further increased the risk exposure. Lewis and Pickren (2003) pointed out that disaster recovery is receiving increasing attention as firms grow because it is more dependent on uninterrupted information system functioning.

As modern business becomes more and more dependent on its underlying IT infrastructure, business continuity issues have been argued not only from technological, but from the business (executives) perspectives as well. BC activities need to be carefully planned and managed by both IT department' and business levels. Arduini and Morabito (2010) argued that the financial sector sees business continuity not only as a technical or risk management issue, but as a driver towards any discussion on mergers and acquisitions. Stanton (2007) highlighted the premise "*Fail to Plan, Plan to Fail*". Wan (2009) argues that in current business-aligned IT operations, the continuity plan needs to be integrated with IT service continuity management if an organization is going to be able to manage fault realization and return to normal business operations. BC initiatives require heavy investments and need to be aligned with IT governance. Spremic (2009) argued about the role of IT governance concept, especially in applying the IT risk management procedures at executive levels. As organizations are becoming increasingly dependent upon IT in order to achieve their corporate objectives and meet their business needs, the necessity for implementing widely applicable IT governance best practices standards and methodologies, offering high quality services is evident. The issue of managing the IT risks in general becomes less and less a technical problem, and more and more the problem of the whole organization i.e. a "business problem" and many companies nowadays formally nominate executive directors for such activities. Therefore, it is highly recommendable that BC Strategy becomes a part of IT governance procedures and that companies have a BC manager that is outside the IT department. DeHaes and Grembergen (2009) suggest that there is a clear relationship between the use of IT governance practices and better business/IT alignment.

Lin et al. (2013) argued that company must have a comprehensive contingency plan that is fully integrated into the organization as an embedded management system. Such a contingency plan must be developed for the entire organization – from senior management to the bottom level. There were some research evidences of the impact of BC in the business. Jarvelainen (2013) extended the concepts of data availability, disaster recovery, business continuity and introduced the concept of "information system continuity management (ISCM)". The framework was validated in a survey of IT managers and chief information officers in organizations operating in Finland. Their results suggest that the embeddedness of continuity practices has perceived business impacts whereas there is no such direct relation in case of organization alertness and preparedness. Kollowitz et al. (2012) investigated the need for an information system that allows critical organizational workflows to continue when these systems are unavailable due to either scheduled or unscheduled downtimes. Leitch (2016) argued that downtime has reached an estimated cost of $700 billion per year to US businesses in 2016.

With regard to senior management's attitudes and awareness of business continuity, authors approached this issue from both quantitative and qualitative methods. The quantitative methods are used by Liu et al. (2012) Lavastre et al. (2012), Corey, and Deitch (2011), Karim (2011), Chow and Wai (2009), Craighead et al. (2007), while qualitative approach is used in Wol (2011), Omar et al. (2011) and Lindstrom (2012). Liu et al. (2012) used Social Cognitive Theory (SCT) and confirmatory factor analysis (CFA). Lavastre et al. (2012) introduced the term of "supply chain continuity planning framework" within the concept of Supply Chain Risk Management (SCRM). Craighead et al. (2007) considered business continuity issues within the supply chain mitigation capabilities and supply chain disruption severity. They proposed a multiple-source empirical research method and presented six propositions that relate the severity of supply chain disruptions. Wolf (2011) presented a qualitative analysis of the German manufacturing industry within the context of sustainable Supply Chain Management integration and relation to long-term business continuity. Lindstrom (2012) presented the business contingency process model that has been developed based on the three cases that included senior management, IT managers and employees in the three case organizations (corporations and state agencies).Recently, Niemimaa (2015) created an up-to-date review of articles addressing business continuity from the information systems perspective. Though the review identified the business continuity perspective on information systems as "a timely question", the results indicate that leading IS journals publish few contributions in this area.

CASE STUDY

A number of circumstances can influence BCM activities in a real business environment. For example, strict and rigorous IT governance regulations in Republic of Croatia may imply that business continuity management procedures are on very mature level in almost all commercial banks operating in the country (Spremic, 2012). We decided to conduct a case study followed by series of comprehensive and in-depth interviews with the key people involved in the BCM processes.

We found case study a good method for investigating the usage of BCM activities in real business environment. As Yin (1994) defined, "*a case study is an empirical inquiry that investigates a contemporary phenomenon within its real-life context, especially when the boundaries between phenomenon and context are not clearly evident*".

One of the most important phases in a case study based research is defining a case and how they are to be selected (Ragin, 1992; Romano, 1989). The case companies for this research were selected based on theoretical sampling, in which the cases are selected such that they represent the problem of the study (Yin, 1994). In order to cover H3 we started to look for companies in financial sector (namely banks, credit institutions and insurance companies). Also, to assess H1 and H2 we choose mature companies with a prevailing international stakeholder structure. Essentially we started with a list of 15 companies and ended up with 3 we gained access to (two banks and one insurance company). All three companies were involved in BCM activities on different levels. The research instrument includes series of in-depth interviews with CIOs, CEOs and BC managers of selected companies and the research model was constructed around following BCM elements:

- Do the analyzed companies have IS Strategy aligned with business strategy, IT Steering Committee and IT investment policy?
- Do the surveyed companies have IT risk management methodology and policy?
- Do the selected companies have Business Continuity Plan (BCP) and Disaster Recovery Plan (DRP)?

- Do the surveyed companies have defined metrics to control key IT processes, for example, Recovery Point Objective (RPO) and Recovery Time Objective (RTO) as key metrics for BCP initiatives?

The selections of interviewees were based on their competencies, knowledge and skills in the area of BCM and IT governance and their involvement in decision making process around it (Table 2).

To address the research's objectives, firstly we draw a survey questionnaire to be able to collect general information about BCM practices during years. Then we narrowed our focus to selected companies and finally conductedseries of comprehensive and in-depth interviews.

The survey resulted with some important responses which gave us crucial information about the growing maturity of BCM activities over the last ten years. After sending the survey to interviewees, we organized visits to selected companies and spent a week or so having in-depth dedicated discussions about BCM practices defined in the research model. Such activities are regular IS auditing procedures in which we were engaged. Selected companies employ 120, 350 and 400 employees, respectively. They have adequate organizational structure according to its size with IT department as strategic business function directly responsible to CEO and/or Board member responsible for IT. IT departments in all companies typically have three units: application support, system support, business support. Specific functions such as CISO (Chief Information Security Officer), BC manager and internal IS auditor are extracted from IT department and represent autonomous organizational units. In company A and company C, CEO is the member of the Board responsible for IT, while in B this function is controlled by other nominated Board member. All companies have various committees who help CIO in IT governance procedures, such as IT Steering Committee, IT Project Management Committee (company C) Business Continuity Board (company B and C), IT Change Management Committee (company A and company C).

Table 2. Interviewees'demographics

Interviewees	BCM Experience	Work Related IT Experience in Years
1. CIO	5 years	> 15
2. BC Manager	10 years	> 7
3. CIO	7 years	> 20

The questions addressed in the in-depth interviews were as follows:

Q1: IS strategy (governance focuses)
Q2: IT risk policy (prerequisite for BCM)
Q3: BCP and DRP (key organizational procedures)
Q4: RPO and RTO (Key metrics for BCM)

All three companies were asked to assess their IT policies, procedures and metrics in BCM over the period of the last three years. This period was characterized by significant efforts on imposing the regulations related to IT/IS governance in Croatia.

With regard to the IS strategy (governance focuses - question 1), it turned out that only one company had this strategy. However, after a period of only three years, all of them had the IS strategy implemented. Some of the answers related to the existence of IT/IS strategy confirm such situation, e.g. "*Confirmed at executive level*", "*CIO reports directly to CEO*", "*CIO member of the Board*".

As for the second question ("IT risk policy as a prerequisite for BCM"), all three companies said that they didn't have such a policy ("*No, individual efforts only*", "*No, in preparation*", "*No IT risk mitigation plan*"). After three years, all answers were as follows: "*Yes, regularly updating*", "*IT risk measure calculated*", "*IT risk register in place, risks are identified*".

The third question Q3 asked for the existence of BC plans and DR plans and existence of these key plans and policies as organizational procedures. The answers were as follows:

Company 1: *No, employees not aware of the importance.*
Company 2: *No, employees not aware of the problem, apart from regulation obligation, Board not aware of the importance.*
Company 3: *No, the issue is not a business priority, regulation provisions are waiting to come into force.*

After a three year period, the answers were as follows:

- Yes, regularly tested and updated.
- Yes, but just for the "show-off" regulation purposes.
- Yes, document (paper) based, no testing procedures, not clear what will happen in the situation of incident.

The fourth question was related to RPO and RTO being key metrics for BCM, with the "*No*" answer to the questions addressing the existence of RPO and RTOas key BCM metrics. However, at the end of this period, the answers were mainly "*Yes*"with some additional details explaining the ways how this metrics was implemented: prescribed for all business processes, RTO < 30 min, RPO < 30 min, CobIT used;RTO < 1 sec, RPO < 1 sec, CobIT and ISO 27000 used; business process owners aware of IT-associated risk in that area.

QUANTITATIVE APPROACH

Methodology

Since the adequate measurement model for BCP couldn't be found in the available literature, development and/or validation of such model imposed as important objective of the chapter. However, LBCP model (logistical business continuity planning) developed by Ojha and Gokhale (2009) was identified as possible foundation for developing a model that would be applicable to all functions and organizational processes and not just for the logistical operations. In addition, the findings of qualitative research have contributed to the understanding of the concept of BCP in other industries and for other operations and organization in general. Specifically, it should be identified if all elements of BCP identified for logistic operations stand for all other business operations.

Ojha & Gokhale (2009) identified nine key complimentary elements that underlie LBCP:(1) awareness of contact points (CP); (2) awareness of roles and responsibilities (RR); (3) awareness of risk levels (RL); (4) awareness of continuity and recovery service levels (CRSL); (5) institution of business continuity reviews (BCR); (6) development of business continuity processes (BCPR); (7) effective failure reporting and documentation (FRD); (8) testing of continuity plans (TEST); and (9) training of employees (TRAIN) to create and execute BCP. However, results of their study showed that the structure of LBCP construct is second-order multidimensional with the seven first-order factors: awareness of contact points; awareness of RR; awareness of business CRSL; use of BCR; institution of BCPR; FRD; and testing and training. Following the finding of the previous qualitative analysis, we decided to adapt LBCP scale in a way to reword its indicators changing "*your business unit*" part with the "*your organization*" and "*for the business continuity planning teams for your logistical operations*" part with the "*for the business continuity planning*". After data collection, scale will be tested for the psychometrically validation. For this purpose, CFA will be used.

SPSS 22 and Lisrel 8.8 are used for the data analysis.

Data Collection and Sample

A questionnaire was prepared as an online survey using Lime survey software and distributed to companies using mailing lists. The sample was statistically relevant and unbiased and consisted of 101 companies in Bosnia and Herzegovina.

Data analysis on respondents shows that 80% of companies which participated in this survey are those with annual income of more than 1 million BAM, while 75% of these were companies with more than 100 employees. 24% of companies were from public administration, while the smallest percentage of participating companies is engaged in production. When it comes to ownership structure, 41.7% of companies are state owned, 25% are private, while 33.4% have a foreign equity share.

Scales Measuring the Business Continuity: Reliability and Validity Control

In the phase of data analysis, prior to hypotheses testing, we analyzed the measurement model for psychometrical characteristics using CFA. After the first model specification, it didn't reveal good fit. Therefore, in order to get acceptable fit and by assessing modification indices we had to exclude some of the items. It

Table 3. Companies' Demographics

Factor	Category	Frequency
Number of employees	up to 10 11-50 51-250 over 250	**6.9** **26.7** **28.7** **37.6**
Annual income (000)	up to 100 101-500 501-1000 1001-5000 over 5000	**6.6** **3.3** **9.9** **19.8** **60.4**
Ownership type	Domestic private Domestic state Foreign Combined domestic /foreign	**25.0** **41.7** **16.7** **16.7**
Industrial sector	Production Trading Services Finance Education Public administration Telecommunications Banks Other	**4.0** **11.2** **12.0** **6.4** **5.6** **24.0** **13.6** **5.6** **17.6**

was necessary to consider the justification of this procedure. Anderson and Gerbin (1988) stated that re-specification of measurement models is most commonly required. However, the re-specification decision cannot be based solely on statistics, but must be based on theory as well. Therefore, we tried not to disrupt the conceptualization and content of the measuring concepts when removing items and concluded that re-specification is not a problem for further analysis. Specifically, BCP is defined as a process that should address three interdependent objectives:

1. Identify major risks of business interruption.
2. Develop a plan to mitigate or reduce the impact of the identified risk.
3. Train employees and test the plan to ensure that it is effective (Cerullo & Cerullo, 2004).

Cerullo and Cerullo (2004) identified the three basic components of a BCP to achieve these objectives: Business Impact Analysis (BIA); Disaster Contingency Recovery Plan(DCRP); and Training and Testing. Thus, in order to get the appropriate measurement model, it should cover these processes. Therefore, it is necessary to consider the definitions of the components in order to match the indicators with the components taking into account the contents of both.

The BIA identifies critical functions a business must perform to stay in business; identifies risks to critical business functions and rates those risks according to probability of occurrence and impact on the business; recommends avoidance, mitigation, or absorption of the risk; and identifies ways to avoid or mitigate the risk (Cerullo & Cerullo, 2004). Furthermore, to develop a disaster recovery plan means to specify procedures to enact when a disaster occurs which includes identification of team members and roles and procedures during the disaster. Finally, training employees and testing the plan on regular basis are important elements of successful BCP.

To capture complete picture of organizational BCP processes, we conducted the analysis and matching of qualitative research results presented in the previous section, BCP components proposed by Cerullo and Cerullo (2004) and LBCP items. Thus, in accordance with the conceptual content of BCP components, our findings and the LBCP model, the measurement model that is proposed in this chapter consists of:

- **BIA:** Awareness of risk level in organization and awareness of continuity and recovery service levels in organization constructs from the LBCP;
- **DRP:** Awareness of roles and responsibilities in organization and documentation and reporting of failures in business unit constructs from the LBCP.
- **TT:** Training and testing from the LBCP.

Figure 1.

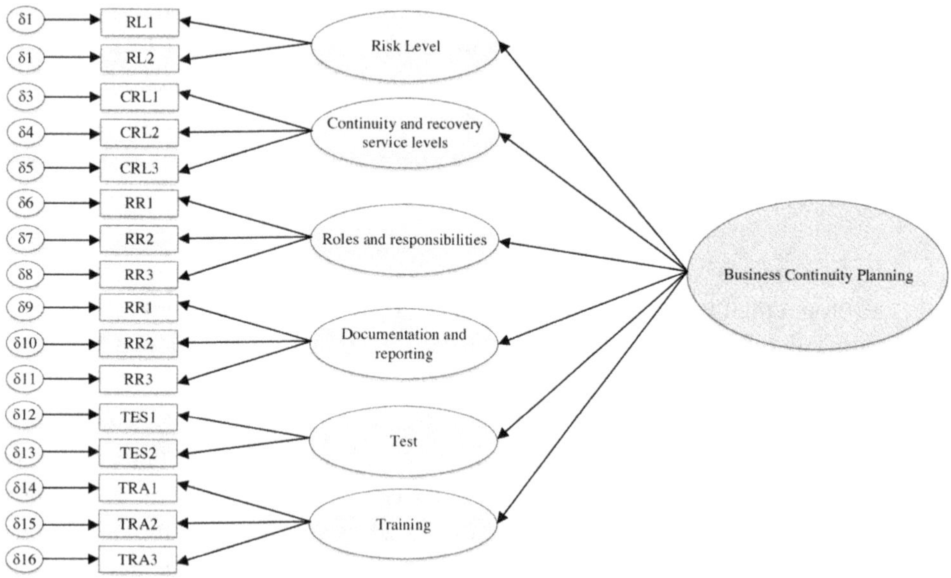

Proposed measurement model is presented in the Figure 1.

Cronbach Alpha coefficient (values above 0.7 are indicating the high level of reliability) was used to analyze the reliability of the constructs. The results have been summarized and presented in Table 4.

The validity analysis was done using CFA. The Maximum Likelihood (ML) estimation method was used. The final model indicates good level of representativeness. Although χ2gof for CFA is significant ($\chi 2 = 160.054$; $N = 101$;$df = 96$, $p<0.01$), all other indicators are indicating that this isa representative (well-fitting) model: CFI = 0.988; RMSEA = 0.0817; SRMR = 0.0378.

Using a validity assessment methodology (Hair et al., 2010) we confirmed the convergent and discriminant validity for all of the six business continuity constructs.

Table 4. Reliability Analysis Results

Construct	Cronbach Alpha
Awareness of risk levels	0.921
Awareness of continuity and recovery service levels	0.933
Awareness of roles and responsibilities	0.902
Documentation and reporting of failures	0.947
Testing of business continuity plans	0.937
Training of employees	0.971

Table 5. Validity Analysis Results

Constructs	CR	AVE	RL	CRL	RR	FRD	TES	TRA
Awareness of risk levels	0.922	0.856	**0.925**					
Awareness of continuity and recovery	0.934	0.825	0.583	**0,908**				
Awareness of roles and responsibilities	0.904	0.759	0.610	0.858	**0.871**			
Documentation and reporting of failures	0.948	0.858	0.524	0.737	0.771	**0.926**		
Testing of business continuity plans	0.937	0.882	0.524	0.736	0.771	0.827	**0.939**	
Training of employees	0.971	0.919	0.533	0.749	0.784	0.674	0.782	**0.958**

Composite reliability (CR) is used to test the convergent validity, and all CR values are greater than 0.7. At the other side, all Average Variance Extracted (AVE) values are greater than 0.5. In addition, right side of Table 5 represents the square root AVE at the diagonal line while correlations between constructs are presented below. In order to prove the discriminant validity, square root AVE value of corresponding construct should be greater than correlation of that construct with all other constructs (Hair et al., 2010). All constructs meet this criteria indicating discriminant validity of the measurement model.

Finally, all items kept in the model are presented in the Table 6.

To summarize, this section has provided the CFA results of the measurement model for the business continuity planning. By using CFA, we confirmed the reliability as well as both convergent and discriminant validity of the model. Proposed model is completely in compliance with the conceptual determination of BCP as a process that consists of BIA, DRP, employees training and plans testing.

Hypotheses Testing and Results Discussion

In this section, a more detailed interpretation of survey's quantitative results is provided. The comments will primarily be presented according to the order in which the hypotheses were defined.

H1: *Size of the organization positively influence the awareness and level of BCP implementation.*

We used structural equation modeling (SEM) technique and ML estimation method to test the relation between the company's size which is expressed as a continuous variable, i.e. number of employees and attitudes of respondents regarding business continuity. Results are presented in Table 7.

Table 6. Measurement Model Indicators

		Variable tag	St. loading
Awareness of risk levels in organization (RL)	Your organization is aware of the magnitude of risk its business operations are exposed to.	/RL1/	0.956
	Your organization is aware of the types of risk its business operations are exposed to.	/RL2/	0.893
Awareness of continuity and recovery service levels in organization (CRLS)	Your organization knows how much time is acceptable for responding to threats to its business operations.	/CRL1/	0.870
	Your organization knows how much time is acceptable for implementing business continuity plans for its logistical operations.	/ CRL2/	0.939
	Your organization knows how much time is acceptable for recovering from disruptions in your business operations.	/ CRL3/	0.914
Awareness of roles and responsibilities in organization (RR)	Your organization has a well-defined organizational structure for the business continuity planning teams for your business operations.	/RR1/	0.923
	Your organization has a well-defined organizational structure to quickly recover after a disruption in your business operations.	/RR2/	0.805
	Employees in your organization unit are aware of their roles in times of emergency relating to your business operations.	/RR3/	0.882
Documentation and reporting of failures in business unit (FRD)	Your organization has in place methods of documenting disruptions in your business operations.	/FRD1/	0.876
	Your organization has in place methods of recording responses to disruptions in your business operations.	/FRD2/	0.932
	Your organization has in place methods of documenting impact of response to disruptions in your business operations.	/FRD3/	0.968
Testing of business continuity plans (TEST)	Your organization has formulated acceptance criteria for the business continuity plan for its business operations.	/TES1/	0.925
	Your organization has formulated the testing requirements for the business continuity plan for its business operations.	/TES2/	0.953
Training of employees for business continuity and failure recovery in firm (TRAIN)	Your organization has provided adequate training for staff involved in preparing business continuity plans for its business operations.	/TRA1/	0.944
	Your organization has provided adequate training for staff involved in failure recovery processes for its business operations.	/TRA2/	0.970
	Your organization has provided adequate training for staff involved in testing the business continuity plans for its business operations.	/TRA3/	0.961

Table 7. SEM results for hypotheses testing

	Estimates	Standardised Estimates	t - value	p-value[1]	Result
H1: SIZE → BCP	0.177	0.182	1.767	0.039	Accepted
	Chi-Square=168.223; df=111; RMSEA=0.0718; SRMR=0.0391; CFI=0.989				

[1]one-tailed

The results suggest that there is significant impact of company's size on the level of BCP at the significance level of 5% (β=0.180; t=1.786; p=0.039).

H2. The level of application and implementation of the business continuity concept is higher in companies with foreign shares compared to those that are fully owned by domestic stakeholders (private or state owned).

H2 is tested using t – test. Companies from the sample were divided into two groups: Group 1 – companies strictly owned domestically (privately or state owned) and Group 2 – companies that are fully foreign-owned or have foreign equity share. Table 8 shows the averages of responses between these two groups according to the BCP variable, along with the t-test statistics.

Table 6. shows that the companies from Group 2 have a higher average score (3.67) compared to companies from Group 1 (3.39). The difference between these two groups is not statistically significant (p = 0.06) at the significance level of 5%. Therefore we cannot confirm this hypothesis at a 5% level of significance. However, if we use a significance level of 10% for causality test, H2 can be confirmed.

***H3:** Banks and other financial institutions are on the higher level of BCP implementation.*

Table 8. t-test results

Variable	N	Mean	SD	t	df	p*
Business continuity summary scale				-1.522	98	.06
Group 1 (exclusively domestically owned)	65	3.39	.83			
Group 2 (foreign or combined ownership)	35	3.67	.96			

* one-tailed

Table 9. t - test results

Variable	N	Mean	SD	t	df	P*
Business continuity summary scale				1.890	99	0.03
Group 1 (banks and finances)	15	3.87	.812			
Group 2 (other)	86	3.42	.874			

* one-tailed

Companies from the sample were divided into two groups: Group 1 – banks and companies offering financial services and Group 2 – all other companies. Table 8 shows the averages of answers between these two groups according to the BCP variable, along with the t-test statistics.

As can be seen from Table 7, the companies from Group 1 show higher average score (3.88) compared to those from Group 1 (3.43) and that there is a statistically significant difference between these two groups ($p = 0.03$). The expected effect size $d = 0.53$ is medium or common. The hypothesis H3 thus can be accepted.

CONCLUSION

Within an organizational context, business continuity management has developed into an organizational process that identifies the proneness of an organization to external and internal threats and provides guidelines for an effective prevention and recovery. An important aspect of the success of the overall business continuity management system is an understanding of a wide range of threats. If an organization is not capable of recovering quickly, the impact of given crisis to its image could last far longer than the impact of crisis itself.

Although strategic planners are focusing on ways in which organizations can improve their organizational efficiency, thus, by a clear understanding of their competitive, political and organizational environment, planning for possible events that could jeopardize business operations becomes, more than ever, a part of strategic planning. Furthermore, the BCM still has high development potential, especially considering the constant increase in terms of number of crisis worldwide, starting from earthquakes, fires, etc. to mass riots and terrorist threats and attacks.

The objective of this study was to analyze conditions within the business environment of transition economy with regard to planning and maintenance of business continuity and to provide comparative analysis of the level of application of the business continuity management concept among the companies of different size and different ownership structure.

The results have shown that there is a statistically significant difference in terms of attitudes of respondents regarding business continuity planning depending of the companies size, i.e. that the larger companies show higher level of application of the business continuity planning. In addition, there is a statistically significant difference in respondents' attitudes depending of the sector, i.e. the higher level of coherence and application of the business continuity planning concept is seen in the financial than in other sectors. When it comes to the ownership type, results didn't reveal statistically significant difference in attitudes of respondents regarding BCP at the 5% level of significance, while it is significant at the 10% level of significant.

The analysis of the comprehensive in-depth interviews conducted over the 3-year time reflects that all the companies in the sample have implemented an IS strategic plan as a part of overall strategic plan, strengthen the position of CIO as executive manager and nominated the Board member who is responsible for IT. Also, the implementation of the procedures and internal acts was not satisfactory in first and even in the second year of the research, but as a company grows and as regulation provisions were about to put into the force, effectiveness of the BCM procedures and its governance, organizational and technical aspects were improved.

Business continuity plan (BCP) and disaster recovery plan (DRP) were only IT governance areas that were last prescribed and implemented in practice. The reason for that may be found in the fact that BCP and DRP are very expensive to implement especially for small companies. Accordingly, all companies have implemented governance, organizational and technological activities which are prerequisite for valid BCM. Major governance activities investigated include prescribing IS strategy which is aligned with business strategy and CIOs organizational position (reports to CEO). Important organizational prerequisite for appropriate BCM which revealed from case study research include performed business impact analysis (BIA), IT risk management methodology which is put up in place and valid BCP and DRP. Finally, technical activities include regular BCP and DRP testing, replication software procedures, data restore routines and prescribing and managing key metrics for BCM such as RTO and RPO.

Finally, comparative analysis of answers from the financial and from other sectors led us to a conclusion that the financial sector is in all of BCM segments more coherent than other sectors. A reason for such a state probably lies in a fact that the issue of business continuity, when it comes to banks, is prescribed by international (Basel III, Sarbanes-Oxley) and national regulations and supported by various world-wide used framework and methodologies (CobiT, BS25999, ISO 27001, etc.)

It would be interesting to explore in more detail the situation when it comes to the application of the concept in light of a cyclical approach to business continuity management development(Botha & Von Solms, 2004), although the results could, to a certain degree, be forecasted based on a research conducted. Recommendations in terms of further actions in this area refer primarily to the adoption of detailed legislation dealing with the business continuity management.

When interpreting the results of this study it is necessary to bear in mind that they relate to the transition economies. Besides, proposed measurement model is based on the earlier proposed items for logistics operations to suit all business operations, so it is necessary to validate the second sample. In other words, analysis is not exclusively confirmatory so it is to cross-validate the final model on another sample drawn from the population to which the results are to be generalized (Anderson &Gerbin, 1988). However, this study sets the great foundation to development of the BCP measurement model. In addition, it gives a concise presentation of the BCM concept evolving process and confirms that e-business environment increases awareness on the business continuity management.

REFERENCES

Aberdeen Report. (2014). *Preventing Virtual Application Downtime*. Available at www.aberdeen.com

Anderson, J. C., & Gerbing, D. W. (1988). Structural equation modeling in practice: A review and recommended two-step approach. *Psychological Bulletin, 103*(3), 411–423. doi:10.1037/0033-2909.103.3.411

Arduini, F., & Morabito, V. (2010, March). Business Continuity and the Banking Industry. *Communications of the ACM, 53*(3), 121–125. doi:10.1145/1666420.1666452

Asgary, A., & Naini, A. S. (2011). Modelling The Adaptation Of Business Continuity Planning By Businesses Using Neural Networks, Intelligent Systems. In *Accounting, Finance And Management 18* (pp. 89–104). Wiley.

Avery Gomez, E. (2011). Towards Sensor Networks: Improved ICT Usage Behavior for Business Continuity. *Proceedings of SIGGreen Workshop, Sprouts: Working Papers on Information Systems, 11*(13). Retrieved from http://sprouts.aisnet.org/11-13

Bajgoric, N. (2006). Information technologies for business continuity: An implementation framework. *Information Management & Computer Security, 14*(5), 450–466. doi:10.1108/09685220610717754

Bielski, R. (2008). *Extreme Risks, American Bankers Association*. ABI/INFORM Global.

Blackhurst, J., Dunn, K. S., & Craighead, C. W. (2011). An Empirically Derived Framework of Global Supply Resiliency. *Journal of Business Logistics*, *32*(4), 374–391. doi:10.1111/j.0000-0000.2011.01032.x

Botha, J., & Von Solms, R. (2004). A cyclic approach to business continuity planning. *Information Management & Computer Security*, *12*(4), 328–337. doi:10.1108/09685220410553541

Brenes, E. R., Madrigal, K., & Requena, B. (2011). Corporate governance and family business performance. *Journal of Business Research*, *64*(3), 280–285. doi:10.1016/j.jbusres.2009.11.013

Broder, J. F., & Tucker, E. (2012). *Business Continuity Planning, Risk Analysis and the Security Survey* (4th ed.). Elsevier.

Cerullo, V., & Cerullo, M. J. (2004). Business continuity planning: A comprehensive approach. *Information Systems Management*, *21*(3), 70–78. doi:10.1201/1078/44432.21.3.20040601/82480.11

Chow, W. S., & Wai, O. H. (2009). Determinants of the critical success factor of disaster recovery planning for information systems. *Information Management & Computer Security*, *17*(3), 248–275. doi:10.1108/09685220910978103

Csaplar, D. (2012). *The Cost of Downtime is Rising*. Available at: http://blogs.aberdeen.com/it-infrastructure/the-cost-of-downtime-is-rising/

De Haes, S., & Grembergen, W. V. (2009). An Exploratory Study into IT Governance Implementations and its Impact on Business/IT Alignment. *Information Systems Management*, *26*(2), 123–137. doi:10.1080/10580530902794786

Finch, P. (2004). Supply Chain Risk management, *Supply Chain management. International Journal (Toronto, Ont.)*, *9*(2), 183–196.

Forrester Report. (2011). *State Of Enterprise Disaster Recovery Preparedness, Q2 2011, May 2011*. Available on: http://i.zdnet.com/whitepapers/Forrester_Analyst_White_Paper_The_State_of_Enterprise.pdf

Gerber, M., & Solms, R. (2005). Management of risk in the information age. *Computers & Security*, *24*(1), 16–30. doi:10.1016/j.cose.2004.11.002

Gibb, F., & Buchanan, S. (2006). A framework for business continuity management. *International Journal of Information Management*, *26*(2), 128–141. doi:10.1016/j.ijinfomgt.2005.11.008

Greening, P., & Rutherford, C. (2011). Disruptions and supply networks: A multi-level, multi-theoretical relational perspective. *The International Journal of Logistics Management*, *22*(1), 104–126. doi:10.1108/09574091111127570

Hair, J. F., Anderson, R. E., Babin, B. J., & Black, W. C. (2010). *Multivariate data analysis: A global perspective* (Vol. 7). Upper Saddle River, NJ: Pearson.

Herbane, B., Elliott, D., & Swartz, E. M. (2004). Business Continuity Management: Time for a strategic role? *Long Range Planning*, *37*(5), 435–457. doi:10.1016/j.lrp.2004.07.011

IDC White Paper. (2009). *Reducing Downtime and Business Loss: Addressing Business Risk with Effective Technology*. IDC.

IDC Report. (2016). *Cut costs, reduce complexity and drive Availability for the Always-On Enterprise*. Available on: https://go.veeam.com/wp-2016-idc-executive-brief.html

Jarvelainen, J. (2013). IT incidents and business impacts: Validating a framework for continuity management in information systems. *International Journal of Information Management*.

Karim, A.J. (2011). Business Disaster Preparedness: An Empirical Study for measuring the Factors of Business Continuity to face Business Disaster. *International Journal of Business and Social Science*, 2(18).

Kim, Y. G., & Cha, S. (2012). Threat scenario-based security risk analysis using use case modeling in information systems. *Security Comm. Networks*, *5*, 293–300.

King, D. L. (2003). *Moving Towards a Business Continuity Culture. In Network Security* (pp. 12–17). Elsevier.

Kolowitz, B.J., Lauro, G.R., Barkey, C., Black, H., Light, K., & Deible, C. (2012). Workflow Continuity—Moving Beyond Business Continuity in a Multisite 24–7 Healthcare Organization. *Journal of Digital Imaging*, *25*, 744-750.

Koronis, E., & Ponis, S.T. (2012). Introducing Corporate Reputation Continuity To Support Organizational Resilience Against Crises. *Journal of Applied Business Research*, *28*(2), 283.

Leitch, G. (2016). *The True Cost of Downtime in 2016*. Available at: http://flexitcenter.dataresolution.net/index.php/2016/06/09/true-cost-downtime-2016/

Lewis, W. R., & Pickren, A. (2003). An Empirical Assessment of IT Disaster Risk. *Communications of the ACM*, *46*(September), 201–206. doi:10.1145/903893.903938

Lin, C. S., Kao, S., & Chen, L. S. (2012). A Proactive Operational Framework for Business Continuity in the Semiconductor Industry. *Quality and Reliability Engineering International*, *28*(3), 307–320. doi:10.1002/qre.1246

Lindstrom, J. (2012). A model to explain a business contingency process. *Disaster Prevention and Management*, *21*(2), 269–281. doi:10.1108/09653561211220052

Lindstrom, J., Samuelson, S., & Hagerfors, A. (2010). Business continuity planningMethodology. *Disaster Prevention and Management*, *19*(2), 243–255. doi:10.1108/09653561011038039

Lump, . (2008). From high availability and disaster recovery to business continuity solutions. *IBM Systems Journal*, *47*(4), 605–619. doi:10.1147/SJ.2008.5386516

Martin, N. (2011). *The true costs of data center downtime*. Available on: http://itknowledgeexchange.techtarget.com/data-center/the-true-costs-of-data-center-downtime/

McNaughton, B., Ray, P., & Lewis, L. (2010). Designing an evaluation framework for IT service management. *Information & Management*, *47*, 219–225.

Melton, A., & Trahan, J. (2009, December). Business Continuity Planning. *Risk Management*, *56*(10), 46–48.

Niemimaa, M. (2015). Interdisciplinary Review of Business Continuity from an Information Systems Perspective: Toward an Integrative Framework. *Communications of the Association for Information Systems*, *37*, 69–102.

Nollau, B. (2009). Disaster Recovery and Business Continuity. *Journal of GXP Compliance*, *13*(3), 51.

Oyha, D., & Gokhale, D. A. (2009). Logistical business continuity planning-scale developmentand validation. *The International Journal of Logistics Management*, *20*(3), 342–359. doi:10.1108/09574090911002814

Omar, A., Alijani, D., & Mason, R. (2011). Information Technology Disaster Recovery Plan: Case Study. *Academy of Strategic Management Journal*, *10*(2), 2011.

Pollard, C., & Cater-Steel, A. (2010). Justifications, Strategies, and Critical Success Factors in Successful ITIL Implementations in U.S. and Australian Companies: An Exploratory Study. *Information Systems Management*, *26*(2), 164–175. doi:10.1080/10580530902797540

Ponemon Institute Report. (2016). *Cost of Data Center Outages*. Available on: http://www.emersonnetworkpower.com/en-US/Resources/Market/Data-Center/Latest-Thinking/Ponemon/Documents/2016-Cost-of-Data-Center-Outages-FINAL-2.pdf

Ragin, C. C. (1992). Introduction: Cases of "What is a Case". In C. C. Ragin & H. S. Becker (Eds.), *What is a case?* (pp. 1–17). Cambridge, UK: Cambridge University press.

Rebman, T., Wang, J., Swick, Z., Reddick, D., & Rosario, J. L. (2013). Business continuity and pandemic preparedness: US health care versus non-health care agencies. *American Journal of Infection Control*, *41*(4), e27–e33. doi:10.1016/j.ajic.2012.09.010 PMID:23337305

Romano, C. (1989). Research Strategies for Small Business: A Case Study. *International Small Business Journal*, *7*(4), 35–43. doi:10.1177/026624268900700403

Sapateiro, C., Baloian, N., Antunes, P., & Zurita, G. (2011). Developing a Mobile Collaborative Tool for Business Continuity Management. *Journal of Universal Computer Science*, *17*(2), 164–182.

Spremic, M. (2009). IT Governance Mechanisms in Managing IT Business Value. *WSEAS Transactions on Information Science and Applications*, *6*(6), 906–915.

Spremić, M. (2012). Measuring IT Governance Performance: A Research Study on CobiT-Based Regulation Framework Usage. *International Journal of Mathematics and Computers in Simulation*, *1*(6), 17-25.

Stanton, R. (2007, Nov.). Fail to plan, plan to fail. *Infosecurity*, 24–25.

Symantec Report. (2011). *Symantec 2011 SMB Disaster Preparedness Survey*. Available on: http://www.symantec.com/content/en/us/about/media/pdfs/symc_2011_SMB_DP_Survey_Report_Global.pdf?om_ext_cid=biz_socmed_twitter_facebook_marketwire_linkedin_2011Jan_worldwide_dpsurvey

Tammineedi, R. L. (2010). Business Continuity Management: A Standards-Based Approach. *Information Security Journal: A Global Perspective*, *19*, 36-50.

Turetken, O. (2008). Is Your Backup IT-Infrastructure in a Safe Location – A Multi-Criteria Approach to Location Analysis for Business Continuity Facilities. *Information Systems Frontiers*, *10*, 375–383. doi:10.1007/s10796-008-9081-8

Veeam Report. (2014). *The Veeam Data Center Availability Report 2014*. Available at: https://www.veeam.com/wp-availability-report-2014.html

Winkler, U., Fritzsche, M., Gilani, W., & Marshall, A. (2010). A Model-Driven Framework for Process-centric Business Continuity Management. *Proceedings of the 2010 Seventh International Conference on the Quality of Information and Communications Technology*, 248-252. doi:10.1109/QUATIC.2010.46

Wolf, J. (2011). Sustainable Supply Chain Management Integration: A Qualitative Analysis of the German Manufacturing Industry. *Journal of Business Ethics*, *102*(2), 221–235. doi:10.1007/s10551-011-0806-0

Yin, R. K. (1994). *Case Study Research. Design and Methods* (2nd ed.). Newbury Park, CA: Sage Publications.

Zhu, Z., Nakata, C., Sivakumar, K., Grewal, D. (2013). Fix It or Leave It? Customer Recovery from Self-service Technology Failures. *Journal of Retailing, 89*, 15–29.

Zobel, C. (2011). Representing perceived tradeoffs in defining disaster resilience. *Decision Support Systems*, *50*(2), 394–403. doi:10.1016/j.dss.2010.10.001

Chapter 9
The Role of Information System Monitoring in Improving System Availability

Semir Ibrahimović
Bosna Bank International d.d. Sarajevo, Bosnia and Herzegovina

Nijaz Bajgoric
University of Sarajevo, Bosnia and Herzegovina

ABSTRACT

The IS availability is an essential requirement that business presents to its IT departments. Ibrahimovic (2016) concluded that, with a very low investment in "monitoring of the relevant components", it is possible to achieve a significant improvement in IS availability. This chapter starts with a brief introduction of the IS availability. Authors provide a short definition of BBN modeling and address different aspects of IS monitoring, particularly: network monitoring, server monitoring, application, security and business process monitoring. As main artifact of this chapter authors proposed the monitoring. Since the framework emphases importance of governance and management layer, chapter contains overview of COBIT 5 and ITIL V3 from the IS monitoring aspect. In the final part of the chapter, authors address the challenges that a monitoring tool needs to address in modern information systems, especially but not limited to DevOps, Cloud and Hybrid IT architectures.

DOI: 10.4018/978-1-5225-3704-5.ch009

INTRODUCTION

Modern information systems (IS) are expected to be always-on by providing services to end-users, regardless of time and location. This is particularly important for organizations and industries where information systems support real-time operations and mission-critical applications that need to be available on "24x7x365" basis. Examples of such organizations include process industries, telecommunications, healthcare, energy, banking, electronic commerce and a variety of cloud services.

Information technologies enable modern business, while, at the same time, a success of an organization is becoming increasingly dependent on the appropriate use of information technologies and managing risks associated with IT. The availability of information system is an essential requirement that business presents to its IT departments. Most commonly, IS availability is referred to be part of the of the CIA information security triangle (confidentiality, integrity, availability). There are many factors influencing information systems availability identified in the relevant literature. Among the others, Franke et. al (Franke, Johnson, König, & Marcks von Würtemberg, 2012) identified 16 factors, by using an expert elicitation, they found that "monitoring of the relevant components" is the second most influential factor, closely following "change management". Ibrahimovic (2016) extended Franke's model with an investment aspect, and concluded that, with a very low investment in implementing best practices in "monitoring of the relevant components", compared to the investments in other factors, it is possible to achieve a significant improvement in information system availability.

Information system monitoring refers to several activities of observing system and detecting changes that occur during operations. Monitoring helps to analyze the status and utilization of various services and infrastructure components, facilitates optimal use of resources and proactive management, supports capacity planning, trend analysis, and root cause/impact analysis. As the business grows, monitoring helps to optimize the use of infrastructure resources. In addition, the monitoring process includes infrastructure's environmental controls and controls of the operating environments for key components such as network components, storage arrays, and servers(Gnanasundaram & Shrivastava, 2012)

The chapter starts with a brief introduction of the IS availability and presents necessary definitions and formulas used for measuring the availability of complex information system. We use formulas for complex systems availability calculation presented in Ibrahimovic and Bajgoric (Ibrahimovic & Bajgoric, 2016). They identified overall system availability as an average availability of each service weighted by a factor of importance of a service. Accordingly, in this chapter, we discuss monitoring at the service level, as well as monitoring of the infrastructure components which are important for proper functioning of the service. We provide a short definition of BBN modeling techniques, with a brief description of factors influencing information system availability. The main section of the chapter addresses "information system monitoring" and explores the best practices in this field.. We will address different aspects of information system monitoring, particularly: network monitoring, server monitoring and application monitoring. We argue that new paradigm for safety engineering, presented by Zio (2016), which proactively integrates the accident preventive tasks of anticipation (imagining what to expect) and monitoring (knowing what to look for), the accident tasks of responding (knowing what to do and being capable of doing it) and learning (knowing what has happened), the mitigative tasks of absorbing (damping the negative impact of the adverse effect) and the recovery tasks of adaptation (making intentional adjustment to come through a disruption), restoration (returning to the normal state) can be applied in information systems field, by going beyond standard definition of monitoring.

In the second part of the chapter, we will address the challenges that a monitoring tool needs to address in modern information systems, especially but not limited to DevOps, Cloud, Hybrid IT, and BYOD architectures. We will analyze how major market players provide responses to best practices prescribed by IT-standards. . We will tackle user experience and data visualization aspect as well as the need for learning from collected data.

Information System Availability: Definition, Factors and BBN Approach

In today's world, most of the business activities are associated with the use of information technology (IT). Information technologies enable and facilitate business, while, at the same time, business success is becoming increasingly dependent on the adequate use of information technologies and on risks associated with this dependence. The availability of information system (IS) is an essential requirement that business presents to IT departments. According to ITIL, availability is the characteristic of the IS to perform its agreed action at the request of an authorized user (Taylor, Vernon, & Rudd, 2007). Availability in the broader sense implies that the information system is ready to serve end users, even in the event of unforeseen and catastrophic events, and that, at the same time, it is protected from various security threats.

In this study, an information system is defined in a broader sense, as a combination of interrelated components that through interaction deliver the desired output. That means, information system, besides hardware and software, includes people, processes, culture and environment, which are all crucial for understanding, explaining and modeling availability and risk (Fenton, 2012). From the availability perspective, in this study, the system was regarded as a set of services that are available to end users. The total availability of the IS is the result of summarizing the availability of individual services which make up the system. It is assumed that each service has an agreed-upon operation time (if service is to be continuously available 24x7 or only 8x5). The percentage of users affected by the outage of individual systems is also considered.

Availability is measured by the ratio of the time in which the system was available and the total time in which system is supposed to be running according to service level agreements:

$$Availability = \frac{Systemuptime}{Systemuptime + Systemdowntime} \quad (1)$$

The usual way to represent the IS availability is "number of nines". For instance, the 99.999% availability is called "five nines" (Singh, 2009).

System availability can be defined as the average availability of each service weighted by a factor of importance of a service as represented by the equation (2)

$$A = \frac{\sum_i A_i * k_i}{\sum_i k_i} \quad (2)$$

where A represents overall system availability, Ai is the availability of service s_i and k_i is a coefficient signifying the importance of service s_i.

For calculating availability of a particular service, it is important to take into account the service operating time, defined in the service level agreement, as well as the number of end users affected by the service interruption as represented by the formula (3)

$$A_i = \frac{t_i}{t_i + T_i * \frac{N_i}{n_i}} \quad (3)$$

In this formula, t_i is the total time that service s_i was available under service level agreement, T_i is the total time for which the system was unavailable, n_i is the total number of the service users, N_i is the number of service users who experienced service interruption during time T_i.

In this chapter, we extend the two works presented by Ibrahimovic (2016) and Ibrahimovic and Bajgoric (Ibrahimovic & Bajgoric, 2016) which introduced BBN model for justifying IT availability investment. They used the framework defined by Franke et al. (2012) based on the BBN approach for IS availability modelling. Their choice of variables was based on "the index of availability" (Marcus & Stern, 2003).

After a thorough literature review, Ibrahimovic and Bajgoric (2016) suggested making some changes in the variables set. They proposed a model that consists of thirteen variables representing thirteen domains affecting information systems availability namely: physical environment, availability requirements management, operations management, change management, backup management, storage redundancy, avoiding errors in internal applications, avoiding errors in external services, network management, equipment and location of the Disaster Recovery (DR) data center, resilient client/server systems, monitoring of relevant components, human resources management. They argued that, if the best practices are implemented in one of those domains, IS unavailability could be reduced. The probability elicitation used for determining model parameters was done by interviewing 23 relevant experts with adequate experience in the availability of IT systems in the financial sector in Bosnia-Herzegovina. During the elicitation, most experts agreed that the selection of variables in the model is adequate and that the model is comprehensive. Elicitation was conducted through structured interviews. In the first part of interviews, training of experts and the calibration of their predictions was carried out, while in the second part experts filled in the questionnaire. The questionnaire consisted of three sets of questions. Experts first were asked to estimate the impact of individual variables on system availability. In the second question, experts gave their assessment of the situation in the areas described by the variables in the financial sector in BiH. To answer the third question, they estimated the necessary investments to bring the field represented by variable to the level of best practices.

Using the experts answers to questions about the current state of best practice, prior probabilities could be found for every node. Thus, the equation for calculating availability becomes the following:

$$P\left(\mathrm{A}\right)=\left(1-p_{0}\right)\prod_{i\in\left[1,\mathrm{n}\right]}\left(1-p_{i}\right)=\left(1-p_{0}\right)*\prod_{i\in\left[1,n\right]}\left(1-\pm V_{i}*(1-B_{i})\right) \tag{4}$$

(Ibrahimovic & Bajgoric, 2016)

In this formula, n represents the number of variables in the model, V_i is the percentage of the improving system's availability if best practices are applied, B_i is the prior state of implementation of the best practices in different system's components, α is a transformation coefficient, and p_0 is the leak representing the probability that the system is unavailable even in the case where for all domains included in the model, best practices are applied.

V_i and Bi are obtained as a weighted average from expert answers. These parameters represent the fact that the impact of the application of best practice is not the same if it is already applied on, say, 30% or 90% of existing IS. Equation (4) shows that if the best practices are already implemented in some domain i.e. state variable B_i = 1, this variable does not affect the availability, or acts like an activated inhibitor. B_i are modeled in the BBN in CPT for nodes representing causal factors.

Research has shown that the managing availability requirements makes the greatest impact on the availability (23.20%), followed by operations management (20.54%) and the location and equipment of the disaster recovery site (19.52%). The reduction of IS unavailability is least impacted by the physical environment (10.53%), followed by backup management (11.05%) and server platforms (11.81%). Research results showed that the state of implementation of best practices in the areas described by variables ranges from 4.60 to 6.85 on a scale from 1 to 10 depending on the area. The worst situation is in the fields of monitoring (4.6) and availability requirements management (4.94), while the best state in the information systems of financial institutions in BiH is in the primary infrastructure areas, backup management (6.85), network management (6:54), server infrastructure (6.39) and physical environment (6.05).According to the results of this research, the perception of experts is that the state of the essential IS infrastructure elements, including the server room, server and network infrastructure, data redundancy, backup management is much better than the process part, which includes change management, operations management, monitoring and requirements management. The assessment of current maturity level of backup management may explain why the experts estimated that implementing

Table 1. Elicitation results for causal factors(Ibrahimovic & Bajgoric, 2016)

Variable	Impact (%)	Maturity level (scale 1-10)	Investment per mil.KM assets
Operations management	20.54	5.24	430.00
Network management	19.53	6.54	584.81
Equipment and location of the DR data center	19.52	5.28	1,029.17
Avoiding errors in internal applications	17.58	5.93	816.67
Avoiding errors in external services	17.52	5.88	614.00
Change management	17.15	5.56	367.88
Human resources management	15.45	5.44	496.91
Backup management	11.05	6.85	279.82
Availability requirements management	23.2	4.94	75.00
Storage redundancy	17.2	5.76	1,131.24
Resilient client / server systems	11.81	6.39	803.33
Physical environment	10.54	6.05	503.49
Monitoring	12.33	4.60	412.00

best practices in that area would have a small impact on reducing unavailability, as the situation in that field has been assessed as the best compared to all other areas that were part of the model. A similar explanation applies to the physical environment and server infrastructure. The above was the main reason to include assessed states of implementing best practices in the field as the prior probability for each parent node in BBN-based "Leaky Noisy-OR" model. The conditional probability table for the node that represents availability is filled based on a linear transformation of the elicited impact values. The model is set up assuming the initial system availability of 99% and a leak of 0.01%, which represents the unavailability of the system. This occurred under the influence of unmodelled causes. Both of these parameters can be subsequently changed.

The influence diagram, based on the Utility Theory, was developed on top of the BBN model for optimizing IT infrastructure investments. The investment cost, to reach best practice in the particular area, was obtained by expert elicitation. Responses were weighted by dividing investment amount by the size of bank assets, to be independent of the bank size. The utility function, which has ben used in the model, is a linear function that represents the total loss due to the unavailability of the system and investments costs necessary to bring variables to the level of best practices. Increasing investment reduces the loss due to unavailability.

Unavailability values below 97% were not modeled due to the assumption that if an IS of a financial institution is not available 11 days in a year, that organization

Figure 1. Influence diagram(Ibrahimovic, 2016)

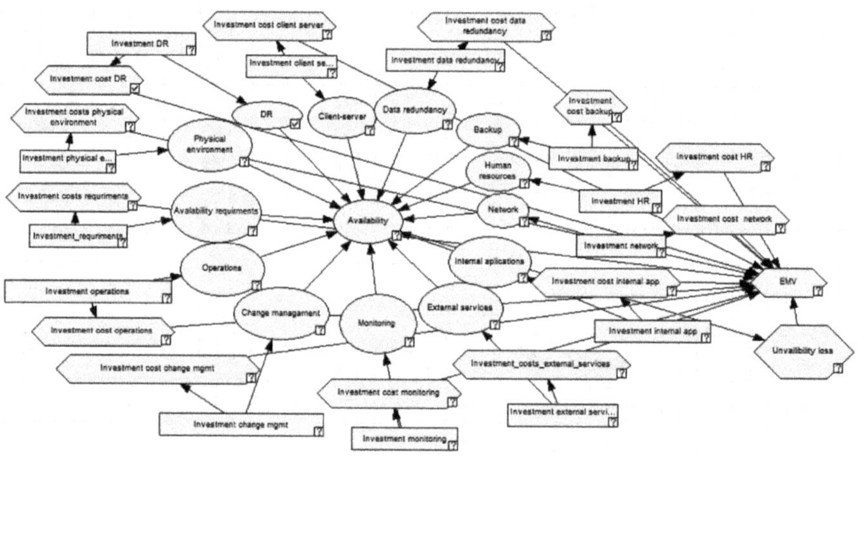

cannot survive on the market. The formula for calculating the total loss is presented below

$$EL = R \text{ for } A<97\%$$

$$EL = (1\text{-}A)*R + \sum I_i \quad (5)$$

EL is the total expected loss due to unavailability and investment costs, A is system availability as a percentage, R is the maximum loss in the case of the total system unavailability, and I_i is the investment needed to bring individual variable i to the level of best practice.

The goal of the model is to maximize the expected utility, with the restrictions imposed by the desired level of availability. As result of the solvin the model without limit imposed to the availability level, the optimal level of investment was very low (in this case only investment in requirements management and monitoring). Main reasons for that were relatively high (99%) initial level of IS availability, and diminishing return for investments made to raise availability level above 99.5%.

From results of this research we can see that with relatively low investment in monitoring, IS availability level can be significantly increased and that's the main reason to continue research in that direction.

Table 2. Crystal Ball optimization results(Ibrahimovic & Bajgoric, 2016)

Variable	Impact (%)	Maturity level (scale 1-10)	Investment per mil.KM assets
Operations management	20.54	5.24	430.00
Network management	19.53	6.54	584.81
Equipment and location of the DR data center	19.52	5.28	1,029.17
Avoiding errors in internal applications	17.58	5.93	816.67
Avoiding errors in external services	17.52	5.88	614.00
Change management	17.15	5.56	367.88
Human resources management	15.45	5.44	496.91
Backup management	11.05	6.85	279.82
Availability requirements management	23.2	4.94	75.00
Storage redundancy	17.2	5.76	1,131.24
Resilient client / server systems	11.81	6.39	803.33
Physical environment	10.54	6.05	503.49
Monitoring	12.33	4.60	412.00

Information System Monitoring: Literature Review

The area of information system monitoring has been treated by international IT standards such as ITIL, COBIT, NIST. Several authors addressed this issue. As already cited, Zio (2016)introduced a new paradigm for safety engineering, which proactively integrates the accident preventive tasks of anticipation (imagining what to expect) and monitoring (knowing what to look for), the in-accident tasks of responding (knowing what to do and being capable of doing it) and learning (knowing what has happened), the mitigative tasks of absorbing (damping the negative impact of the adverse effect) and the recovery tasks of adaptation (making intentional adjustment to come through a disruption), restoration (returning to the normal state). Abrams et al. (2007), argued that most companies initially focus on improving the efficiency of their compliance and control procedures to minimize cost by standardizing procedures throughout the enterprise and adding automated status monitoring. Bajgoric (2008), while citing the main technologies that are used to provide high availability, identified predictive system-monitoring capabilities as toll aimed at eliminating failures before they occur.

Chiasson & Davidson (2005) focused on IT-enabled monitoring of employees is integrated into the IT artifacts as a tool for improving governance systems, such as managerial controls.

Fatema et al. (2014) dealt with monitoring of complex cloud systems with regard to how existing monitoring tools fit in the cloud computing paradigm. They identified some practical capabilities that an ideal monitoring tool should possess to serve the objectives in these operational areas. Based on these identified capabilities, they presented a taxonomy of the monitoring tools to determine their strength and weaknesses.

Hernantes & Gallardo (2015) identified the features that software monitoring tools have to cover and compared main infrastructure monitoring tools in respect with those features. Rusu & Manolache (2004) dealt with monitoring of networks which superpose multiple sets of services belonging to different participants on the same communication infrastructure. They proposed a model that illustrates the way a participant should organize and manage its network presence with minimum investment and maximum efficiency based on a structure named Distributed Virtual NOC. Jia et al. (2007) proposed an Integrated Network Management System. They presented an analysis of the requirements and key enabling technologies for the development of integrated network management system. They proposed a new integrated network management system (INMS) architecture including a monitoring component as well. Khan et al. (2013) presented an effective and automatic network monitoring system that continuously monitors all network switches and informs the administrator by email or SMS when any of the network switches goes down.

Their system refers to the problem location in the network topology and its effect on network stability. Prathamesh & Mayekar(2016) raised the question "Is prevention always better ?" by using a case of IT service management. They pointed out the increasing focus on cost reduction, as essential to revisit the trade-off between costs and other primary ITSM objectives such as service availability and quality. Among other variables they included monitoring cost as well. Cedillo et al. (2015) suggested a definition of an SLA compliance monitoring infrastructure which is based on the use of "models@run.time", its main components and artifacts, and the interactions among them. Sharma et al. (2015) dealt with diagnosing faults in OpenStack and presented HANSEL, a system that leverages non-intrusive network monitoring to expedite root cause analysis of such faults manifesting in OpenStack operations. Patra et al. (2011) addressed monitoring of service based e-Governance systems and proposed a framework for monitoring the compliance of SBS for which a set of requirements have been pre-specified. They developed a Monitor Specification Language, a language that has to specify the properties of the system to be monitored at run-time. Chan & Chieu (2003) proposed an approach to fix the problem that lies in those applications where source code is not available and therefore is virtually impossible to modify the application code to include monitoring functions. Or, the application code is too tangled with other components which make modification difficult. Tang et al. (2013) developed an integrated framework for optimizing automatic monitoring systems in large IT infrastructures. Their framework define a set of monitoring conditions and optimal corresponding delay times based on an off-line analysis of historical alerts and incident tickets. Gómez-Iglesias et al. (2016) presented a tool designed to provide the information that is most critical for running an application on HPC systems. Kutare et al. (2010) studied Online monitoring and analytics for managing large scale data centers. They coined the term 'monalytics' to refer to the combined monitoring and analysis systems used for managing large-scale data center systems. Comuzzi & Spanoudakis (2010) presented a framework that supports the dynamic assessment of "monitorability" of SLAs' terms and the dynamic setup of an appropriate infrastructure for monitoring them following such changes. Meng (2013) in his awarded dissertation research tackled critical challenges in providing Monitoring as Service (MaaS) with a layered approach that systematically addresses monitoring efficiency, scalability, reliability and utility at the monitoring infrastructure level, the monitoring functionality level and the monitoring data utility level.

As a summary, all papers analyzed in the literature review are characterized by focusing on a partial dimension or technology. None of them addresses this issue from systemic (holistic) perspective, a perspective which will include all subsystems of information system, including IS monitoring as well.

The Framework

When thinking about IS monitoring, it is very important to approach it strategically, from a holistic (systemic/top-down) approach. The main point in such an approach is based on creation of new value for business stakeholders. New value can be created by: benefits realization, risk creation and resource optimization (Isaca, 2012). If we start from the bottom, we will end in having a number of siloed monitoring solutions, as shown in Fig. 2.

However, we propose a monitoring framework which is presented on Fig. 3

Figure 2. Siloed monitoring solution (CATechnologies, 2016)

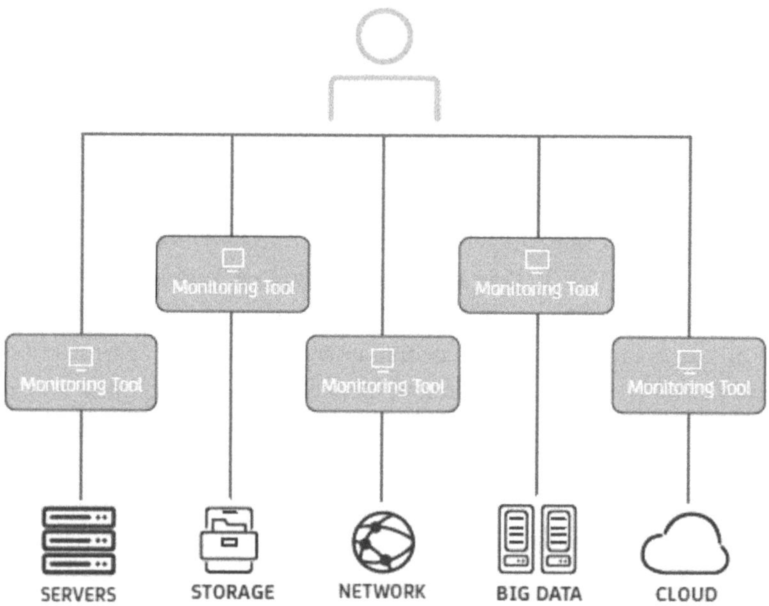

Table 3. IS monitoring: A Conceptual holistic framework

<table>
<tr><td colspan="5">Governance and management Layer COBIT – ITIL – NIST- ISO 27001
• Business Goals
• IT- related goals
• Processes and procedures
• Actions
• Metrics
• Assurance</td></tr>
<tr><td>Security</td><td>Network</td><td>System</td><td>Application performance</td><td>Business process performance</td></tr>
<tr><td colspan="5">Tools</td></tr>
</table>

Figure 3. Monitoring framework technical scheme modified from (Turnbull, 2016)

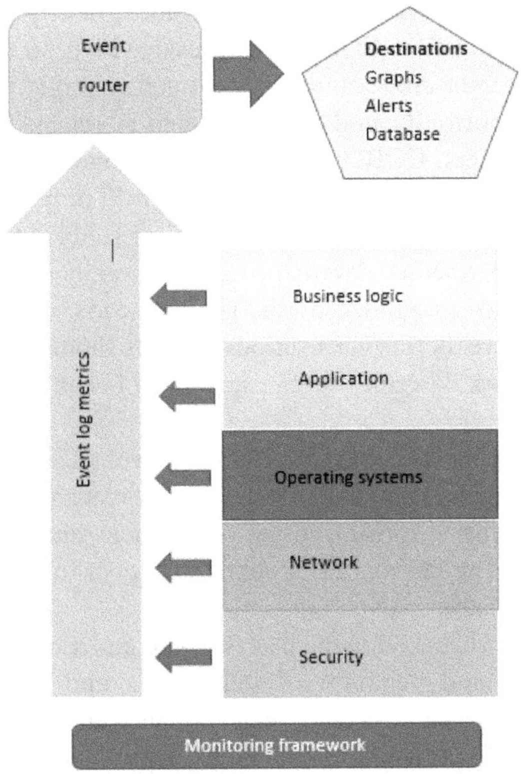

The first layer in this model is made of governance and management layers, where the goals, both business and IT -related, processes and procedures, actions, metrics and assurance, are defined.

On the second level, we define methods for monitoring each specific area of IS monitoring system such as: Security, Network, System, Application performance and Business process performance. Output s from the first layer are inputs for this layer. This fact ensures that we have an integrated, instead of siloed monitoring system

From technical implementation perspective, we adopt a model shown in Fig.4, which is a modified version of model suggested by Turnbull (, 2016). As can be seen, the framework imposes single monitoring tool which takes inputs from different IS parts, processes them, contextualizes them and stores them into a single event database and generate alerts. Using this events database, various visualizations can be created for real time IS component status and performance monitoring.

The two most prominent IT standards from the first layer of the proposed framework (Cobit 5 and ITIL V3) suggest comprehensive frameworks with regard to IS monitoring. **COBIT 5** provides a framework that helps businesses achieve their goals for governance and IT management. In short, it helps companies to create optimal value from IT finding balance between realizing benefits and optimizing risk levels and resource utilization. COBIT 5 ensures that IT is governed and managed in a holistic manner for the entire company, considering end-to-end business and IT functional areas responsibility, and having in mind IT-related interests of internal and external stakeholders. COBIT 5 is a generic framework and can be used in companies of all sizes, whether commercial, non-profit or public sector.

COBIT introduce concept of enablers in terms of factors that, individually and collectively, influence whether governance and management will work across the enterprise IT. Enablers are guided by the goals cascade, meaning that related a higher level IT objectives define what various enablers should achieve.(Isaca, 2013)

COBIT 5 framework describes seven categories of enablers(Isaca, 2013):

1. The principles, policies and frameworks are a vehicle to translate the desired behavior into practical guidance for day-to-day management.
2. Processes describe an organized set of practices and activities to achieve certain goals and produce a set of output in support of the accomplishing of the overall IT-related goals.
3. Organizational structures are the places where key decision are made.
4. Culture, ethics and behavior of individuals and companies are often underestimated as a success factor in governance and management activities.
5. Information is ubiquitous throughout any organization, and includes all of the information produced and used by the company. Information is needed to keep the organization running and well managed, and at the same time, at the operational level, information is often the key products of the company.
6. Services, infrastructure and applications include infrastructure, technology and applications that provide company with IT processing and services.
7. People skills and competencies associated with people are necessary for the successful completion of all activities and for making the right decisions and taking corrective measures.

COBIT 5 defines three monitoring processes:

- MEA01 Monitor, Evaluate and Assess Performance and Conformance
- MEA02 Monitor, Evaluate and Assess the System of Internal Control
- MEA03 Monitor, Evaluate and Assess Compliance with External Requirements**MEA03 Monitor,**

MEA01- Collect, validate and evaluate business, IT and process goals and metrics. Monitor that processes are performing against agreed-on performance and

Figure 4. Cobit 5 enterprise enablers(Isaca, 2013)

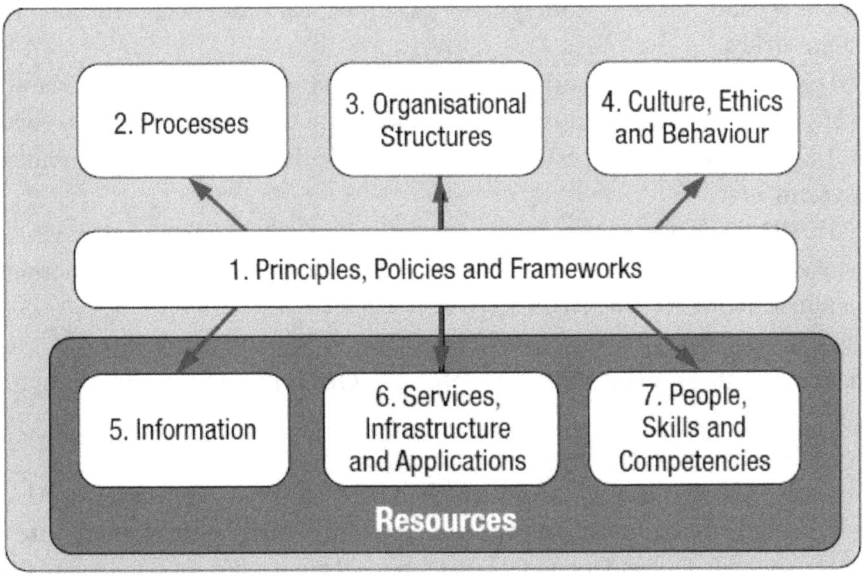

conformance goals and metrics and provide reporting that is systematic and timely. This process is closely related with ISO 27001 and ITIL V3 Continual Service Improvement standards.

It support the following IT- related goals

- Managed IT-related business risk
- Delivery of IT services in line with business requirements
- Optimization of IT assets, resources and capabilities
- IT compliance with internal policies

It consists of the following management practices:

- **MEA01.01 Establish a Monitoring Approach:** Engage with stakeholders to establish and maintain a monitoring approach to define the objectives, scope and method for measuring business solution and service delivery and contribution to enterprise objectives. Integrate this approach with the corporate performance management system.
- **MEA01.02 Set Performance and Conformance Targets:** Work with stakeholders to define, periodically review, update and approve performance and conformance targets within the performance measurement system.

- **MEA01.03 Collect and Process Performance and Conformance Data:** Collect and process timely and accurate data aligned with enterprise approaches.
- **MEA01.04 Analyze and Report Performance:** Periodically review and report performance against targets, using a method that provides a succinct all-around view of IT performance and fits within the enterprise monitoring system.
- **MEA01.05 Ensure the Implementation of Corrective Actions:** Assist stakeholders in identifying, initiating and tracking corrective actions to address anomalies.(Isaca, 2012)

For each of these management practices, COBIT defines inputs, outputs and activities.

- **In the IS-Availability Context, MAE02 is Very Important:** MAE02 -Continuously monitor and evaluate the control environment, including self-assessments and independent assurance reviews. Enable management to identify control deficiencies and inefficiencies and to initiate improvement actions. Plan, organize and maintain standards for internal control assessment and assurance activities.

Even at the first glance assurance does not have direct connection with IS availability, it is confirmed in practice that IS audit can improve governance and management practices and indirectly help in in achieving higher IS availability

It supports following IT- related goals:

- IT compliance and support for business compliance with external laws and regulations
- Managed IT-related business risk (this one is particularly important for IS availability)
- IT compliance with internal policies

MAE02 consists of the following management practices (Isaca, 2012):

- **MEA02.01 Monitor Internal Controls:** Continuously monitor, benchmark and improve the IT control environment and control framework to meet organizational objectives.
- **MEA02.02 Review Business Process Controls Effectiveness:** Review the operation of controls, including a review of monitoring and test evidence, to ensure that controls within business processes operate effectively. Include

activities to maintain evidence of the effective operation of controls through mechanisms such as periodic testing of controls, continuous controls monitoring, independent assessments, command and control centres, and network operations centres. This provides the business with the assurance of control effectiveness to meet requirements related to business, regulatory and social responsibilities.

- **MEA02.03 Perform Control Self-Assessments:** Encourage management and process owners to take positive ownership of control improvement through a continuing programme of self-assessment to evaluate the completeness and effectiveness of management's control over processes, policies and contracts.
- **MEA02.04 Identify and Report Control Deficiencies:** Identify control deficiencies and analyses and identify their underlying root causes. Escalate control deficiencies and report to stakeholders.
- **MEA02.05 Ensure That Assurance Providers are Independent and Qualified:** Ensure that the entities performing assurance are independent from the function, groups or organizations in scope. The entities performing assurance should demonstrate an appropriate attitude and appearance, competence in the skills and knowledge necessary to perform assurance, and adherence to codes of ethics and professional standards.
- **MEA02.06 Plan Assurance Initiatives:** Plan assurance initiatives based on enterprise objectives and strategic priorities, inherent risk, resource constraints, and sufficient knowledge of the enterprise.
- **MEA02.07 Scope Assurance Initiatives:** Define and agree with management on the scope of the assurance initiative, based on the assurance objectives.
- **MEA02.08 Execute Assurance Initiatives:** Execute the planned assurance initiative. Report on identified findings. Provide positive assurance opinions, where appropriate, and recommendations for improvement relating to identified operational performance, external compliance and internal control system residual risk.(Isaca, 2012)

ITIL is a set of concepts and policies for managing IT infrastructure, development and operations. The development of ITIL started in the eighties of the twentieth century at the request of the British Government, by Central Computer & Telecommunication Agency as a response to the growing dependence on information technology and the increasing complexity of IT systems. ITIL v1 was published between 1989 and 1996 in the form of a collection of more than 30 books. In 2000, the UK Office of Government Commerce released ITIL v2 as a set of eight books, each covering a specific topic of IT management. Although simplified, ITIL2 has been criticized as too confusing and complex. In response to criticism, ITIL3 was released in 2007. ITIL3 reduced the number of publications on five: service strategy, service design, service transition, service operation, and continual service improvement. The enhanced version of ITIL3 was published in 2011.

ISO/IEC20000 is an international standard for quality assurance of IT services - IT services management. By implementing the requirements defined by this standard, the organization introduce the system of IT services management which can be certified under the same norms to provide proof of the quality of IT services. It has almost completely taken over all the ITIL terminology and scope so ITIL can be considered as *de facto* standard, since the ISO 20000 is the only valid standard for IT service management today (Spremić & Kostic, 2008). However, it is important to note that ITIL could not be implemented, but organization can benefit from a variety of recommendations and best practices contained in it (Sučić, 2012). ITIL is a set of best practices for IT service management that emphasize the central role of service users. ITIL is published in a number of books which cover various areas of IT management services. This section provides a brief overview of all modules with a little more extensive attention to security management.

The main tasks to which is ITIL dedicated to are:

- Operation and maintenance of the existing system;
- Development of the new system;
- Constant adaptation in order to provide services according to the changing demands of business.

ITIL framework is based on the five stages of the life cycle of services: service strategy, service design, service transition, service operation, and continual service improvement. In the center of this life cycle is a service strategy, followed by the service design, service transition, and service operation. Continual service improvement (CSI) surrounds and supports all phases of the life cycle. Both phases influence each other and are mutually supportive in terms of input and output information. The purpose of CSI life cycle is to align IT services to changing business needs by identifying and implementing improvements to IT services that support business processes (Taylor, 2007).

According to ITIL definition monitoring is "repeated observation of a Configuration Item, IT Service or Process to detect Events and to ensure that the current status is known". ITIL also defines monitoring control loop as "monitoring the output of a Task, Process, IT Service or Configuration Item; comparing this output to a predefined

Norm; and taking appropriate action based on this comparison". Monitoring loop is the most common model for defining control in a Service Management Lifecycle .

In service operation context (and thereby providing service availability) ITL implies:

- Using tools to monitor the status of key system components and key operational activities
- Generating notifications and distributing them to the responsible persons, when defined conditions are met.
- Ensuring that the system's performance or component state is within a specified range (e.g., disk space and memory usage)
- Detection of abnormal activity types or activity levels in infrastructure (e.g. a potential security threat). Detecting unauthorized changes (e.g. unauthorized software installation)
- Ensuring compliance with the organizational policies of (e.g. inappropriate use of e-mail)
- Monitoring of service output and ensuring that they meet quality requirements
- Monitoring of the information used to measure key performance indicators (KPI).

ITIL defines the control process as well as management process of using of device, system, or service. It is worth noting, however, that control is broader concept then the manipulation of the device. Control requires three conditions:

- Action must be conducted following the defined standard or norm
- Circumstances that trigger the action must be defined, clear and confirmed
- Action must be defined, approved and proper for given circumstances.

In an availability context, control means the following:

- Use tools to define the circumstances which represent normal operation or abnormal operation
- Regulate the performance of the device, system or service
- Measurement of availability
- Initiation of corrective measures, whether they are automated (e.g. To restart the device remotely or run the script) or manually (e.g. To inform the supervisory staff on the status) (Taylor, Cannon & Wheldon, 2007).

CURRENT TRENDS AND FUTURE DIRECTIONS IN MONITORING TOOLS DEVELOPMENT

There are a number of tools for network and systems monitoring available on the market. Some of them are developed for specific purpose, for example for HPC (High Performance Computing) cluster monitoring. Most of them are being improved in a way that they can support new developments in the IT industry like virtualization, cloud computing and containerization. General purpose infrastructure monitoring tools typically utilize a client–server model by installing an agent in every system to be monitored. Monitoring agents measure the metric values from monitored components and send them to the monitoring server. The server stores the collected metrics into a database, analyses them, and sends alerts generate graphs, trending reports and SLA reports based on the monitored metrics retrieved from the database (Fatema et al., 2014). Some of those tools are Nagios, SolarWinds, Hyperic, Zabix, ManageEngine, OpManager, IBM Tivoli, HP Operations Manager, WahtsUP Gold.

Within the new monitoring paradigm, some general purpose tools are still widely used, and new tools for application performance monitoring, metrics collection and visualization are appearing, as can be seen in Fig. 6.

Figure 5. Tools used for monitoring (Williams, 2016)

Analysis of Monitoring Status Quo Circa 2015

Survey Results	Analysis
Nagios was the most widely used tool, followed by Amazon CloudWatch and New Relic. A second tier of products included Incinga, Sensu, Zabbix, Datadog, Riemann and Microsoft System Center Operations Manager.	The data confirms a conventional approach, with Nagios used for monitoring infrastructure and New Relic used for application performance monitoring. Since the survey was conducted, we expect that Datadog and AWS CloudWatch usage has increased.
Server infrastructure was monitored by 81 percent of the respondents. Cloud infrastructure, network infrastructure, and applications were monitored less often.	Although DevOps practitioners care about infrastructure, they will not use the same metrics as those valued by traditional IT operations teams.
collectd, StatsD and New Relic were the most common products used to collect metrics. That data is being stored most often with Graphite. Although used less often, time series databases InfluxDB and OpenTSDB were also represented in the study.	We expect that container-related agents like Sysdig will show up more often. New monitoring tools like Prometheus have a custom-built time series database at their core.
Grafana was most used for visualization, followed by Graphite.	Notably absent from the list is Kibana, which is a commonly used part of the ELK Stack, now called Elastic Stack by its corporate parent.

The three important directions in monitoring tools development can be identified:

1. Unified view of all events generated by various infrastructure elements
2. Focusing on end user experience instead of state of particular IS component
3. Using artificial intelligence to identify patterns and detect anomalies

Unified view of all events generated by various infrastructure elements means that tool has to provide holistic, end-to-end picture of all IS services. To achieve that, the starting point has to be business services, which is decomposed to IS-related services, and on the lowest level to the IT infrastructure components. For each component, the KPI set has to be defined which are translated into alerts and dashboards.

Focusing on end user experience instead of state of particular IS component - New monitoring parading is not just about bringing data together in a unified view. It is also about bringing data together in a tool that can quickly identify an element failure and intuitively understand the impact of that failure on a business service and end-user experience. Proactively tracking end-user experience along with infrastructure key performance metrics enables:

Proactive 3 Experience Reporting STEP

- Superior customer experience as focus is shifted on improved experience versus availability.
- Proactive issue resolution as resolve bottlenecks before they happen is enabled.
- Fewer service desk tickets because streamlined support operations.

To support that, the monitoring system has to: a) Identify relevant customer or business data sources, b) Build unified business and IT reports/views, c) Correlate IT and non-IT data to find meaningful patterns, d) Use information to proactively pinpoint bottlenecks.("Infrastructure Monitoring Necessary for a Customer-Driven World Fueling the Application Experience," n.d.)

Using artificial intelligence to identify patterns and detect anomalies - a few of the companies that use artificial intelligence to identify patterns and detect anomalies result is that much of the noise created by older monitoring approaches gets suppressed.

Some of the challenges in the field of IS-monitoring are listed below:

- Most small organizations don't have automated monitoring — instead, they focus on minimizing downtime and managing physical assets. Big businesses, mainly replace the manual approach with automated monitoring systems that utilizes dashboards. (Turnbull, 2016)

- As concepts and processes of digital economy and business digitalization are becoming ubiquitous, pressure on IT systems, especially on their availability and reliability, is growing. To respond to the pressure IT architecture landscape is rapidly changing.
- More and more businesses are moving their IT systems to the cloud. Other companies are choosing to move only certain IS components into cloud and use various types of hybrid architectures. Since companies can choose among different cloud architectures: infrastructure as service (IaaS), Platform as Service (PaaS) and Software as Service (SaaS), from the monitoring point of view, situation becomes even more complex. Besides public cloud providers such as Amazon Web Services -AWS and Microsoft Azure, some companies decided to build their own private clouds.
- Cloud services introduced new demands for dynamic infrastructure management. First, IT operations must monitor the cloud environments themselves and then the applications and services that run on top of them. These cloud technologies are inherently dynamic, so monitoring tools must be elastic and responsive to changes in cloud infrastructure. (ENTERPRISE MANAGEMENT ASSOCIATES, 2016)
- As most monitoring tools have implemented monitoring of virtual machines as standard featured With the introduction of containers and microservices they exposed to the new challenge. Not only are there more objects to manage, but they're generating more pieces of information. Collecting data from environments composed of so many moving parts has become increasingly complex. As an example, we can consider number of metrics needed to monitor a standard host: 100 about the operating system and 50 about an application. With containers, we have an additional 50 metrics per container and 50 metrics per orchestrator on the host. Considering a scenario where there a cluster is running 100 containers on top of two underlying hosts, there would be over 10,000 metrics to track (Williams, 2016).
- Another challenge for IS monitoring system is emerging DevOps paradigm. Central to the idea of DevOps is collaboration between all of the teams involved in IT applications and infrastructure. Developers, Operations, Quality Assurance, Security, and more, all have stakes in the delivery of a product or service. So, what does collaboration mean when it comes to monitoring in the world of DevOps. In DevOps focus of monitoring shifting from infrastructure monitoring to an application monitoring which requires some special tools.

CONCLUSION

Applying the best practices in the field of monitoring IS is an important role in enhancing the levels of IS availability. In this paper, we tried to figure out the role of the best practices in monitoring IS in ensuring high system availability. We made a literature review including numerous industry white papers and best practices recommendation. We proposed a holistic (top-down) framework which includes the leading industry standards Cobit 5 and ITIL V3 in the layered form as a foundation for monitoring governance and management framework. The chapter also presents the current situation and future trends in monitoring tools, as well as main challenges in monitoring modern information systems based on new IT-platforms such as cloud computing, hybrid environment, containerization and DevOps.

REFERENCES

Abrams, C., Von Kanel, J., & Muller, S. (2007). Optimized enterprise risk management. *IBM Systems, 46*(2), 219–234. Retrieved from http://ieeexplore.ieee.org/xpls/abs_all.jsp?arnumber=5386607

Analysis, I. (2016). *CA Unified Infrastructure Management Deepens its Visibility Into Cloud and Hybrid IT With Comprehensive New Capabilities CA Unified Infrastructure Management Deepens its Visibility*. Academic Press.

Bajgoric, N. (2008). *Continuous Computing Technologies for Enhancing Business Continuity*. IGI Global. doi:10.4018/978-1-60566-160-5

CATechnologies. (2016). *Agile Infrastructure Monitoring for the Application Economy The Application Economy Is Here — Is Your IT Monitoring Approach Ready*. CA Technologies.

Cedillo, P., Gonzalez-Huerta, J., Abrahao, S., & Insfrán, E. (2015). A Monitoring Infrastructure for the Quality of Cloud Services. *24th International Conference on Information Systems Development (ISD2015-Harbin).*

Chan, H., & Chieu, T. C. (2003). An Approach to Monitor Application States for Self-managing (Autonomic) Systems. *Companion of the 18th Annual ACM SIGPLAN Conference on Object-Oriented Programming, Systems, Languages, and Applications*, 312–313. doi:10.1145/949344.949428

Chiasson, M., & Davidson, E. (2005). Taking industry seriously in information systems research. *Management Information Systems Quarterly, 29*(4), 591–605. Retrieved from http://dl.acm.org/citation.cfm?id=2017276

Comuzzi, M., & Spanoudakis, G. (2010). Dynamic set-up of monitoring infrastructures for service based systems. *Of the 2010 ACM Symposium on*, 2414–2421. doi:10.1145/1774088.1774591

Fatema, K., Emeakaroha, V. C., Healy, P. D., Morrison, J. P., & Lynn, T. (2014). A survey of Cloud monitoring tools: Taxonomy, capabilities and objectives. *Journal of Parallel and Distributed Computing*, *74*(10), 2918–2933. doi:10.1016/j.jpdc.2014.06.007

Franke, U., Johnson, P., König, J., & Marcks von Würtemberg, L. (2012). Availability of enterprise IT systems: An expert-based Bayesian framework. *Software Quality Journal*, *20*(2), 369–394. doi:10.1007/s11219-011-9141-z

Gnanasundaram, S., & Shrivastava, A. (Eds.). (2012). *Information Storage and Management (2nd ed.)*. John Wiley & Sons, Inc.

Gómez-iglesias, A., Rosales, C., & Evans, T. (n.d.). *Practical Monitoring of Resource Utilization for HPC Applications. Academic Press.*

Hernantes, J., & Gallardo, G. (2015). *IT Infrastructure- Monitoring Tools*. Academic Press.

Ibrahimovic, S. (2016). Optimizicija ulaganja u raspoloživost it infrastrukture korištenjem bayesian belief networks modela. University of Sarajevo.

Ibrahimovic, S., & Bajgoric, N. (2016). Modeling Information System Availability by Using Bayesian Belief Network Approach. *Interdisciplinary Description of Complex Systems*, *14*(2), 125–138. doi:10.7906/indecs.14.2.2

ISACA. (2012). *Enabling Processes*. ISACA. Retrieved from papers3://publication/uuid/24E0C493-40C6-4495-946E-A25765C97BF1

ISACA. (2013). *COBIT: A Business Framework for the Governance and Management of Enterprise IT*. ISACA.

Jia, L., Zhu, W., Zhai, C., & Du, Y. (2007). Research on an Integrated Network Management System. *Software Engineering, Artificial Intelligence, Networking, and Parallel/Distributed Computing, 2007. SNPD 2007. Eighth ACIS International Conference on, 2*, 311–316. doi:<ALIGNMENT.qj></ALIGNMENT>10.1109/SNPD.2007.203

Khan, , Khan, , & Zaheer, , & M. I. B. (2013). An Efficient Network Monitoring and Management System. *International Journal of Information and Electronics Engineering*, *3*(1), 122. doi:10.7763/IJIEE.2013.V3.280

Kutare, M., Eisenhauer, G., Wang, C., Schwan, K., Talwar, V., & Wolf, M. (2010). Monalytics: Online Monitoring and Analytics for Managing Large Scale Data Centers. *Proceeding of the 7th International Conference on Autonomic Computing - ICAC '10*, 141. http://doi.org/ doi:10.1145/1809049.1809073

Meng, S., & Liu, L. (2013). Monitoring-as-a-service in the cloud. *Proceedings of the ACM/SPEC International Conference on International Conference on Performance Engineering - ICPE '13*, 373. doi:10.1145/2479871.2479929

Patra, M. R., Tripathy, A. K., & Das, R. K. (2011). Monitoring of service based e-governance systems. *Proceedings of the 5th International Conference on Theory and Practice of Electronic Governance - ICEGOV '11*, 353. doi:<ALIGNMENT.qj></ALIGNMENT>10.1145/2072069.2072138

Prathamesh & Mayekar. (2016). Is prevention always better? A case of IT service management. *Pacific Asia Conference on Information Systems.*

Rusu, O. (n.d.). *Network Management Framework: A Distributed Virtual NOC Architecture NOCs APMs*. Academic Press.

Sharma, D., Poddar, R., Mahajan, K., Dhawan, M., & Mann, V. (2015). HANSEL: Diagnosing Faults in OpenStack. *Sigcomm*, *2015*, 421–434. doi:10.475/123

Singh, J. (2009). Modeling application availability. In *Proceedings of the 2009 Spring Simulation Multiconference* (pp. 1–4). Retrieved from http://dl.acm.org/citation.cfm?id=1639932

Spremić, M., & Kostić, D. (2008). Upravljanje kvalitetom informatičke usluge: Studije slučaja primjene ITIL metode. *Poslovna Izvrsnost*, *2*(1), 37–58.

Tang, L., Li, T., Shwartz, L., Pinel, F., & Grabarnik, G. Y. (2013). An Integrated Framework for Optimizing Automatic Monitoring Systems in Large IT Infrastructures. *Proc. of KDD*, 1249–1257. doi:10.1145/2487575.2488209

Taylor, S., Vernon, L., & Rudd, C. (2007). *ITIL Service Design*. The Stationary Office, TSO. <ALIGNMENT.qj></ALIGNMENT>10.1002/0471744719.ch1

Turnbull, J. (2016). *The art of monitoring*. Academic Press.

Williams, A. (Ed.). (2016). Monitoring & management with docker & containers (Vol. 5). Academic Press.

Chapter 10
Always-On Enterprise Information Systems With Service-Oriented Architecture and Load Balancing

Serdal Bayram
Siemens, Turkey

ABSTRACT

In today's digital age, it is essential for a business to provide a seamless and continuous service to its customers and other stakeholders like providers. Such an always-on service is required, not only for the strong competitive environment but also because of the fact that most the stakeholders also have to offer seamless and continuous service to their own stakeholders. In this chain, failure of one of the systems and components even for a short time can result in a disaster in the entire service chain. A wise approach to provide a continuous service should consider all possible failure areas in a computer-based information system. Since hardware and software are vulnerable to a myriad of problems that can halt the normal operation of a system, an ideal solution should not only consider both of these two components, but also should seek to find ways for them to work in support of each other against a malfunction. This chapter is an attempt to develop a model that provides this functionality. Service Oriented Architecture (SOA) is implemented in the model due to its tenets that are suitable for such functionality.

DOI: 10.4018/978-1-5225-3704-5.ch010

INTRODUCTION

Due to the ever-increasing reliance of the society on the Enterprise Information Systems (EIS), these systems need to be up and running all the time. Malfunction even for a short time can have disastrous consequences in many environments such as banks where almost all of the processes are performed through the IS round-the-clock. This situation is aggravated by the competitive environment where service consumers have the power of shifting into another service provider in the slightest flaw of satisfaction. The activities and services can be easily imitated by competitors thanks to the ever-increasing standardization of IS that perform these activities and services.

Hence, offering a continuous service is of utmost importance for today's businesses where undisruptive service means lack of failure of IS on which the services depend. However, due to the inherent fragility of IS, there are myriad of factors that have the potential of disrupting the smooth running of these systems. Since IS have mainly two distinct components, namely hardware and software, it is plausible to scrutinize potential failure reasons in these two distinct components where potential failure areas are different from each other. This chapter proposes a model that aims continuous EIS operation in terms of hardware and software components where these components work in tandem. The model uses Service Oriented Architecture (SOA) as an important component of the software side of the model. This chapter is organized as follows: SOA, which is implemented as the main software component of the model is described in the following section. That section will also cover the Quality of Service (QoS) and Enterprise Service Bus (ESB) concepts of SOA due to their relevancy to the proposed model. Hardware component of the model and the Load Balancer will be described in the following section which will be followed by the section which describes the tandem working of SOA and Load Balancer. A case study that has been developed by the model will be explained next and the chapter will terminate with the conclusion.

SOFTWARE COMPONENT: SERVICE ORIENTED ARCHITECTURE

Service-oriented architecture (SOA) and its paradigms provide efficient IT environment for business processes to run and manage them effectively and efficiently. SOA is a framework to address the requirement of loosely coupled, standards-based and protocol-independent distributed computing, mapping enterprise information systems to the overall business process flow (Gong and Janssen, 2012). A SOA-enabled business process uses IT services also called as eservices which are distributed, virtualized and can be consumed 24*7 by overcoming geographic limitations. SOA provides dynamical business processes that can also run across different organizations and are able to be constructed to achieve a higher flexibility and agility. As stated by Aalst *et al.* 2007, for the last 20 years enterprise information systems have been becoming more "process-aware" instead of "data-aware". This forces EIS to be designed with business process perspective. Business processes and their mature EIS implementation bring successful results. Business processes of the enterprises are lacking of efficient and successful integration of IT applications to the other key processes. This problem results in time and money consuming issues because data integrity, repeatable and inconsistent tasks and challenging maintenance problems are faced.

Although SOA can be defined in several ways, all definitions can be categorized in two main perspectives, namely business perspective and technical perspective. Business perspective can be analyzed in terms of business processes and business services, whereas technical perspective can be analyzed in terms of software components and operational resources. The two perspectives, their components, and their interrelationships are illustrated in the Figure 1.

Figure 1. SOA with Technical and Business Perspective (OMG, nodate)

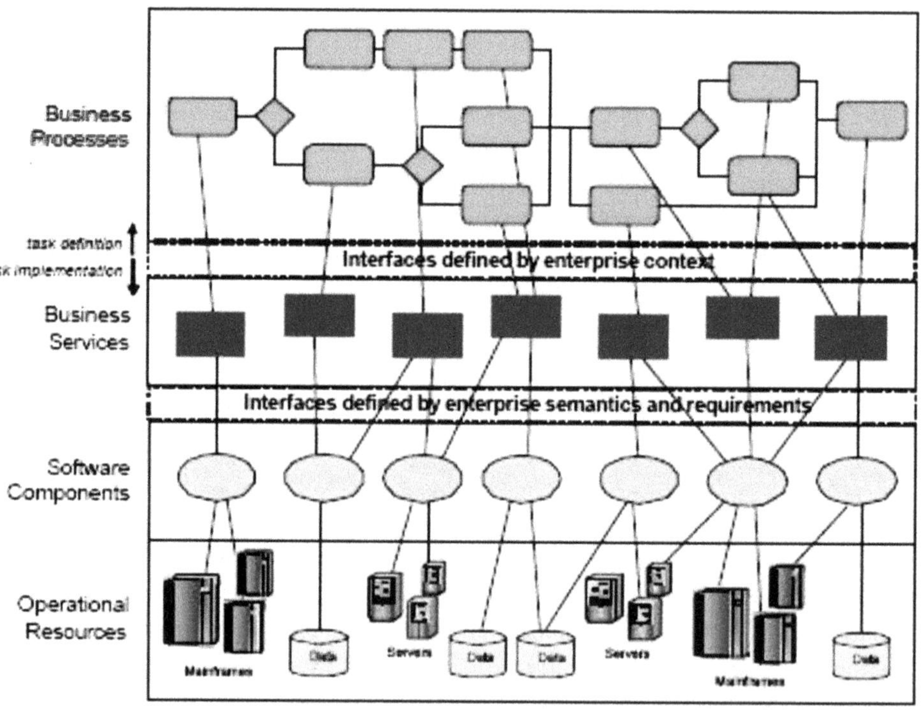

From the business perspective, which is seen as top level in the figure, SOA is an architectural style that guides all aspects of creating and using business processes (Newcomer & Lomow, 2005). In this view, business processes and their management are highlighted and Business Process Management (BPM) concept arises. BPM can be defined as the method of efficiently aligning an organization with the wants and needs of clients. Business perspective contains the interaction between business services and business processes. A business process can contain one or more business services, and a business service can be used in one or more business processes.

The technical perspective is depicted in the lower half of the figure. According to this perspective, SOA can be defined as a kind of distributed computing that is designed to allow the communication of software components, namely services, across a network. In this view, services are performed by software components and SOA contains interactions of these software components in a distributing computing environment. Under services, there are some operational resources such as database servers or mainframes. At a higher level of abstraction, business processes and services are implemented through the technical level which contains software components and operational resources.

In this environment, SOA can be defined as follows:

A service-Oriented Architecture (SOA) is a software architecture that is based on the key concepts of an application frontend, service, service repository, and service bus. A service consists of a contract, one or more interfaces, and an implementation. (Krafzig, Banke & Dirk, 2005, p.57)

According to this definition, there are four main elements of SOA: Application frontend, service, service repository, and service bus. Application frontend is the component that is used to initiate, control, and receive the results. For example, it can be the interfaces that have been designed through GUI concepts or batch program triggers which invoke the services. It can also be used for controlling the execution of services.

The second element in definition of SOA is the service. A service can be described as "a component capable of performing a task" (Sprott & Wilkes, 2004, p.2). Although a service can be seen as a task or an activity, it is more complicated than these concepts. This is due to the fact that every service has a contract, an interface, and an implementation routine. Josuttis (2007) argues that a service has the following attributes:

- **Self-Contained:** Self-contained means independent and autonomous. Although there can be exceptions, a service should be self-contained. In order for the services to be self-contained, their inter-dependencies should be kept in a minimum level.

- **Coarse-Grained:** This indicates the implementation detail level of services for consumers. Implementation details are hidden for a service consumer because the consumer doesn't care about such details.
- **Visible/Discoverable:** A service should be visible and easily reachable. This is also important for reusability which means that a service can be used multiple times in multiple systems.
- **Stateless:** Services, ideally, but not always, should be stateless. This means that a service request does not affect another request because service calls don't hold invocation parameters and execution attributes in a stateless service. On the other hand, sometimes a service can be statefull, such as shopping-chart services because they have to hold service invocation sticky attributes, like products that are put in to the shopping-basket.
- **Idempotent:** This means the ability of redo or rollback. In some case, while a service is executing, a bad response can be returned to the service consumer. In such a case service consumers can rollback or redo the service execution.
- **Composable:** For a composable service, the service can contain several sub-services where they can be separated from the main service. A composable service can call another composable service.
- **QoS and Service Level Agreement (SLA)-Capable:** A service should provide some non-functional requirements such as runtime performance, reliability, availability, and security. These requirements are important for QoS and SLA.
- **Pre- and Post-Conditions:** These specify the constraints and benefits of the service execution. Pre-condition represents the state before the service execution. Post-condition represents the state after the service execution.
- **Vendor Diverse:** SOA is neither a technology nor a product. It is also platform (or vendor) independent. This means that a SOA platform can be implemented by different products and one does not need to be familiar with the technology used for the service.
- **Interoperable:** Services should be highly interoperable. They can be called from any other systems. Interoperability provides the ability of different systems and organization to work together. In other words, services can be called from any other system regardless of the types of environment for them.

The third element of SOA is the Service Repository. As explained above, a service should be easily discoverable. This requirement is realized by the Service Repository. All required information when calling a service such as arguments, operation service provider, access rights, and QoS values can be retrieved from the Service Repository. Service Repository holds meta-data about services and it provides service dictionary to the systems.

The last element of SOA is the Service Bus. Service Bus is used to connect the service consumer and service provider. Through the Service Bus, the concepts of connectivity (interconnections between the components of an SOA system) and heterogeneity of technology (communication of a variety of technologies among themselves) are achieved.

SOA offers several advantages some of which are explained below:

- **Distributed Computing:** Distributed Computing is an old concept that has been developed in the last 30 years. Goff (2004) describes a distributed system as "embedded in a single device or can operate within cluster of devices in which the nodes work together to appear as a single node, offering a unified view of system resources to the application". In the SOA perspective, a service does not need to reside on the same physical machine as the calling client (frontend). The capability of calling a program (or service) from another service which is located on a different server in another physical location is one of the main tenets of SOA. From this point of view, SOA is well-suited to dealing with complex distributed systems which are becoming more and more common in today's world.
- **Loose Coupling:** This is another key concept in SOA which is essential to minimize the impact of modifications and failures on the whole system which is usually made up of several components. Coupling refers to degree of dependency between any two systems (Papazoglou, 2008). In a loosely coupled system failure of a component has minimal effect on other components thereby preventing the failure of the entire system. This concept is also useful in a dynamic business environment where existing requirements often change and frequently new requirements are introduced. The minimal level of coupling between the components is a real advantage in such an environment, because it provides easy maintainability and flexibility. In the SOA, modules and services are loosely coupled by using physical connections via a mediator. On the contrary, physical connections are established with point-to-point communication in a tightly coupled system.
- **Heterogeneous Systems:** An important tenet of today's complex world is the heterogeneity of components in a software system. A complex distributed system should be able to run across a range of different platforms such as different operating systems, databases, and application servers. Although interoperability of heterogeneous systems is not a goal in SOA *per se*, SOA provides an excellent environment for such a system through the concept of loose coupling.

Quality of Service in Service Oriented Architecture

According to Choi *et al.* (2007), QoS is determined by non-functional requirements of service such as availability, performance, reliability, usability, discoverability, adaptability, and composability (Figure 2).

These attributes are ideally included in the service contract. Although QoS attributes are hidden to service consumers due to the black-box nature of SOA, they are important to provide the continuity and smooth running of the system. Availability and reliability are of utmost importance in providing the continuity of the system and performance is important due to its relation with service quality. Hence, these three particularly important attributes for an always-on system will be elaborated:

- **Availability:** Is the degree accessibility for a service by the service requestors. In order for a service to be available, it must be operational as a prerequisite. Relation between these two concepts can be formulated as follows:

$$Availability\ of\ Service = \frac{Service\ Operating\ Time}{Service\ Operating\ Time + Service\ \mathrm{Re}\,paring\ Time}$$

In this formula Service Operating Time is up-time of the service and Service Repairing Time is down-time. The range of availability is 0..1 where higher value means higher availability of service.

Figure 2. Service Quality Model in SOA Environment (Choi et al., 2007)

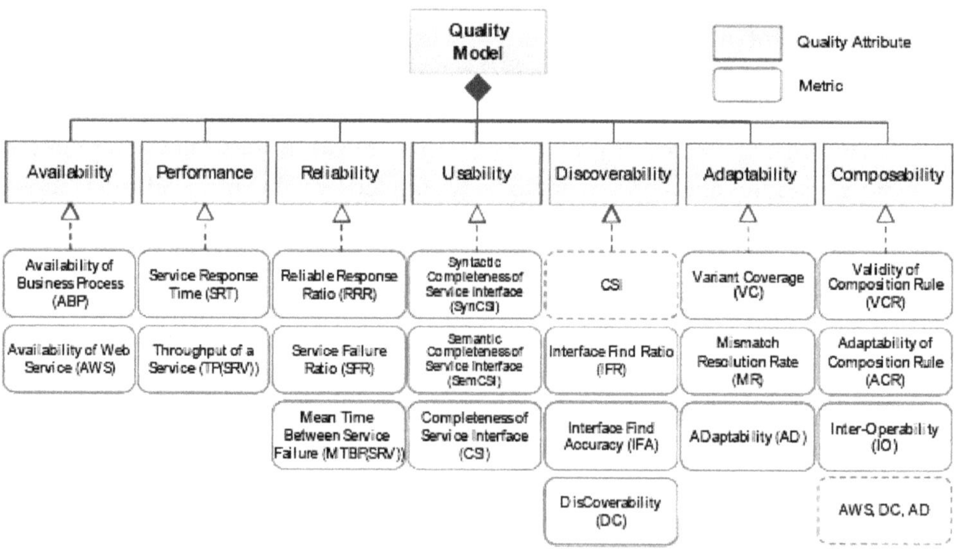

- **Performance:** Is the capability of service to provide appropriate response and processing times and throughput rates when performing its function under stated conditions. Service Response Time (SRT) and Throughput (TP) of a service are the metrics of the performance. SRT is calculated as follows:

SRT = (Time when service consumer finishes sending request to the service) – (Time when service consumer starts receiving response from service)

SRT is always greater than zero and a low SRT means high performance.

The other performance metric, Throughput represents the number of service requestsat unit time and it can be calculated as follows:

$$Thoughput\,(TP) = \frac{Number\ of\ Completed\ Service\ \mathrm{Re}\,quests}{Unit\ Time}$$

High Throughput indicates high performance.

- **Reliability:** Is the ability of a service to keep operating with specified level of performance over time. Since services are reusable and can be used in multiple applications in a SOA environment, the reliability of a service can affect several applications. The metrics of reliability are Reliable Response Ratio (RRR), Service Failure Ratio (SFR), and Mean Time Between Service Failure (MTBSF).

RRR can be calculated as:

$$RRR = \frac{Number\ of\ \mathrm{Re}\,liable\ \mathrm{Re}\,sponse}{Total\ Number\ of\ \mathrm{Re}\,quests}$$

SFR can be calculated as:

$$SFR = \frac{Number\ of\ Failures}{Time\ Period}$$

Lower SFR means higher reliability. The third metric, MTBSF, can be calculated as:

$$MTBSF = \frac{Summation\ of\ Time\ Between\ Failures}{Time\ Number\ of\ Failures}$$

MTBSF represents the average time between two failures and high MTBSF means higher reliability.

Enterprise Service Bus in Service Oriented Architecture

ESB is a kind of SOA based software infrastructure for business application integration (or Enterprise Application Integration (EAI)). As seen in the Figure 3, main responsibility of ESB is to enable service consumers to call the services provided. Today's complex business structures demand several platforms to interoperate. This means that ESB should provide an environment where the system would be technology-independent. In other words, ESB should work like a medium for smooth operation of services originating from a diverse range of sources. Josuttis (2007) lists some functionalities of ESB:

- **Providing Connectivity:** As explained before, the main purpose of the ESB is to provide connectivity. Not only different hardware and software platforms but also distinct implementation of services can be connected via ESB. The ESB works like a universal language.
- **Data Transformation:** The ESB can also be used for data transformation. In some cases, extracted data from the source is not fit to the destination system because formats are different. ESB deals with this problem and it translates the data as required. For example, let's say that a source service

Figure 3. Example of Enterprise Service Bus

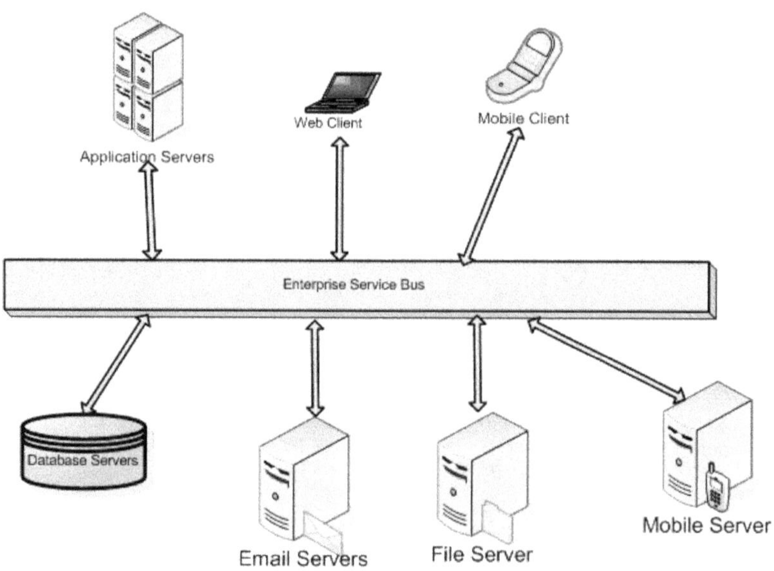

has the Name and Surname as different fields and the destination service has these combined. In such a case ESB concatenates the fields as:

"Name", "Surname" → *(ESB transformation)* → "Name, Surname"

- **Intelligent Routing:** The ESB routes requests to the service according to predefined rules. According to data from the service requester, a service provider can be chosen via the ESB. This is an important capability for providing a continuous operation because through Intelligent Routing the load might be shifted from an ailing unit to another one automatically when required. This can be possible by making the Intelligent Routing work in tandem with the Load Balancer. Whenever a service fails or has too much load, ESB routes the request to another service or unit according to the load balancing algorithm. In order for this to be realized, there should be replicated services in the system. As illustrated in the Figure 4, whenever a service consumer requests a service, ESB invokes the Load Balancer which directs the request to the idle service. The Load Balancer also continuously monitors the availability of each service and whenever a service that is consumed is down for any reason it directs the request to another service that is available at that time. In such a case the interrupted work is rolled-back and restarted by the new available service.

ESB also provides additional functionalities for security, service management, service monitoring and logging.

Figure 4. An ESB with a load balancer for provided services (Josuttis, 2007)

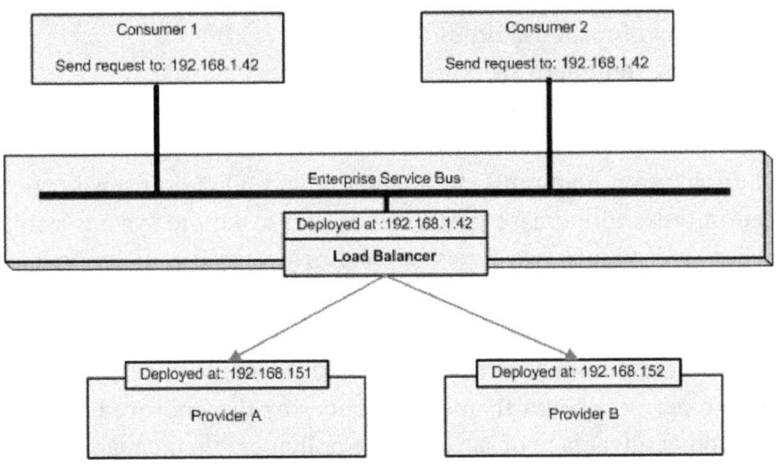

HARDWARE COMPONENTS

The responsiveness is the most important health factor of a SOA system. Responsiveness is the level of availability and timeliness of a service when requested. In order to achieve a high level of responsiveness hardware resources must be utilized effectively. The key for effective hardware utilization is to have a series of resource units such as servers and individual processors in these servers. The load must be distributed evenly to these resources not only for getting the full power of the hardware, but also for providing a continuous service in case of a hardware malfunction. In the proposed system this is achieved through a software component called Load Balancer.

Load Balancer

SOA enables a distributed system. Like all distributed systems it is likely that some components are more heavily loaded when some others are lightly loaded or even idle. In the SOA terminology unit in the above sentence can be translated as a service. Since it is desirable to distribute the workload evenly among all the services, an agent responsible for this task is required. Effective operation of such a service will not only increase the overall performance of the system but it will also increase its reliability by eliminating the probability of system malfunctioning as a result of malfunctioning of an individual unit or service.

The Load Balancer agent has the following objectives each of which might have some implications on the design strategy:

- Increased Reliability
- Minimization of response time
- Maximization of throughput
- Predictability of response times
- Balanced distribution of work load
- Shifting the process to other resources in case of a malfunction

A load distribution plan must decide where and when a given service should be executed in order to increase performance and make the system available and reliable. There are mainly two types of load distribution policies, namely static policy and dynamic policy. In static polices, load is distributed without taking into consideration of the current state of the system. On the other hand, dynamic policies use the system-state information to make load distribution decisions, so they have the potential to perform better than static polices by the improved quality of their decisions. Another advantage of the dynamic policies is their capability to perform through monitoring the long-term status of the components and deciding accordingly so that they are not affected by short-term load surges. Although dynamic policies consume some system resources for such a monitoring task, this cost can be justified when compared by the advantages provided.

In order to realize the objectives of the Load Balancer there are several commonly used algorithms of load distribution such as Round Robin Algorithm (RRA), Random Load Balancing Algorithm (RLBA), Weight-Based Algorithm (WBA), and Hardware-Awareness Minimum Load Algorithm (HAMLA). Although these algorithms are mainly used for load distribution among particular servers, they can also be used for load distribution among particular services in a SOA environment. Since the proposed model uses all these algorithms they need to be explained:

- **RRA:** In the Round-Robin Algorithm, where static load distribution policy is employed, there is a list of server resources and they are selected one at a time in order. The advantages of the round-robin algorithm are that it is simple, cheap, and very predictable. None of the servers have priority to the others. RRA is advantageous in cases where the work loads of the tasks and capacities of servers are close to each other. In cases where opposite is true, i.e., where there are major variations in workloads and server capacities RRA might not be effective. For example, the tasks executed on a comparably less powerful server will take more time than the others, resulting in the overall degrade of the system performance.
- **RLBA:** In Random Load Balancing Algorithm service requests are routed to servers randomly. The algorithm is also good in cases where the power of servers is close to each other. Otherwise, the problem described in the RRA is also applicable for RLBA. RLBA also employs static load distribution policy.
- **WBA:** Weight-Based Load Balancing bears a resemblance to the RRA and it also employs static load balancing policy. The only difference with the RRA is that a pre-assigned weight for each server is taken into account when distributing the load. The weight usually varies between 1 and 100 and it determines the load capacity of each server compared to the others. Load distribution is made according to the weight, i.e., a server that has twice the weight of another one can bear twice as much as the other. Hence, WBA is finely applicable for heterogeneous systems where server capacities vary.
- **HAMLA:** In Hardware-Awareness Minimum Load Algorithm the Load Balancer selects the minimum loaded server to route the request. In order to perform this, the balancer has to consider several hardware parameters such as CPU usages, memory usages, and/or I/O operations. This algorithm is more complicated than the others and it uses some models such as Service

Level Checker (Polling System) and Service Status Monitoring System. These models are as follows:

- **Service Level Checker System:** In order to have real-time information about the work load of individual servers they are continuously monitored by a polling system. This system produces historical availability information that can be used by the Load Balancer to gain an insight for the behavior of the system. This information can be used as a basis for the Service Level Agreement (SLA) between service requestor and service provider in the SOA.
- **Service Status Monitoring System:** Service Status Monitoring System provides the following system information for the Load Balancer:
  - **CPU Idle Ratio:** Calculated as 1-CPU usage ratio. The load balancer tends to choose the server that has the maximum CPU idle ratio for the next request.
  - **Available Memory Ratio:** Calculated as available memory divided by the system maximum memory. The load balancer tends to choose the server that has the maximum AMR for the next request.
  - **Disk I/O Intensity:** Defines the disc usage at real time with information such as read bytes and write bytes. Load Balancer tends to choose the server that has the minimum disk I/O for the next request.
  - **Open Sessions:** The number of connected users at a specific time. When the number of active (open) sessions increases, server consumption increases. Load Balancer tends to choose the server that has the minimum open session number for the next request.

Parameters of Service Level Checker System and Service Status Monitoring System are used by HAMLA not only for diverting the requests to the idle services, but also for informing the operators about the problems of the services.

SOA AND LOAD BALANCER WORKING IN TANDEM FOR CONTINUITY

As explained in the previous sections, SOA has the capability of providing continuity from the software side and Load Balancer can do that from the hardware side. This section will explain the suggested model that uses these components that work in tandem to provide an environment where probability for failure will be minimum.

In order to explain the main tenets of the model, consider the following simple scenario: We have a small service organization where only four roles exist. Let this be an accounting company which lodges tax files for individual customers. The first role is the customer to be served. The second role is the one that is performed by the experts of the company who actually fill in the tax forms for the client. The third role is performed by the manager that assigns tasks to the experts who perform the second task. The last role is performed by the supervisor who continuously monitors the current and the future work load of the experts. In other words, the supervisor is knowledgeable for the tax files of each expert that is currently processed as well as that are waiting in the queue. The supervisor is also knowledgeable about the competence level of each expert in terms of speed and accuracy.

According to the sample scenario, as illustrated in the Figure 5 below, the customer sends the tax lodging request to the manager. After accepting the task, the manager then asks the supervisor which expert is most suitable for the new task in terms of work load. The supervisor checks the experts' current workload and the works of each that wait in the queue. S/he then chooses the most suitable expert for the new

Figure 5. The scenario for Load Balancing with SOA

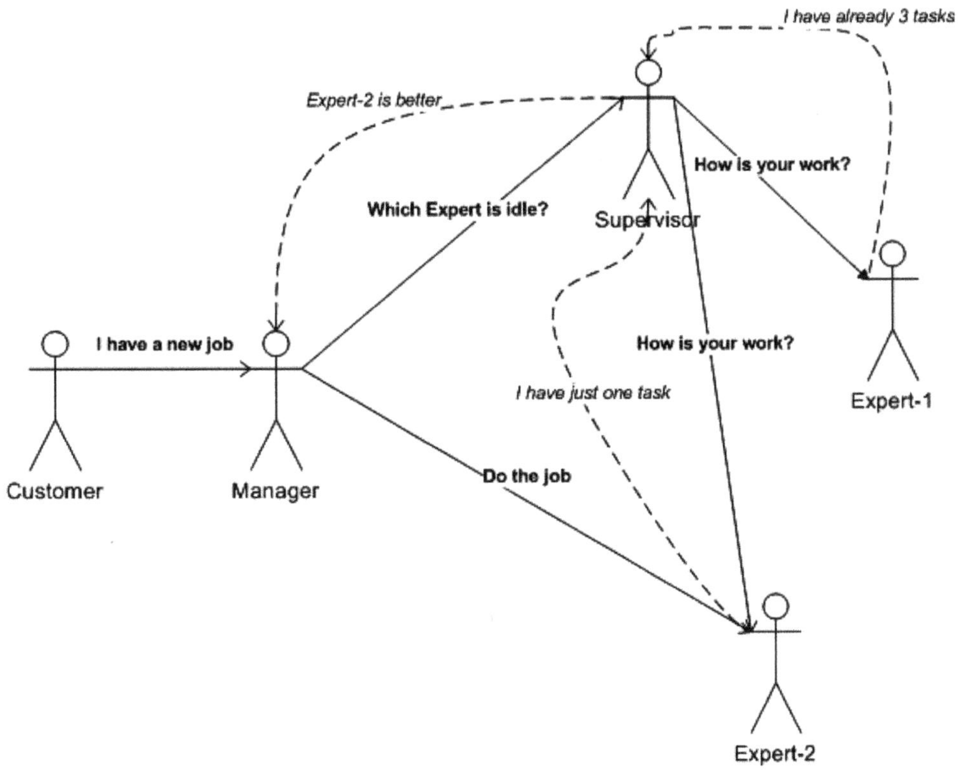

task and informs the manager about it. The process of choosing the most suitable expert for the new task is performed by the supervisor through a specific algorithm. The manager then assigns the new task to the expert pointed by the supervisor.

Translating this scenario to the SOA terminology, the customer is the service consumer, the manager is the ESB, and the experts are individual services. The supervisor performs the task of the Load Balancer in the model. In other words, the three roles of the model are performed in terms of SOA concept and the fourth one, which is the supervisor's role, is performed outside SOA.

This scenario can further be elaborated in terms of the proposed model in Figure 6. Service Consumers correspond to customers of Figure 5, the main ESB performs

Figure 6. The proposed model with SOA roles and Load Balancer

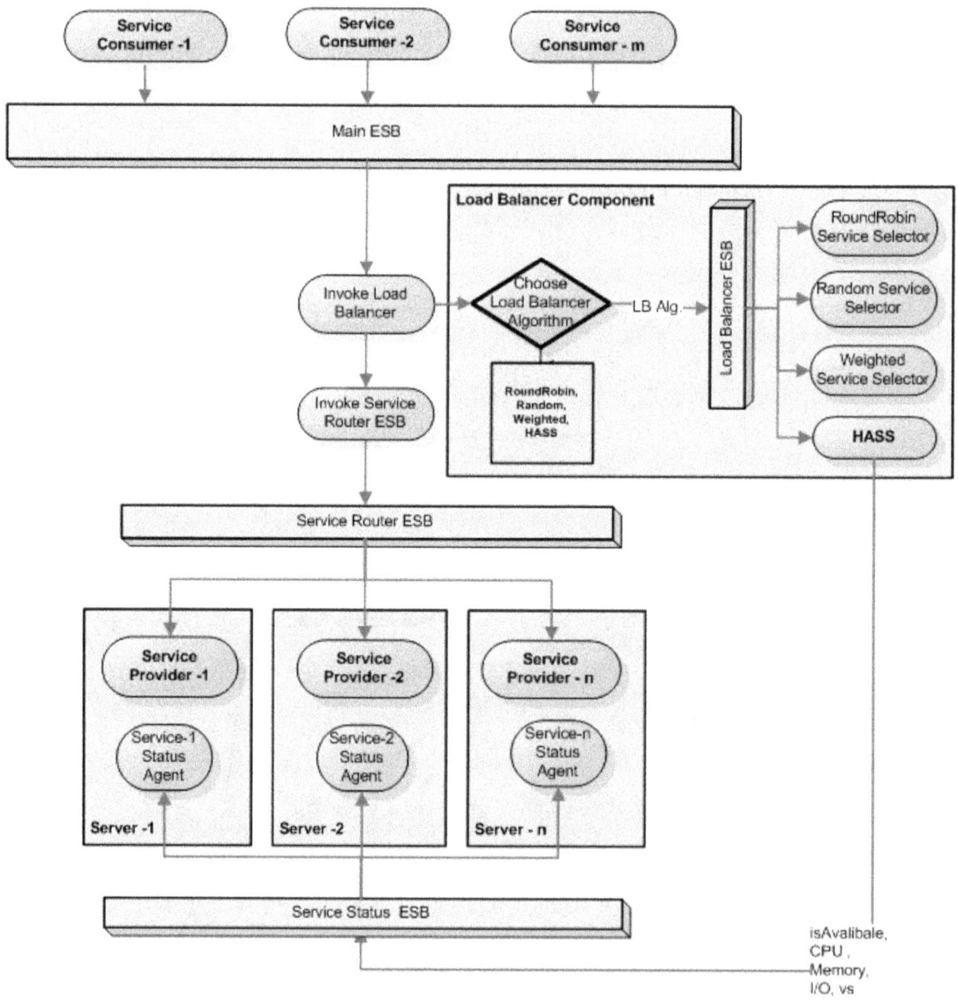

the task of the manager, Service Providers correspond to the tax experts, and Load Balancer Component corresponds to the supervisor.

In the model, the requests of the service consumers are first confronted by the main ESB at the top. The key task performed here by the main ESB is to route the requests to the most convenient algorithm. In order to accomplish this task, the main ESB invokes the Load Balancer Component which is responsible for selecting the most suitable algorithm. Load Balancer then selects the appropriate service through that algorithm. This process is performed by invoking the Service Router ESB which is responsible by routing the task to the previously selected service provider.

Although choosing the most appropriate Load Balancer algorithm can be performed through Artificial Intelligence methods, the proposed model currently does not support such a method. Instead, this task is currently performed manually.

The four service selectors in the Load Balancer component are based on the four algorithms explained above. They are as follows:

Round Robin Service Selector (RRSS): This service selector is based on RRA which means that all requests are distributed to the services equally without regarding the size of the task and the power of the service provider. When service resources and tasks are homogenous RRSS is a good alternative.

Random Service Selector (RSS): Random Service Selector runs the RLBA. A service request is routed to a random service provider. This selector also works best when service resources and tasks are homogeneous.

Weighted Service Selector (WSS): This selector is based on WBA described in Load Balancer algorithms. Every service has a pre-defined weight as load factor. The requests are routed according to this weight. For example, if the weight ratio is 1:2 for two services the number of requests that are routed to the second service will be as twice as the number for the first service provided that both tasks are of equal size. WSS is suitable for both heterogonous and homogonous capacity resources.

Hardware Awareness Service Selector (HASS): This is based on HAMLA explained above. It chooses the most appropriate service provider according to the parameters of the hardware like CPU, memory, and I/O. Additionally, availability of the service provider is also considered. This relationship is shown in Figure 6 with the connection between Service Status ESB and HASS. As an example, if all of service providers are available but memory of the server of the first service provider is higher than the others and all other system values are equal then the selector chooses this service for routing the next request. The service selector gets the service state information from Service Status ESB that collects the status information from service agents.

After getting the right service for the current request from Load Balancer Component, Service Router ESB (SR-ESB) is invoked. SR-ESB is used to direct the request to the relevant service. Each candidate service runs on a different server container. This is an essential requirement for the proposed model, because as explained above, a computer system may cease to function as a result of either hardware or software resources.

On the software side services are monitored by Service Status Agents. The agents contain Service Status Monitoring and Service Level Checker Systems which are explained in Load Balancer. The agents are aware of the availability and work load of their relevant services through the Service Level Checker and the Service Status Monitoring Systems. When a service selector like HASS needs this information, SS-ESB makes this information available to the service selector.

If the system did not use the SOA concept, all connections would be point-to-point where there would be tight coupling among different components of the system. In such a case malfunction of a single unit would have adverse effects on the entire system. SOA and the concept of ESB in load balancing process provides loose coupling where malfunction of a unit (other than ESB, of course) simply results in shifting the load to another unit.

Additionally, loose coupling enables easier maintenance and enhancement of the system when business conditions dictate such cases. In essence, loose coupling can only be possible by a modular approach where hardware and software resources are self-contained in an SOA environment.

This environment is quite suitable for providing not only continuity, but also flexibility and agility in business. When requirements change, as it is frequent in a business environment, it is easy to insert a new load balancer selector service. It is also flexible with the "Choose Load Balancer Algorithm" decision activity which can be easily made. For example, a day can be divided into time slices where peak hours, normal workload hours, and idle hours are identified. In these slices different Load Balancer algorithms which fit best to each slice can be used. Most probably, HASS would be more suitable in peak hours where many heavy requests have to be responded and system resources have to be used in a most effective way. On the contrary RRA would probably be more convenient for idle hours such as midnight.

The proposed model offers the SOA's QoS attributes such as availability, performance, and reliability. Each of these attributes is crucially important in providing business continuity and they deserve further elaboration:

- **Increased Availability:** Replicated services can continue to function even in the face of server down time due to hardware failure or maintenance. With a simple calculation, if there are three replicated services and all services have the same availability of 95%, overall system availability can be calculated as

$$(1 - overall\ system\ failure)$$

which is

$$(1 - 0.05 * 0.05 * 0.05) = 99.9875\%$$

provided that the services are stateless, i.e., they do not interfere with each other.

In cases where even higher availability is required this can be simply accomplished by adding new hardware which hosts additional services.

- **Increased Performance:** The service requests which have to be processed simultaneously can easily be performed by the proposed model. Since there are several hardware resources, each of which supporting a service stateless tasks can be processed in parallel by services. This results in reduced processing time for large tasks which involve several sub-tasks.
- **Increased Reliability:** As stated above, the degree of reliability can be measured by MTBSF. Reliability of a system is strongly related with the availability of it. The main difference between these concepts is the unit of measure where availability is measured in terms of ratio of time and reliability is measured in terms of time. Since reliability is measured as total time between failures (up time) divided by number of failures, reduced failures through higher availability will result in higher reliability.

CASE STUDY

The proposed model is applied in a case study. The study employs Oracle SOA Suite which makes use of graphical symbols for service activities and processes. Without actually writing code, Oracle SOA Suite provides tools and techniques to develop a service-based system graphically.

The case study implements the Business Process Execution Language (BPEL) which is a language for specifying business processes in SOA environment. BPEL is an XML-based flow language for the formal specification of business processes and interaction protocols (Papazoglou, 2008).

Normally, service consumers directly connect to service providers in a SOA environment. The difference of the proposed model in this aspect is that the connection is established through the Load Balancer. The implementation of the proposed model is seen in the Figure 7. The figure illustrates the main process of the model which contains the activities of services. There are totally seven activities in the model. The process starts with the Service Consumer's request that targets the

Receive_Input activity. Control is then transferred into the Assign_LB_Algorithm activity which is, in the BPEL terminology, an assign activity. These activities are used for assigning values to variables. Assign_LB_Algorithm is used for manually assigning the name of the Load Balancer algorithm intended to be used. The model contains a number of load balancer algorithms which are explained above as RRSS, RSS, WSS, and HASS. After the Load Balancer algorithm is selected, the algorithm is notified to the Load Balancer ESB which is responsible for calling the previously preferred Load Balancer algorithm. This task is accomplished by the Invoke_LB-ESB activity which is an invoke activity in BPEL terminology. Invoke activities are used for calling or invoking a service, LoadBalancerESB service in the model (Figure 8).

Figure 7. Service Routing and Load Balancer

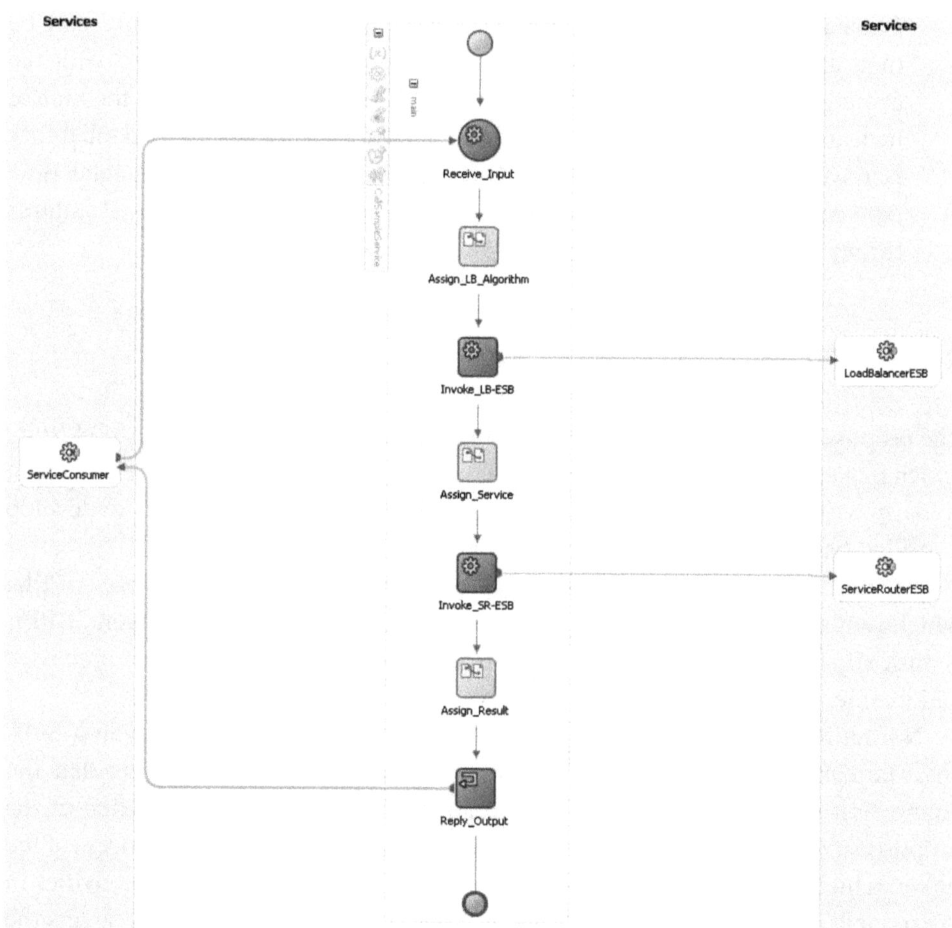

LoadBalancerESB connects the service selectors to the main process. The service selectors choose the service based on their own algorithms. For example, if the selected algorithm in the Assign_LB_Algorithm activity is the Round-Robin then RRSS service will be invoked by the LoadBalancerESB (Figure 8). The LoadBalancerESB also has an output for the selected service name which will be used for routing the request to the relevant service. This output is used as an input for the Assign_Service activity which starts the Invoke_SR-ESB activity which, in turn, invokes the ServiceRouterESB service. This service is used to connect the Service Providers to the model (Figure 8). There are two Service Providers in the model and each of them uses different hardware resources. The Service Status Monitoring System explained above continuously monitors the health of the hardware resources and in case of a malfunction of one of the resources the second one replaces it. This is accomplished by the HASS service explained above. The ServiceRouterESB gets the result of the execution of the service from the relevant

Figure 8. Load Balancer and Service Router ESBs

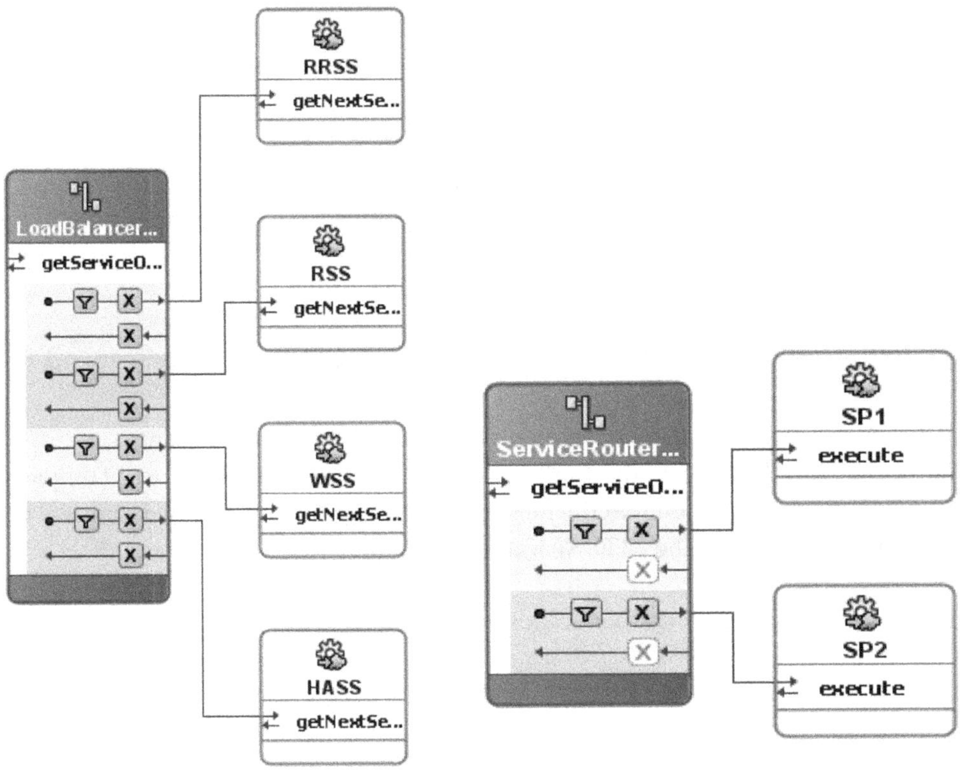

service provider and transfers this value to the Assign_Result activity. The process ends with the transfer of this value to the consumer via the Reply_Output activity.

In order to show the expediency of the model, it was tested with test data. Two rounds of tests were performed, first without the Load Balancer and with only one service working on a single server. The second round was performed with the Load Balancer and in that test two servers were used. Both tests were performed according to the following scenario: An average of five service requests in a second were sent to the system. The requests involved loading some dummy data into the memory through the CPU by a loop. The loop iterated 100 to 1000 times at each request depending on the load factor of 1 to 10 respectively. Each request was assigned a random load factor. Each test lasted 24 hours which is 1440 minutes. The tests aim to find out the number of failures in a given time due to insufficiency of resources such as memory. The requests load data into the memory and the Garbage Collection service continuously deletes the data loaded by the requests. Failure occurs whenever the system attempts to load data into the memory that is full. In such a case the computer cannot respond to the service requests and the system is regarded to be down until the Garbage Collector clears the memory. Results of the tests in terms of Availability of Service and MTBSF, explained above, are as follows:

In the first test where no Load Balancer was used the down-time of the system was 171 minutes and 87 failures were encountered. This means that uptime of the system was 1269 minutes and the Availability of Service and MTBSF values were calculated as follows:

Availability of Service = 1269 minutes / (1269 minutes +171 minutes) = 0.881

which means that the system was 88.1% available in this case.

MTBSF = 1269 minutes / 87 failures =14.59 minutes / failure.

In the second round the system was tested with the Load Balancer and two separate servers. In this case the down-time of the system was reduced to 39 minutes and 20 failures were encountered which means that uptime was 1401 minutes. The Availability of Service and MTBSF values were calculated as follows:

Availability of Service = 1401 minutes / (1401 minutes + 39 minutes) = 0.973

which means that the system was 97.3% available in this case.

MTBSF = 1401 minutes / 20 failures = 70.05 minutes / failure

The improvement provided by the Load Balancer is from 88.1% to 97.3% in terms of Availability of Service and from 14.59 minutes/failure to 70.05 in MTBSF. These figures will be much better with increasing number of additional servers. Although it is impossible to provide 100% availability in theory by this method an acceptable level of high availability can be accomplished.

CONCLUSION AND FUTURE WORKS

Availability and reliability of a computer system depend on both of the components of the system, namely hardware and software and both of these components are prone to malfunctions and failures. This chapter asserts that one of the ways of developing a highly available and reliable system is to consider the potential failure possibilities not only in hardware or not only in software, but in both of them. Although hardware failures are inevitable, the most plausible way to reduce their impact is to backup them so that if one piece of hardware fails some other can assume its workload. SOA can be helpful in this aspect by having a number of identical services each working on separate hardware. This provides an ideal environment for substituting the service of a healthy hardware instead of an ailing one. SOA can also be helpful in the software side by some its main tenets. Unlike the traditional software where components are tightly coupled in a point-to-point architecture, SOA is based on distributed and heterogeneous architecture and offers loose coupling. Distributed computing allows services to be distributed to different resources thereby enhancing the backup logic, and loose coupling minimizes the impact of modifications and failures on the whole system when there is a problem in one component. The support of SOA for heterogeneous systems is also important in today's world where systems are increasingly large and involving heterogeneous components. In short, the main tenet of model proposed in this chapter is to backup hardware and to support this task with the software. SOA provides an ideal environment for this support.

These arguments are supported by the case study where notable improvements in availability and reliability are achieved by using additional hardware and a SOA-based Load Balancer. However, it must also be acknowledged that using the proposed approach for every task is impossible because the requirement for additional hardware becomes unacceptable after some point. Hence, only key services that allocate main part of the system can be modeled.

The model uses a manual command for choosing the Load Balancing algorithm. As a future work, this may be done automatically through a software agent which has learning capability from the effectiveness of past choices. Such a component should increase the usability of the model.

REFERENCES

Aalst, W. M. P., Benatallah, B., Casati, F., Curbera, F., & Verbeek, E. (2007). *Business process management: Where business processes and web services*. Retrieved July 08, 2017 from https://wwwis.win.tue.nl/~wvdaalst/publications/p371.pdf

Choi, S. W., Her, J. S., & Kim, S. D. (2007). Modeling QoS Attributes and Metrics for Evaluating Services in SOA Considering Consumers' Perspective as the First Class Requirement. In *The 2nd IEEE Asia-Pacific Services Computing Conference* (pp. 398-405). Seoul, South Korea: IEEE Computer Society.

Goff, M. K. (2004). *Network Distributed Computing: Fitscapes and Fallacies*. Santa Clara, CA: Prentice Hall.

Gong, Y., & Janssen, M. (2012). From policy implementation to business process mananagement: Principles for creating flexibility and agility. *Government Information Quarterly*, *29*, 61–71. doi:10.1016/j.giq.2011.08.004

Josuttis, N. M. (2007). *SOA in Practice*. Sebastopol, CA: O'Reilly.

Krafzig, D., Banke, K., & Dirk, S. (2005). *Enterprise SOA: Service-Oriented Architecture Best Practices*. Upper Saddle River, NJ: Prentice Hall.

Newcomer, E., & Lomow, G. (2005). *Understanding SOA with Web Services*. Upper Saddle River, NJ: Pearson Education.

OMG. (n.d.). *The OMG and Service-Oriented Architecture*. Retrieved July 10, 2017, from http://www.omg.org/attachments/pdf/OMG-and-the-SOA.pdf

Papazoglou, M. P. (2008). *Web Services: Principles and Technology*. Harlow, UK: Pearson Education Limited.

Sprott, D., & Wilkes, L. (2004). *Understanding Service-Oriented Architecture*. CBDI Forum. Retrieved July 10, 2017, from https://msdn.microsoft.com/en-us/library/aa480021.aspx

Compilation of References

Aalst, W. M. P., Benatallah, B., Casati, F., Curbera, F., & Verbeek, E. (2007). *Business process management: Where business processes and web services*. Retrieved July 08, 2017 from https://wwwis.win.tue.nl/~wvdaalst/publications/p371.pdf

Aberdeen Report. (2014). *Preventing Virtual Application Downtime*. Available at www.aberdeen.com

Abrams, C., Von Kanel, J., & Muller, S. (2007). Optimized enterprise risk management. *IBM Systems, 46*(2), 219–234. Retrieved from http://ieeexplore.ieee.org/xpls/abs_all.jsp?arnumber=5386607

AIRMIC. (2010). *A structured approach to enterprise risk management (ERM) and the requirements of ISO 31000*. Retrieved February 23, 2015, from https://www.theirm.org/media/886062/ISO3100_doc.pdf

Aktas, M. S. (2010). Principles And Experiences: Designing and Building Enterprise Information Systems. In N. Bajgoric (Ed.), *Always-On Enterprise Information Systems for BusinessContinuance: Technologies for Reliable and Scalable Operations* (pp. 58–77). IGI Global. doi:10.4018/978-1-60566-723-2.ch004

Alcantara, P., & Riglietti, G. (2017). *Business Continuity Institute Horizon Scan Report 2017*. Caversham: BCI.

Ambrose, C., Spencer, J., & Weinstein, E. (2016). Magic quadrant for IT vendor risk management. *Gartner*. Retrieved January 22, 2017, from https://www.gartner.com/doc/reprints?id=1-2ZVRYZA&ct=160229&st=sb

Analysis, I. (2016). *CA Unified Infrastructure Management Deepens its Visibility Into Cloud and Hybrid IT With Comprehensive New Capabilities CA Unified Infrastructure Management Deepens its Visibility*. Academic Press.

Anderson, J. C., & Gerbing, D. W. (1988). Structural equation modeling in practice: A review and recommended two-step approach. *Psychological Bulletin, 103*(3), 411–423. doi:10.1037/0033-2909.103.3.411

Anderson, M., Banker, R., Menon, N., & Romero, J. (2011). Implementing Enterprise Resource Planning Systems: Organizational Performance and the Duration of the Implementation. *Information Technology Management*, *12*(3), 197–212. doi:10.1007/s10799-011-0102-9

Aon Risk Solutions. (2014). *2014 software survey*. Retrieved February, 27, 2015, from https://www.theirm.org/media/1163669/software_survey.pdf

Arduini, F., & Morabito, V. (2010). Business continuity and the banking industry. *Communications of the ACM*, *53*(3), 121–125. doi:10.1145/1666420.1666452

Ašenbrener, M., Šimunović, D., & Dovedan Han, Z. (2013). Model informacijskogsustavaplaniranja TV emisija. *Culture and Public Relations*, *4*(1), 61–69.

Asgary, A., & Naini, A. S. (2011). Modelling The Adaptation Of Business Continuity Planning By Businesses Using Neural Networks, Intelligent Systems. In *Accounting, Finance And Management 18* (pp. 89–104). Wiley.

Ashurst, C., Freer, A., Ekdahl, J., & Gibbons, C. (2012). Exploring IT-enabled innovation: A new paradigm? *International Journal of Information Management*, *32*(4), 326–336. doi:10.1016/j.ijinfomgt.2012.05.006

Austin, A., Barnard, J., Hutcheon, N., & Parry, D. (2015). *Media Consumption Forecast*. London: ZenithOptimedia.

Avaya Report. (2014). *Network Downtime Results in Job, Revenue Loss, March, 2014*. Available at: http://www.avaya.com/usa/about-avaya/newsroom/news-releases/2014/pr-140305/

Avery Gomez, E. (2011). Towards Sensor Networks: Improved ICT Usage Behavior for Business Continuity. *Proceedings of SIGGreen Workshop, Sprouts: Working Papers on Information Systems, 11*(13). Retrieved from http://sprouts.aisnet.org/11-13

Baird, D., & Fisher, M. (2005). Neomillennial User Experience Design Strategies: Utilizing Social Networking Media to Support Always On Learning Styles. *Journal of Educational Technology Systems*, *34*(1), 5–32. doi:10.2190/6WMW-47L0-M81Q-12G1

Bajgoric, N. (2008). Continuous Computing Technologies for Enhancing Business Continuity. IGI Global.

Bajgoric, N. (2005, October-December). Continuous Computing Technologies for Improving Performances of Enterprise Information Systems. *International Journal of Enterprise Information Systems*, *1*(4), 70–89. doi:10.4018/jeis.2005100105

Bajgoric, N. (2006). Information Systems for E-Business Continuance: A Systems Approach, Kybernetes. *The International Journal of Systems and Cybernetics*, *35*(5), 632–652. doi:10.1108/03684920610662377

Bajgoric, N. (2006). Information technologies for business continuity: An implementation framework. *Information Management & Computer Security*, *14*(5), 450–466. doi:10.1108/09685220610717754

Bajgoric, N. (2007). Toward Always-On Enterprise Information Systems. In A. Gunasekaran (Ed.), *Modeling and Analysis of Enterprise Information Systems - Advances in Enterprise Information Systems* (pp. 250–284). IGI Global.

Bajgoric, N. (2008). *Continuous Computing Technologies for Enhancing Business Continuity*. IGI Global. doi:10.4018/978-1-60566-160-5

Bajgoric, N. (2010). Server Operating Environment for Business Continuance: Framework for Selection. *Int. J. Business Continuity and Risk Management*, *1*(4), 317–338. doi:10.1504/IJBCRM.2010.038622

Bajgoric, N. (2014). Business continuity management: A systemic framework for implementation. *Kybernetes*, *43*(2), 156–177. doi:10.1108/K-11-2013-0252

Bajgoric, N. (Ed.). (2010). *Always-On Enterprise Information Systems for Business Continuance: Technologies for Reliable and Scalable Operations*. IGI Global. doi:10.4018/978-1-60566-723-2

Bajgoric, N., & Moon, Y. B. (2009). Enhancing systems integration by incorporating business continuity drivers. *Industrial Management & Data Systems*, *109*(1), 74–97. doi:10.1108/02635570910926609

Bannister, J. E., & Bawcutt, P. A. (1981). *Practical risk management*. London: Witherby & Co.

Bano, M., & Zowghi, D. (2013). User involvement in software development and system success: A systematic literature review. In *Proceedings of the 17th International Conference on Evaluation and Assessment in Software Engineering* (pp. 125–130). doi:10.1145/2460999.2461017

Bardhan, I., Krishnan, V., & Lin, S. (2013). Business Value of Information Technology: Testing the Interaction Effect of IT and R&D on Tobins Q. *Information Systems Research*, *24*(4), 1147–1161. doi:10.1287/isre.2013.0481

Baron, N. S. (2010). *Always On: Language in an Online and Mobile World*. New York: Oxford University Press.

Baskerville, R., & Sainsbury, R. (2005). Securing against the possibility of an improbable event: Concepts for managing predictable threats and normal compromises. In *4th European Conference on Information Warfare and Security 2005, ECIW 2005* (pp. 29–38). Academic Press.

Bayram, S., Kirlidog, M., & Vayvay, O. (2010). Always-On Enterprise Information Systems With Service Oriented Architecture And Load Balancing. In N. Bajgoric (Ed.), *Always-On Enterprise Information Systems for Business Continuance: Technologies for Reliable and Scalable Operations* (pp. 91–108). IGI – Global. doi:10.4018/978-1-60566-723-2.ch006

BCI. (2005). Retrieved from http://www.thebci.org/Glossary.pdf

Bell, R., & Gomez, E. A. (2011). Business Continuity for Small Business Owners : Do the Tools Fit Their Need?. *Proceedings of the 8th International ISCRAM Conference – Lisbon, Portugal, May 2011*, 1–5.

Beranek, L. (2011). Risk analysis methodology used by several small and medium enterprises in the Czech Republic. *Information Management & Computer Security*, *19*(1), 42–52. doi:10.1108/09685221111115854

Bharosa, N., Lee, J. K., & Jansen, M. (2010). Challenges and obstacles in sharing and coordinating information during multi-agency disaster response: Propositions from field exercises. *Information Systems Frontiers*, *12*(1), 49–65. doi:10.1007/s10796-009-9174-z

Bhatt, G., & Grover, V. (2005). Types of Information Technology Capabilities and their Role in Competitive Advantage: An Empirical Study. *Journal of Management Information Systems*, *22*(2), 253–277. doi:10.1080/07421222.2005.11045844

Bielski, R. (2008). *Extreme Risks, American Bankers Association*. ABI/INFORM Global.

Blackhurst, J., Dunn, K. S., & Craighead, C. W. (2011). An Empirically Derived Framework of Global Supply Resiliency. *Journal of Business Logistics*, *32*(4), 374–391. doi:10.1111/j.0000-0000.2011.01032.x

Blos, M. F., Quaddus, M., Wee, H., & Watanabe, K. (2009). Supply chain risk management (SCRM): A case study on the automotive and electronic industries in Brazil. *Supply Chain Management: An International Journal*, *14*(4), 247–252. doi:10.1108/13598540910970072

Botha, J., & Von Solms, R. (2004). A cyclic approach to business continuity planning. *Information Management & Computer Security*, *12*(4), 328–337. doi:10.1108/09685220410553541

Brands. (2013). *8 Step Process Perfects New Product Development*. Retrieved March 01, 2017, from http://innovationexcellence.com/blog/2013/05/27/8-step-process-perfects-new-product-development/

Braun, T., & Martz, B. (2007). Business Continuity Preparedness and the Mindfulness State of Mind. *AMCIS 2007 Proceedings*. Cerullo, M. V., & Cerullo, M. J. (2004). Business Continuity Planning: A Comprehensive Approach. *Information Systems Management*, *21*(3), 70–78.

Brende, N., & Markov, I. (2013). Risk perception and risk management in cloud computing: Results from a case study of Swiss companies. *International Journal of Information Management*, *33*(5), 726–733. doi:10.1016/j.ijinfomgt.2013.05.004

Brenes, E. R., Madrigal, K., & Requena, B. (2011). Corporate governance and family business performance. *Journal of Business Research*, *64*(3), 280–285. doi:10.1016/j.jbusres.2009.11.013

Bresnahan, T., Brynjolfsson, E., & Hitt, L. (2002). Information Technology, Workplace Organization, and the Demand for Skilled Labor: Firm-Level Evidence. *The Quarterly Journal of Economics*, *117*(1), 339–376. doi:10.1162/003355302753399526

Broder, J. F., & Tucker, E. (2012). *Business Continuity Planning, Risk Analysis and the Security Survey* (4th ed.). Elsevier.

Brooks, F. (1987). No silver bullet: Essence and accidents of software engineering. *IEEE Computer*, *20*(4), 10–19. doi:10.1109/MC.1987.1663532

Buckl, S., & Schweda, C. M. (2013). A Systemic View on Enterprise Architecture Management. In P. Saha (Ed.), *A Systemic Perspective to Managing Complexity with Enterprise Architecture* (pp. 237–254). IGI Global.

Bush, G. W. (2007). *National Security and Homeland Security Presidential Directive.* Retrieved from https://georgewbush-whitehouse.archives.gov/news/releases/2007/05/20070509-12.html

Butler, B. (2013). Amazon.com suffers outage: Nearly $5M down the drain?. *Network World.* Available at: http://www.networkworld.com/article/2163191/cloud-computing/update--amazon-com-suffers-outage--nearly--5m-down-the-drain-.html

Butler, B. S., & Gray, P. H. (2006). Reliability, Mindfulness, And Information Systems. MIS Quarterly, 30(2), 211-224.

Calero, A. (2015). *6 Ways to Use Live Streaming Video for Business.* Retrieved March 01, 2017, from http://www.socialmediaexaminer.com/live-streaming-video-for-business

Calzolari, G., & Scarpa, C. (2007). *Regulating a Multi-Utility Firm.* Centre for Economic Policy Research (CEPR) (No. 5516).

Carr, N. (2004). *Does IT Matter? Information Technology and the Corrosion of Competitive Advantage.* Cambridge, MA: Harvard Business School Press.

Carvalho, M. M. D., & Rabechini Junior, R. (2015). Impact of risk management on project performance: The importance of soft skills. *International Journal of Production Research, 53*(2), 321–340. doi:10.1080/00207543.2014.919423

Castillo, C. (2004). Disaster preparedness and business continuity planning at Boeing: an integrated model. *Journal of Facilities Management, 3*(1), 8-26.

CATechnologies. (2016). *Agile Infrastructure Monitoring for the Application Economy The Application Economy Is Here — Is Your IT Monitoring Approach Ready.* CA Technologies.

Cecchinato, M. E., Cox, A. L., & Bird, J. (2017, May). Always On (line)?: User Experience of Smartwatches and their Role within Multi-Device Ecologies. *Proceedings of the 2017 CHI Conference on Human Factors in Computing Systems,* 3557-3568. doi:10.1145/3025453.3025538

Cedillo, P., Gonzalez-Huerta, J., Abrahao, S., & Insfrán, E. (2015). A Monitoring Infrastructure for the Quality of Cloud Services. *24th International Conference on Information Systems Development (ISD2015-Harbin).*

Cerullo, V., & Cerullo, M. J. (2004). Business continuity planning: A comprehensive approach. *Information Systems Management, 21*(3), 70–78. doi:10.1201/1078/44432.21.3.20040601/82480.11

Chalupnik, M. J., Wynn, D. C., & Clarkson, P. J. (2013). Comparison of ilities for protection against uncertainty in system design. *Journal of Engineering Design, 24*(12), 814–829. doi:10.1080/09544828.2013.851783

Chambers, M. (2016). Risk software survey 2015: Speed, compliance and valuation. Risk. Retrieved March 02, 2017, from http://www.risk.net/risk-management/2440870/risk-software-survey-2015-speed-compliance-and-valuation

Chan, H., & Chieu, T. C. (2003). An Approach to Monitor Application States for Self-managing (Autonomic) Systems. *Companion of the 18th Annual ACM SIGPLAN Conference on Object-Oriented Programming, Systems, Languages, and Applications*, 312–313. doi:10.1145/949344.949428

Chander, M., Jain, S. K., & Shankar, R. (2013). Modeling of information security management parameters in Indian organizations using ISM and MICMAC approach. *Journal of Modelling in Management*, *8*(2), 171–189. doi:10.1108/JM2-10-2011-0054

Chatman, C. (2010, May). How Cloud Computing is changing the Face of Health Care Information Technology. *Journal of Health Care Compliance*, 37-70.

Chen, I., & Popovich, K. (2003). Understanding Customer Relationship Management (CRM) People, Process, and Technology. *Business Process Management Journal*, *9*(5), 672–688. doi:10.1108/14637150310496758

Chen, J. (2009). An exploratory study of alignment ERP implementation and organizational development activities in a newly established firm. *Journal of Enterprise Information Management*, *22*(3), 298–316. doi:10.1108/17410390910949733

Chesbrough, H., & Rosenbloom, R. (2002). The Role of the Business Model in Capturing Value from Innovation: Evidence from Xerox Corporations Technology Spin-off Companies. *Industrial and Corporate Change*, *11*(3), 529–555. doi:10.1093/icc/11.3.529

Chiasson, M., & Davidson, E. (2005). Taking industry seriously in information systems research. *Management Information Systems Quarterly*, *29*(4), 591–605. Retrieved from http://dl.acm.org/citation.cfm?id=2017276

Choi, S. W., Her, J. S., & Kim, S. D. (2007). Modeling QoS Attributes and Metrics for Evaluating Services in SOA Considering Consumers' Perspective as the First Class Requirement. In *The 2nd IEEE Asia-Pacific Services Computing Conference* (pp. 398-405). Seoul, South Korea: IEEE Computer Society.

Choudhary, V., & Vithayathil, J. (2013). The Impact of Cloud Computing: Should the IT Department Be Organized as a Cost Center or a Profit Center?. *Journal of Management Information Systems*, *30*(2), 67–100. doi:10.2753/MIS0742-1222300203

Choudhuri, B., Maguire, S., & Ojiako, U. (2009). Revisiting learning outcomes from market led ICT outsourcing. *Business Process Management Journal*, *15*(4), 569–587. doi:10.1108/14637150910975543

Chow, W. S., & Wai, O. H. (2009). Determinants of the critical success factor of disaster recovery planning for information systems. *Information Management & Computer Security*, *17*(3), 248–275. doi:10.1108/09685220910978103

Christopher, M., & Peck, H. (2004). Building the resilient supply chain. *International Journal of Logistics Management, 15*(2), 1–13. doi:10.1108/09574090410700275

Cigolini, R., Pero, M., & Sianesi, A. (2016). Reinforcing supply chain security through organizational and cultural tools within the intermodal rail and road industry. *The International Journal of Logistics Management, 27*(3), 816–836. doi:10.1108/IJLM-02-2014-0023

CIO Report. (2013). The Worst Cloud Outages of 2013 (So Far). *InfoWorld.* Available at: http://www.cio.com/slideshow/detail/108561/The-Worst-Cloud-Outages-of-2013--So-Far-?source=CIONLE_nlt_cloud_computing_2013-07-08

Clancy, H. (2013). Most common cause of SMB downtime? The answer may surprise you. *ZDNET.* Available at: http://www.zdnet.com/most-common-cause-of-smb-downtime-the-answer-may-surprise-you-7000011137

Clemons, E., & Row, M. (1991). Sustaining IT Advantage: The Role of Structural Differences. *Management Information Systems Quarterly, 15*(3), 275–292. doi:10.2307/249639

CMI. (2005). *Chartered Management Institute: Business Continuity Management.* Available at: www.managers.org.uk/docs_docs/BCM_20052865.pdf

Committee of Sponsoring Organizations of the Treadway Commission. (2004a). Enterprise risk management—Integrated framework: Executive summary. Retrieved September 15, 2016, from http://www.theiia.org/media/files/virtual-seminars/COSO_ERM_Integrated_Framework.pdf

Committee of Sponsoring Organizations of the Treadway Commission. (2004b). Enterprise risk management—Integrated framework: Application techniques. Retrieved September 15, 2016, from http://www.macs.hw.ac.uk/~andrewc/erm2/reading/ERM%20-%20COSO%20Application%20 Techniques.pdf

Comuzzi, M., & Spanoudakis, G. (2010). Dynamic set-up of monitoring infrastructures for service based systems. *Of the 2010 ACM Symposium on*, 2414–2421. doi:10.1145/1774088.1774591

Connell, C. M. (2002). Jardine, Matheson, & Company: The role of the external organization in risk reduction and learning. Academy of Management Proceedings, 2002(1), B1-B6.

Cooper, R., & Zmud, R. (1990). Information Technology implementation research: A technological diffusion approach. *Management Science, 36*(2), 123–139. doi:10.1287/mnsc.36.2.123

Crnkovic, J. Y. (2013). The Future of CRM is UX. *Business Systems Research, 4*(1), 4–13.

Crockford, N. (1982). The bibliography and history of risk management: Some preliminary observations. The Geneva Papers on Risk and Insurance, 7(23), 169–179. doi:10.1057/gpp.1982.10

Csaplar, D. (2012). *The Cost of Downtime is Rising.* Available at: http://blogs.aberdeen.com/it-infrastructure/the-cost-of-downtime-is-rising/

Cui, Y., Chipchase, J., & Jung, Y. (2007). Personal TV: A Qualitative Study of Mobile TV Users. In P. Cesar, K. Chorianopoulos, & J. F. Jensen (Eds.), Lecture Notes in Computer Science: Vol. 4471. *Interactive TV: a Shared Experience. EuroITV 2007*. Berlin: Springer. doi:10.1007/978-3-540-72559-6_21

De Haes, S., & Grembergen, W. V. (2009). An Exploratory Study into IT Governance Implementations and its Impact on Business/IT Alignment. *Information Systems Management*, *26*(2), 123–137. doi:10.1080/10580530902794786

Delic, K. A., & Riley, J. A. (2009). Enterprise Knowledge Clouds: Next Generation KM Systems?. *International Conference on Information, Process, and Knowledge Management*. IEEE Computer Society. doi:10.1109/eKNOW.2009.28

Deloitte. (2005). *CPM Global Assurance and Deloitte and Touche LLP 5th annual survey of BCM professionals entering the mainstream business continuity planning*. Available at: http://www.deloitte.com/dtt/cda/doc/content/us_ers_Final_DeloitteCPM_BCMSurvey.pdf

Desyllas, P., & Sako, M. (2013). Profiting from Business Model Innovation: Evidence from Pay-As-You-Drive Auto Insurance. *Research Policy*, *42*(1), 101–116. doi:10.1016/j.respol.2012.05.008

Dickinson, G. (2001). Enterprise Risk Management: Its Origins and Conceptual Foundation. *The Geneva Papers on Risk and Insurance*, *26*(3), 360–366. doi:10.1111/1468-0440.00121

Dignan, L. (2011). *Cloud computing market: $241 billion in 2020*. Retrieved from http://www.zdnet.com/blog/btl/cloud-computing-market-241-billion-in-2020/47702

Dinnie, G. (1999). The Second Annual Global Information Security Survey. *Information Management & Computer Security*, *7*(3), 112–120. doi:10.1108/09685229910693812

Dionne, G. (2013). Risk Management: History, Definition, and Critique. *Risk Management & Insurance Review*, *16*(2), 147–166. doi:10.1111/rmir.12016

Doomun, M. R. (2008). Multi-level information system security in outsourcing domain. *Business Process Management Journal*, *14*(6), 849–857. doi:10.1108/14637150810916026

Douglas, B. (1993). The Evolution of Risk Management. *Risk Management*, *40*(4), 38.

Du, M., Kihl, M., Arvidsson, Å., Zhang, H., Lagerstedt, C., & Gavler, A. (2015). Prefetching Schemes and Performance Analysis for TV on Demand Services. *International Journal on Advances in Telecommunications*, *8*(3&4), 162–172.

Duncan, W. J., Yeager, V. A., Rucks, A. C., & Ginter, P. M. (2011). Surviving organisational disasters. *Business Horizons*, *54*(2), 135–142. doi:10.1016/j.bushor.2010.10.005

Dvornik, D. (2000). An investment view on mobile telecommunications market in the Europe with special review of Croatia. *Ekonomski Pregled*, *51*(9-10), 1033–1052.

Dwyer, J. (1993). *The Body at War: The Story of Our Immune System*. London: JM Dent.

Dynes, S., Pixley, S., & Madory, D. (2009). Managing risk of IT disruptions in healthcare settings: A continuity of operations planning process. In *15th Americas Conference on Information Systems 2009, AMCIS 2009* (*Vol. 2*, pp. 1360–1373). Academic Press.

Eden, P., & Matthews, W. (1996). Disaster management in libraries. *Library Management, 17*(3), 5–12. doi:10.1108/01435129610112743

Elliott, D., Swartz, E., & Herbane, B. (2002). *Business Continuity Management: A Crisis Management Approach*. London: Routledge.

Fang, L., Zhang, Y., & Ma, Y. (2005). Business continuity management security module and implementation. *Jisuanji Gongcheng/Computer Engineering, 31*(24).

Fatema, K., Emeakaroha, V. C., Healy, P. D., Morrison, J. P., & Lynn, T. (2014). A survey of Cloud monitoring tools: Taxonomy, capabilities and objectives. *Journal of Parallel and Distributed Computing, 74*(10), 2918–2933. doi:10.1016/j.jpdc.2014.06.007

Ferguson, W. R. (2002). *Remarks by vice chairman of Federal Reserve to Institute of International Bankers*. Available at: www.federalreserve.gov

FERMA. (2016). *FERMA Risk Management Benchmarking Survey 2016* (8th ed.). Retrieved March 29, 2017, from http://www.ferma.eu/app/uploads/2016/09/FERMA-European-Risk-and-Insurance-Report-Full-set-of-results.pdf

Finch, P. (2004). Supply Chain Risk management, *Supply Chain management. International Journal (Toronto, Ont.), 9*(2), 183–196.

Finch, P. (2004). Supply chain risk management. *Supply Chain Management: An International Journal, 9*(2), 183–196. doi:10.1108/13598540410527079

FirstPost. (2014). *Terrorism is like cancer, history won't forgive us if it is not treated now: Nawaz Sharif.* Retrieved April 25, 2017, from http://www.firstpost.com/world/terrorism-like-cancer-history-wont-forgive-us-treated-now-nawaz-sharif-2014153.html

Fontaine, G., Le Borgne-Bachschmidt, F., & Leiba, M. (2010). Scenarios for the Internet Migration of the Television Industry. *Communications & Stratégies, 77*(1), 21–34.

Ford, J. D., Berrang-Ford, L., & Paterson, J. (2011). A systematic review of observed climate change adaptation in developed nations. *Climatic Change, 106*(2), 327–336. doi:10.1007/s10584-011-0045-5

Forrester Report. (2011). *State Of Enterprise Disaster Recovery Preparedness, Q2 2011, May 2011*. Available on: http://i.zdnet.com/whitepapers/Forrester_Analyst_White_Paper_The_State_of_Enterprise.pdf

Forrester Report. (2013). *How Organizations Are Improving Business Resiliency With Continuous IT Availability*. Available on http://www.emc.com/collateral/analyst-report/forrester-improve-bus-resiliency-continuous-it-avail-ar.pdf

Foster, S. P., & Dye, K. (2005). Building continuity into strategy. *Journal of Corporate Real Estate*, *7*(2), 105–119. doi:10.1108/14630010510812530

Franke, U., Johnson, P., König, J., & Marcks von Würtemberg, L. (2012). Availability of enterprise IT systems: An expert-based Bayesian framework. *Software Quality Journal*, *20*(2), 369–394. doi:10.1007/s11219-011-9141-z

Gallagher, R. B. (1956). Risk management: New phase of cost control. *Harvard Business Review*, *34*(5), 75–86.

Gartner. (2014). *The Costs of Downtime, July 2014.* Available at: http://blogs.gartner.com/andrew-lerner/2014/07/16/the-cost-of-downtime

Gartner. (2017). *Reviews for operational risk management.* Retrieved from March 18, 2017,https://www.gartner.com/reviews/market/operational-risk-management

Gerber, M., & Solms, R. (2005). Management of risk in the information age. *Computers & Security*, *24*(1), 16–30. doi:10.1016/j.cose.2004.11.002

Gershman, A. (2002). *Ubiquitous Commerce – Always On, Always Aware, Always Pro-Active.* The 2002 International Symposium on Applications and the Internet SAINT 2002, Nara, Japan.

Giarini, O. (1976). A macro-economicapproach to risk management. *The Geneva Papers on Risk and Insurance*, *1*(2), 5–9. doi:10.1007/BF02420933

Gibb, F., & Buchanan, S. (2006). A framework for business continuity management. *International Journal of Information Management*, *26*(2), 128–141. doi:10.1016/j.ijinfomgt.2005.11.008

Gnanasundaram, S., & Shrivastava, A. (Eds.). (2012). *Information Storage and Management (2nd ed.).* John Wiley & Sons, Inc.

Goff, M. K. (2004). *Network Distributed Computing: Fitscapes and Fallacies.* Santa Clara, CA: Prentice Hall.

Gómez-iglesias, A., Rosales, C., & Evans, T. (n.d.). *Practical Monitoring of Resource Utilization for HPC Applications. Academic Press.*

Gong, Y., & Janssen, M. (2012). From policy implementation to business process mananagement: Principles for creating flexibility and agility. *Government Information Quarterly*, *29*, 61–71. doi:10.1016/j.giq.2011.08.004

Greening, P., & Rutherford, C. (2011). Disruptions and supply networks: A multi-level, multi-theoretical relational perspective. *The International Journal of Logistics Management*, *22*(1), 104–126. doi:10.1108/09574091111127570

Grose, V. L. (2015). *Five weaknesses of enterprise risk management.* Retrieved January 19, 2017, from http://www.omegainc.com/hs-fs/hub/142206/file-23577569-pdf/docs/5_weaknesses_of_enterprise_risk_management.pdf

Gumaer, R. (1996). Beyond ERP and MRPII. *IIE Solutions*, *28*(9), 32–36.

Hair, J. F., Anderson, R. E., Babin, B. J., & Black, W. C. (2010). *Multivariate data analysis: A global perspective* (Vol. 7). Upper Saddle River, NJ: Pearson.

Hair, J. F., Black, W. C., Babin, B. J., & Anderson, R. E. (2010). *Multivariate data analysis* (7th ed.). Upper Saddle River, NJ: Prentice Hall.

Halliday, S., Badenhorst, K., & von Solms, R. (1996). A business approach to effective information technology risk analysis and management. *Information Management & Computer Security*, *4*(1), 19–31. doi:10.1108/09685229610114178

Hamilton, G. (1988). This is risk management. Stockholm, Sweden: Lund.

Haverine, H., Siren, J., & Eronen, P. (2007). Energy Consumption of Always-On Applications in WCDMA Networks. *Vehicular Technology Conference.*

Heikkinen, M. V., Casey, T., & Hecht, F. (2010). Value analysis of centralized and distributed communications and video streaming. *Info*, *12*(5), 42-58.

Hendricks, K., Singhal, V., & Stratman, J. (2007). The Impact of Enterprise Systems on Corporate Performance: A Study of ERP, SCM, and CRM system implementations. *Journal of Operations Management*, *25*(1), 65–82. doi:10.1016/j.jom.2006.02.002

Herbane, B. (2010). The evolution of business continuity management: A historical review of practices and drivers. *Business History*, *52*(6), 978–1002. doi:10.1080/00076791.2010.511185

Herbane, B., Elliott, D., & Swartz, E. M. (2004). Business continuity management: Time for a strategicrole? *Long Range Planning*, *37*(5), 435–457. doi:10.1016/j.lrp.2004.07.011

Hernantes, J., & Gallardo, G. (2015). *IT Infrastructure- Monitoring Tools*. Academic Press.

Hesson, M., & Al-Ameed, H. (2007). Online security evaluation process for new e-services. *Business Process Management Journal*, *13*(2), 223–246. doi:10.1108/14637150710740473

Hiete, M., & Merz, M. (2009). An indicator framework to assess the vulnerability of industrial sectors against indirect disaster losses. In *ISCRAM 2009 - 6th International Conference on Information Systems for Crisis Response and Management: Boundary Spanning Initiatives and New Perspectives*. Information Systems for Crisis Response and Management, ISCRAM.

Hills, M. (2017). On Her Majesty's Service (and beyond): Anthropology's Contribution to an Unconventional Career. In J. MacClancy (Ed.), *Anthropology and Public Service: the UK Experience* (pp. 61–78). Oxford, UK: Berghahn.

Hills, M. (Ed.). (2016). *Why Cyber Security is a Socio-Technical Challenge: New Concepts and Practical Measures to Enhance Detection, Prevention and Response*. New York: Nova Science Publishers.

Houliez, C., & Gamble, E. (2012). Augmented focus groups: On leveraging the peculiarities of online virtual worlds when conducting in-world focus groups. *Journal of Theoretical and Applied Electronic Commerce Research*, *7*(2), 31–51.

Ho, W., Zheng, T., Yildiz, H., & Talluri, S. (2015). Supply chain risk management: A literature review. *International Journal of Production Research*, *53*(16), 5031–5069. doi:10.1080/00207543.2015.1030467

IBM Global Services. (2006). *In the Spotlight: The Human Side of Business Continuity Planning*. New York, NY: Somers.

IBM. (n.d.a). *IBM Threat Protection System*. Retrieved April 26, 2017, fromhttp://www-03.ibm.com/security/uk/en/threat-protection/

IBM. (n.d.b). *4 Ways to Build Your Immunity to Cyber Threats*. Retrieved April 26, 2017, from https://securityintelligence.com/events/4-ways-to-build-your-immunity-to-cyber-threats/?cm_mc_uid=36931390999714782651689&cm_mc_sid_50200000=1478265168

Ibrahimovic, S. (2016). Optimizicija ulaganja u raspoloživost it infrastrukture korištenjem bayesian belief networks modela. University of Sarajevo.

Ibrahimović, S., & Bajgorić, N. (2016). Modeling information system availability by using bayesian belief network approach. *Interdisciplinary Description of Complex Systems*, *14*(2), 125–138. doi:10.7906/indecs.14.2.2

IDC Report. (2015). *High-Value Business Applications on x86: The Need for True Fault -Tolerant Systems*. Available on: http://www8.hp.com/h20195/v2/GetPDF.aspx/4AA5-8631ENW.pdfaccessed

IDC Report. (2016). *Cut costs, reduce complexity and drive availability for the always-on enterprise*. Available on: https://go.veeam.com/wp-2016-idc-executive-brief.html

IDC Report. (2016). *Cut costs, reduce complexity and drive Availability for the Always-On Enterprise*. Available on: https://go.veeam.com/wp-2016-idc-executive-brief.html

IDC White Paper. (2009). *Reducing Downtime and Business Loss: Addressing Business Risk with Effective Technology*. IDC.

IDC White Paper. (2014). *DevOps and the Cost of Downtime: Fortune 1000 Best Practice Metrics Quantified*. AVAILABLE on: http://www.idc.com/getdoc.jsp?containerId=253155

Information Today Report. (2012). *Enterprise Data And The Cost Of Downtime: 2012 IOUG Database Availability Survey*. Available at: http://www.oracle.com/us/products/database/2012-ioug-db-survey-1695554.pdf

Inkster, N. (2016). Information Warfare and the US Presidential Election. *Survival: Global Politics and Strategy, 58*(5), 23-32. Retrieved from https://www.iiss.org/en/politics%20and%20strategy/blogsections/2016-d1f9/november-b3f2/information-warfare-and-the-us-presidential-election-e9ad

International Standards Organisation (ISO). (2009). *ISO31000 Risk Management: Principles and Guidelines*. Geneva: ISO.

ISACA. (2012). *Enabling Processes*. ISACA. Retrieved from papers3://publication/uuid/24E0C493-40C6-4495-946E-A25765C97BF1

ISACA. (2013). *COBIT: A Business Framework for the Governance and Management of Enterprise IT*. ISACA.

Iwatsuki, K. (2016). *Cyberphysical system based on resilient ICT, (2011), 97720J*. Academic Press.

Iyer, R. K., & Bandyopadhyay, K. (2000). Managing technology risks in the healthcare sector: Disaster recovery and business continuity planning. *Disaster Prevention and Management*, *9*(4), 257–270. doi:10.1108/09653560010351899

Jamieson, R., Smith, S., & Jamieson, R. (2005). Key Factors in E-Government Information System Security. *18th BLED 2005 Proceedings*, 1–15.

Jarvelainen, J. (2013). IT incidents and business impacts: Validating a framework for continuity management in information systems. *International Journal of Information Management*.

Järveläinen, J. (2012). Information security and business continuity management in interorganizational IT relationships. *Information Management & Computer Security*, *20*(5), 332–349. doi:10.1108/09685221211286511

Jarvelainen, J. (2013). IT incidents and business impacts: Validating a framework for continuity management in information systems. *International Journal of Information Management*, *33*(3), 583–590. doi:10.1016/j.ijinfomgt.2013.03.001

Jia, L., Zhu, W., Zhai, C., & Du, Y. (2007). Research on an Integrated Network Management System. *Software Engineering, Artificial Intelligence, Networking, and Parallel/Distributed Computing, 2007. SNPD 2007. Eighth ACIS International Conference on*, *2*, 311–316. doi:<ALIGNMENT.qj></ALIGNMENT>10.1109/SNPD.2007.203

Josuttis, N. M. (2007). *SOA in Practice*. Sebastopol, CA: O'Reilly.

Kaasinen, E., Kulju, M., Kivinen, T., & Oksman, V. (2009). User Acceptance of Mobile TV Services. *MobileHCI '09 Proceedings of the 11th International Conference on Human-Computer Interaction with Mobile Devices and Services*, 34-43.

Kahn, M. B. (2012). *Disaster Response and Planning for Libraries*. Chicago, IL: American Library Association.

Kanellopoulos, D. N. (2014). Multimedia networking issues for digital video libraries. *The Electronic Library*, *32*(6), 898–922. doi:10.1108/EL-01-2013-0009

Karim, A.J. (2011). Business Disaster Preparedness: An Empirical Study for measuring the Factors of Business Continuity to face Business Disaster. *International Journal of Business and Social Science*, *2*(18).

Katusic, D., Marcev, A., Vulas, R., & Jezic, G. (2013). Machine-to-Machine: Emerging market and consequences on existing regulatory framework. *Proceedings of the 12th International Conference on Telecommunications*. Zagreb: University of Zagreb.

Khan, , Khan, , & Zaheer, , & M. I. B. (2013). An Efficient Network Monitoring and Management System. *International Journal of Information and Electronics Engineering*, *3*(1), 122. doi:10.7763/IJIEE.2013.V3.280

Kim, Y. G., & Cha, S. (2012). Threat scenario-based security risk analysis using use case modeling in information systems. *Security Comm. Networks*, *5*, 293–300.

King, D. L. (2003). *Moving Towards a Business Continuity Culture. In Network Security* (pp. 12–17). Elsevier.

King, D. L. (2003). Moving towards a business continuity culture. *Network Security*, *2003*(1), 12–17. doi:10.1016/S1353-4858(03)00112-0

Kolowitz, B.J., Lauro, G.R., Barkey, C., Black, H., Light, K., & Deible, C. (2012). Workflow Continuity—Moving Beyond Business Continuity in a Multisite 24–7 Healthcare Organization. *Journal of Digital Imaging*, *25*, 744-750.

Koroleva, D. (2016). Always Online: Mobile Technology and Social Media Usage by Modern Teenagers at Home and at School. Retrieved March 10, 2017 from: https://cyberleninka.ru/article/n/always-online-mobile-technology-and-social-media-usage-by-modern-teenagers-at-home-and-at-school

Koronis, E., & Ponis, S.T. (2012). Introducing Corporate Reputation Continuity To Support Organizational Resilience Against Crises. *Journal of Applied Business Research*, *28*(2), 283.

Krafzig, D., Banke, K., & Dirk, S. (2005). *Enterprise SOA: Service-Oriented Architecture Best Practices*. Upper Saddle River, NJ: Prentice Hall.

Kuo, T.-H. (2011). How to improve organizational performance through learning and knowledge? *International Journal of Manpower*, *32*(5/6), 581–603. doi:10.1108/01437721111158215

Kutare, M., Eisenhauer, G., Wang, C., Schwan, K., Talwar, V., & Wolf, M. (2010). Monalytics: Online Monitoring and Analytics for Managing Large Scale Data Centers. *Proceeding of the 7th International Conference on Autonomic Computing - ICAC '10*, 141. http://doi.org/doi:10.1145/1809049.1809073

Kwok, L., & Longley, D. (1999). Information security management and modelling. *Information Management & Computer Security*, *7*(1), 30–40. doi:10.1108/09685229910255179

Lam, J. C. (2000). *Enterprise-Wide Risk Management and the role of the Chief Risk Officer*. Retrieved June 22, 2013, from http://www.erisk.com/learning/research/011_lamriskoff.pdf

Lam, W. (2002, May). Ensuring business continuity. *IT Pro*, 19-25.

Lawler, C. M., & Szygenda, S. A. (2007). Realities of disaster recovery: IT systems & disaster preparedness. In *WMSCI 2007 - The 11th World Multi-Conference on Systemics, Cybernetics and Informatics, Jointly with the 13th International Conference on Information Systems Analysis and Synthesis, ISAS 2007 - Proc.* (Vol. 3, pp. 33–40). Academic Press.

Lee, A. S., Thomas, M., & Baskerville, R. L. (2015). Going back to basics in design science: From the information technology artifact to the information systems artifact. *Information Systems Journal, 25*(1), 5–21. doi:10.1111/isj.12054

Leitch, G. (2016). *The True Cost of Downtime in 2016*. Academic Press.

Leitch, G. (2016). *The True Cost of Downtime in 2016*. Available at: http://flexitcenter.dataresolution.net/index.php/2016/06/09/true-cost-downtime-2016/

Lewis, W. R., & Pickren, A. (2003). An Empirical Assessment of IT Disaster Risk. *Communications of the ACM, 46*(September), 201–206. doi:10.1145/903893.903938

Liebowitz, S. J., & Margolis, S. E. (1998). *Network externalities (effects)*. The New Palgrave's Dictionary of Economics and the Law.

Li, G., Fan, H., Lee, P. K., & Cheng, T. C. E. (2015). Joint supply chain risk management: An agency and collaboration perspective. *International Journal of Production Economics, 164*, 83–94. doi:10.1016/j.ijpe.2015.02.021

Lin, C. S., Kao, S., & Chen, L. S. (2012). A Proactive Operational Framework for Business Continuity in the Semiconductor Industry. *Quality and Reliability Engineering International, 28*(3), 307–320. doi:10.1002/qre.1246

Lindstrom, J. (2012). A model to explain a business contingency process. *Disaster Prevention and Management, 21*(2), 269–281. doi:10.1108/09653561211220052

Lindstrom, J., Samuelson, S., & Hagerfors, A. (2010). Business continuity planningMethodology. *Disaster Prevention and Management, 19*(2), 243–255. doi:10.1108/09653561011038039

Loudder, M., Khurana, I., & Boatsman, J. (1996). Market Valuation of Regulatory Assets in Public Utility Firms. *Accounting Review, 71*(3), 357–373.

Lump, . (2008). From high availability and disaster recovery to business continuity solutions. *IBM Systems Journal, 47*(4), 605–619. doi:10.1147/SJ.2008.5386516

Machiavelli, N. (2003). *The Prince*. London: Penguin Classics. doi:10.1522/cla.man.pri

Maitland, J. (2011). *A really bad week for Google and Amazon*. Available on: http://searchcloudcomputing.techtarget.com/news/2240035039/A-really-bad-week-for-Google-and-Amazon?asrc=EM_NLN_13718724&track=NL-1324&ad=826828

Mankis, M. (2016, February). Is Technology Really Helping Us Get More Done?. *Harvard Business Review*.

Ma, Q., Johnston, A. C., & Pearson, J. M. (2008). Information security management objectives and practices: A parsimonious framework. *Information Management & Computer Security*, *16*(3), 251–270. doi:10.1108/09685220810893207

Marsh ClearSight. (2016). *Revolutionizing the way risk is viewed and managed: The evolution of risk management information systems*. Chicago, IL: Author.

Marshall, D. (2013). *Cloud storage provider Nirvanix is closing its doors*. Available at: http://www.infoworld.com/d/virtualization/cloud-storage-provider-nirvanix-closing-its-doors-227289

Martin, N. (2011). *The true costs of data center downtime*. Available on: http://itknowledgeexchange.techtarget.com/data-center/the-true-costs-of-data-center-downtime/

Martin, N. (2007). The Asian tsunami: An urgent case for improved government information systems and management. *Disaster Prevention and Management: An International Journal*, *16*(2), 188–200. doi:10.1108/09653560710739513

McGoogan, C. (2017). *Cyber attacks hit half of UK businesses in 2016*. Retrieved 15 May 2017 from http://www.telegraph.co.uk/technology/2017/04/19/cyber-attacks-hit-half-uk-businesses-2016/

McGovern, T. J., & Samuels, H. W. (1998). Our institutional memory at risk: Collaborators to the rescue. *Campus-Wide Information Systems*, *15*(3), 103–107. doi:10.1108/10650749810227170

Mcmanus, D., Carr, H., & Adams, B. (2011). Wireless on the Precipice: The 14th Century Revisited. *Proceedings of the IADIS International Conference Information Systems 2009, IS 2009*, *54*(6), 138–143. doi:10.1145/1953122.1953155

McMurray, A. J., Pace, R. W., & Scott, D. (2004). *Research: A commonsense approach*. Melbourne: Thomson Learning Social Science Press.

McMurray, A. J., Scott, D., & Pace, R. W. (2004). The relationship between organizational commitment and organizational climate in manufacturing. *Human Resource Development Quarterly*, *15*(4), 365–377. doi:10.1002/hrdq.1116

McNaughton, B., Ray, P., & Lewis, L. (2010). Designing an evaluation framework for IT service management. *Information & Management*, *47*, 219–225.

Mehr, R. I., & Hedges, B. A. (1963). *Risk management in the business enterprise*. Homewood, IL: Irwin.

Melton, A., & Trahan, J. (2009, December). Business Continuity Planning. *Risk Management*, *56*(10), 46–48.

Melville, N., Kraemer, K., & Gurbaxani, V. (2004). Review: Information Technology and Organizational Performance: An Integrative Model of IS Business Value. *Management Information Systems Quarterly*, *28*(2), 283–322.

Meng, S., & Liu, L. (2013). Monitoring-as-a-service in the cloud. *Proceedings of the ACM/SPEC International Conference on International Conference on Performance Engineering - ICPE '13*, 373. doi:10.1145/2479871.2479929

Metcalfe, R. (1995, October). Metcalfe's Law: A Network Becomes More Valuable as it Reaches More Users. *InfoWorld*, 2.

Middleton, C. (2007). Illusions of Balance and Control in an Always-On Environment: A Case Study of Blackberry Users. *Continuum (Perth)*, *21*(2), 165–178. doi:10.1080/10304310701268695

Mitchell, R. C., Marcella, R., & Baxter, G. (1999). Corporate information security management. *New Library World*, *100*(5), 213–227. doi:10.1108/03074809910285888

Mitroff, I. I., & Alpaslan, M. C. (2003). Preparing for Evil. *Harvard Business Review*. Retrieved 15 May 2017 from www.hbr.org/2003/04/preparing-for-evil

Muir, A., & Shenton, S. (2002). If the worst happens: The use and effectiveness of disaster plans in libraries and archives. *Library Management*, *23*(3), 115–123. doi:10.1108/01435120210697216

Myers, K. N. (2006). *Business Continuity Strategies* (3rd ed.). Hoboken, NJ: John Wiley & Sons.

Nankervis, A., Compton, R., & Baird, M. (2005). *Human Resource Management*. Melbourne: Thomson.

Naqvi, S., Dallons, G., & Ponsard, C. (2010). Protecting corporate ICT infrastructures by using digital forensics. *2010 International Conference on Computer Information Systems and Industrial Management Applications, CISIM 2010*, 255–258. doi:10.1109/CISIM.2010.5643653

Newcomer, E., & Lomow, G. (2005). *Understanding SOA with Web Services*. Upper Saddle River, NJ: Pearson Education.

Nicholson, J., & Nicholson, D. B. (2010). A stream runs through IT: Using streaming video to teach information technology. *Campus-Wide Information Systems*, *27*(1), 17–24. doi:10.1108/10650741011011255

Nicolle, L. (1999). Countdown to disaster? *Computer Bulletin (London)*, *1*(3), 22–25. doi:10.1093/combul/41.3.22

Niemimaa, M. (2015). Interdisciplinary Review of Business Continuity from an Information Systems Perspective: Toward an Integrative Framework. *Communications of the Association for Information Systems*, *37*, 69–102.

Niemimaa, M. (2017). Information systems continuity process : Conceptual foundations for the study of the " social. *Computers & Security*, *65*, 1–13. doi:10.1016/j.cose.2016.11.001

Noguchi, H., Ohtaki, Y., & Kamada, M. (2015). Design and practice of file backup system taking advantage of remotely distributed campuses. *Proceedings - 2015 18th International Conference on Network-Based Information Systems, NBiS 2015*, 694–697. doi:10.1109/NBiS.2015.105

Nollau, B. (2009). Disaster Recovery and Business Continuity. *Journal of GXP Compliance*, *13*(3), 51.

Nollau, B. (2009). *Disaster Recovery and Business Continuity*. ABI/INFORM Global.

Okuda, K., Ohashi, M., & Hori, M. (2011). On the studies of the disaster recovery and the business continuity planning for private sector caused by Great East Japan earthquake. In *Communications in Computer and Information Science* (Vol. 219, pp. 14–21). CCIS. doi:10.1007/978-3-642-24358-5_2

Omar, A., Alijani, D., & Mason, R. (2011). Information Technology Disaster Recovery Plan: Case Study. *Academy of Strategic Management Journal*, *10*(2), 2011.

OMG. (n.d.). *The OMG and Service-Oriented Architecture*. Retrieved July 10, 2017, from http://www.omg.org/attachments/pdf/OMG-and-the-SOA.pdf

Orgad, S. (2009). Mobile TV. *Convergence (London)*, *15*(2), 197–214. doi:10.1177/1354856508101583

Oyha, D., & Gokhale, D. A. (2009). Logistical business continuity planning-scale developmentand validation. *The International Journal of Logistics Management*, *20*(3), 342–359. doi:10.1108/09574090911002814

Pandit, S., Wasley, C., & Zach, T. (2011). The effect of research and development (R&D) inputs and outputs on the relation between the uncertainty of future operating performance and R&D expenditures. *Journal of Accounting, Auditing & Finance*, *26*(1), 121–144. doi:10.1177/0148558X11400583

Papazoglou, M. P. (2008). *Web Services: Principles and Technology*. Harlow, UK: Pearson Education Limited.

Parise, G., Hesla, E., Parise, L., & Pennacchia, R. (2016). Switching Procedures and Business Continuity Management: The Flock Logic of Multiple Source Systems. *IEEE Transactions on Industry Applications*, *52*(1), 60–66. doi:10.1109/TIA.2015.2463791

Paton, D. (1999). Disaster business continuity: Promoting staff capability. *Disaster Prevention and Management: An International Journal*, *8*(2), 127–133. doi:10.1108/09653569910266175

Patra, M. R., Tripathy, A. K., & Das, R. K. (2011). Monitoring of service based e-governance systems. *Proceedings of the 5th International Conference on Theory and Practice of Electronic Governance - ICEGOV '11*, 353. doi:<ALIGNMENT.qj></ALIGNMENT>10.1145/2072069.2072138

Patterson, T. (2015). *The use of information technology in risk management*. Retrieved March 09, 2017, from http://www.aicpa.org/InterestAreas/FRC/AssuranceAdvisoryServices/DownloadableDocuments/ASEC_Whitepapers/Risk_Technology.pdf

Pejić Bach, M., Zoroja, J., & Jirouš, Ž. (2013). Croatian Telecommunication Market: Concentration Trends in the Period from 2003 to 2008. *Interdisciplinary Description of Complex Systems*, *11*(1), 131–142. doi:10.7906/indecs.11.1.11

Pejic-Bach, M., Draganic, M., & Jakovic, B. (2010). Some Aspects of Implementing Always-on IT-solutions and Standards in Banking Sector: The Case of Croatia. In N. Bajgoric (Ed.), *Always-On Enterprise Information Systems for BusinessContinuance: Technologies for Reliable and Scalable Operations* (pp. 149–174). IGI Global. doi:10.4018/978-1-60566-723-2.ch009

Perez-Floriano, L. R., & Gonzalez, J. A. (2007). Risk, safety and culture in Brazil and Argentina: The case of TransInc Corporation. *International Journal of Manpower*, *28*(5), 403–417. doi:10.1108/01437720710778394

Peterson, C. A. (2009). Business Continuity Management & guidelines. In *Proceedings of the 2009 Information Security Curriculum Development Annual Conference, InfoSecCD'09* (pp. 114–120). Academic Press. doi:10.1145/1940976.1940999

Pink, R. (2004). Looking for continuity. *Corporate Finance*, *135*, 32–35.

Pinta, J. (2011). Disaster recovery planning as part of business continuity management. *Agris On-Line Papers in Economics and Informatics*, *3*(4), 55–61.

Pollard, C., & Cater-Steel, A. (2010). Justifications, Strategies, and Critical Success Factors in Successful ITIL Implementations in U.S. and Australian Companies: An Exploratory Study. *Information Systems Management*, *26*(2), 164–175. doi:10.1080/10580530902797540

Ponemon Institute Report. (2016). *Cost of Data Center Outages*. Available on: http://www.emersonnetworkpower.com/en-US/Resources/Market/Data-Center/Latest-Thinking/Ponemon/Documents/2016-Cost-of-Data-Center-Outages-FINAL-2.pdf

Prathamesh & Mayekar. (2016). Is prevention always better? A case of IT service management. *Pacific Asia Conference on Information Systems*.

PricewaterhouseCoopers. (2015). *How ERM programs evolve*. Retrieved March 09, 2017, from https://www.pwc.com/us/en/risk-assurance-services/publications/assets/pwc-how-erm-programs-evolve.pdf

Protiviti. (2017). *Executive perspectives on top risks for 2017*. Retrieved March 22, 2017, fromhttps://www.protiviti.com/US-en/insights/protiviti-top-risks-survey

Purdy, G. (2010). ISO 31000:2009—Setting a new standard for risk management. *Risk Analysis*, *30*(6), 881–886. doi:10.1111/j.1539-6924.2010.01442.x PMID:20636915

Quorum Report. (2013). *Quorum Disaster Recovery Report, Q1 2013*. Available at: http://www.quorum.net/news-events/press-releases/quorum-disaster-recovery-report-exposes-top-causes-of-downtime

Raats, T., Evens, T., & Ruelens, S. (2016). Sustaining local audiovisual ecosystems.Analysis of financing and production of domestic TV fiction in small media markets. *Journal of Popular Television*, *4*(1), 129–147. doi:10.1386/jptv.4.1.129_1

Rabaey, M. (2013). Complex Adaptive SystemsThinking Approach toEnterprise Architecture. In P. Saha (Ed.), *A Systemic Perspective to Managing Complexity with Enterprise Architecture* (pp. 99–149). IGI Global.

Ragin, C. C. (1992). Introduction: Cases of "What is a Case". In C. C. Ragin & H. S. Becker (Eds.), *What is a case?* (pp. 1–17). Cambridge, UK: Cambridge University press.

Rappa, M. (2004). The Utility Business Model and the Future of Computing Services. *IBM Systems Journal, 43*(1), 32–42. doi:10.1147/sj.431.0032

Razali, A.R., Tahir, I.M. (2011). Review of the Literature on Enterprise Risk Management. *Business Management Dynamics, 1*(5), 8-16.

Rebman, T., Wang, J., Swick, Z., Reddick, D., & Rosario, J. L. (2013). Business continuity and pandemic preparedness: US health care versus non-health care agencies. *American Journal of Infection Control, 41*(4), e27–e33. doi:10.1016/j.ajic.2012.09.010 PMID:23337305

Roblek, V., Pejić Bach, M., Meško, M., & Bertoncelj, A. (2013). The impact of social media to value added in knowledge-based industries. *Kybernetes, 42*(4), 554–568.

Romano, C. (1989). Research Strategies for Small Business: A Case Study. *International Small Business Journal, 7*(4), 35–43. doi:10.1177/026624268900700403

Romero, J., Menon, N., Banker, R., & Anderson, M. (2010). ERP: Drilling for Profit in the Oil and Gas Industry. *Communications of the ACM, 53*(7), 118–121. doi:10.1145/1785414.1785448

Rosenthal, U., & Pijnenburg, B. (1991). *Crisis Management and Decision Making - Simulation Oriented Scenarios*. Springer-Science+Business Media, B. V.

Rubin, H. (1999). Bracing for zero day. *IT Professional, 1*(3), 73–79. doi:10.1109/6294.774957

Rusu, O. (n.d.). *Network Management Framework: A Distributed Virtual NOC Architecture NOCs APMs*. Academic Press.

Sabolić, D. (2009). Telecommunications reforms in Croatia. *Technology in Society, 31*(1), 11–110. doi:10.1016/j.techsoc.2008.10.005

Saha, P. (2013). Preface, Systemic Enterprise Architecture as Future: Tackling Complexity in Governments in the Cusp of Change. In P. Saha (Ed.), *A Systemic Perspective to Managing Complexity with Enterprise Architecture* (pp. xix–xxiv). IGI Global.

Sahebjamniaa, N., Torabi, S. A., & Mansourib, S. A. (2015). Integrated business continuity and disaster recovery planning: Towards organizational resilience. *European Journal of Operational Research, 242*(1), 261–273. doi:10.1016/j.ejor.2014.09.055

Sanchez, J., Korbin, W., & Viscara, D. (1995). Corporate support in the aftermath of a natural disaster: Effects on employee strains. *Academy of Management Journal, 38*(2), 504–521. doi:10.2307/256690

Sapateiro, C., Baloian, N., Antunes, P., & Zurita, G. (2011). Developing a Mobile Collaborative Tool for Business Continuity Management. *Journal of Universal Computer Science*, *17*(2), 164–182.

Savage, M. (2002). Business continuity planning. *Work Study*, *51*(5), 254–261. doi:10.1108/00438020210437277

Sax, J., & Torp, S. S. (2015). Speak up! Enhancing risk performance with enterprise risk management, leadership style and employee voice. *Management Decision*, *53*(7), 1452–1468. doi:10.1108/MD-10-2014-0625

Sharma, D., Poddar, R., Mahajan, K., Dhawan, M., & Mann, V. (2015). HANSEL: Diagnosing Faults in OpenStack. *Sigcomm*, *2015*, 421–434. doi:10.475/123

Simmons, O. S. S. (2003). The Corporate Immune System: Governance from the Inside Out. *Illinois Law Review*. Retrieved 15 May 2017 from https://illinoislawreview.org/wp-content/ilr-content/articles/2013/3/Simmons.pdf

Šimonová, S., & Šprync, O. (2011). Proactive IT / IS monitoring for business continuity planning. *Ekonomie a Management*, *14*(3), 57–65.

Šimundić, S., & Boban, M. (2008). Business Continuity management systems - challenges of management on the way to business success in digital economy. In *MIPRO 2008 - 31st International Convention Proceedings: Digital Economy - 5th ALADIN, Information Systems Security, Business Intelligence Systems, Local Government and Student Papers* (Vol. 5, pp. 53–56). Academic Press.

Singh, J. (2009). Modeling application availability. In *Proceedings of the 2009 Spring Simulation Multiconference* (pp. 1–4). Retrieved from http://dl.acm.org/citation.cfm?id=1639932

Singh, A., Gupta, M., & Ojha, A. (2014). Identifying factors of organizational information security management.. *Journal of Enterprise Information Management*, *27*(5), 644–667. doi:10.1108/JEIM-07-2013-0052

Smallman, C., & Smith, D. (2003). Managerial risk perceptions: Exploring the dimensions of managers accepted risks. *Risk Management*, *5*(1), 7–32. doi:10.1057/palgrave.rm.8240137

Smith, D. (2005). Business (not) as usual: Crisis management, service recovery and the vulnerability of organisations. *Journal of Services Marketing*, *19*(5), 309–320. doi:10.1108/08876040510609925

Smith, D., & Fischbacher, M. (2009). The changing nature of risk and risk management: The challenge of borders, uncertainty and resilience. *Risk Management*, *11*(1), 1–12. doi:10.1057/rm.2009.1

Snedaker, S. (2013). *Business Continuity and Disaster Recovery Planning for IT Professionals*. Maryland Heights, MO: Elsevier.

Speight, P. (2011). Business Continuity. *Journal of Applied Security Research*, *6*(4), 529–554. doi:10.1080/19361610.2011.604021

Spremić, M. (2012). Measuring IT Governance Performance: A Research Study on CobiT-Based Regulation Framework Usage. *International Journal of Mathematics and Computers in Simulation*, *1*(6), 17-25.

Spremić, M. (2004). *Menadžment i elektroničko poslovanje*. Zagreb: Narodne novine.

Spremic, M. (2009). IT Governance Mechanisms in Managing IT Business Value. *WSEAS Transactions on Information Science and Applications*, *6*(6), 906–915.

Spremic, M. (2010). IT Governance and IT Risk Management Principles And Methods For Supporting 'Always-On' Enterprise Information Systems. In N. Bajgoric (Ed.), *Always-On Enterprise Information Systems for Business Continuance: Technologies for Reliable and Scalable Operations* (pp. 1–16). IGI Global. doi:10.4018/978-1-60566-723-2.ch001

Spremić, M., & Kostić, D. (2008). Upravljanje kvalitetom informatičke usluge: Studije slučaja primjene ITIL metode. *Poslovna Izvrsnost*, *2*(1), 37–58.

Sprott, D., & Wilkes, L. (2004). *Understanding Service-Oriented Architecture*. CBDI Forum. Retrieved July 10, 2017, from https://msdn.microsoft.com/en-us/library/aa480021.aspx

Stanton, R. (2005). Beyond Disaster Recovery: The Benefits of Business Continuity. *Computer Fraud & Security*, *2005*(July), 18–19. doi:10.1016/S1361-3723(05)70234-7

Stanton, R. (2007, Nov.). Fail to plan, plan to fail. *Infosecurity*, 24–25.

Sumner, M. (2009). Information Security Threats: A Comparative Analysis of Impact, Probability, and Preparedness. *Information Systems Management*, *26*(1), 2–11. doi:10.1080/10580530802384639

Swartz, M., Herbane, B., & Elliott, D. (2004). *Business Continuity Management: Time for a strategic role?*. Academic Press.

Symantec Report. (2011). *Symantec 2011 SMB Disaster Preparedness Survey*. Available on: http://www.symantec.com/content/en/us/about/media/pdfs/symc_2011_SMB_DP_Survey_Report_Global.pdf?om_ext_cid=biz_socmed_twitter_facebook_marketwire_linkedin_2011Jan_worldwide_dpsurvey

Tammineedi, R. L. (2010). Business Continuity Management: A Standards-Based Approach. *Information Security Journal: A Global Perspective*, *19*, 36-50.

Tang, L., Li, T., Shwartz, L., Pinel, F., & Grabarnik, G. Y. (2013). An Integrated Framework for Optimizing Automatic Monitoring Systems in Large IT Infrastructures. *Proc. of KDD*, 1249–1257. doi:10.1145/2487575.2488209

Taylor, P., Dani, S., & Deep, A. (2010). International Journal of Logistics Research and Applications : A Leading Journal of Supply Chain Management Fragile food supply chains: reacting to risks. *October*, *5567*, 37–41.

Taylor, S., Vernon, L., & Rudd, C. (2007). *ITIL Service Design*. The Stationary Office, TSO. <ALIGNMENT.qj></ALIGNMENT>10.1002/0471744719.ch1

Tomic, D., & Markic, B. (2010). Continuous Database Availability. In N. Bajgoric (Ed.), *Always-On Enterprise Information Systems for Business Continuance: Technologies for Reliable and Scalable Operations* (pp. 129–148). IGI Global. doi:10.4018/978-1-60566-723-2.ch008

Tripwire. (2017). *Insider Threats as the Main Security Threat in 2017*. Retrieved 15 May 2017 from https://www.tripwire.com/state-of-security/security-data-protection/insider-threats-main-security-threat-2017/

Tucker, E. (2014). *Business Continuity from Preparedness to Recovery: A Standards-Based Approach*. Butterworth-Heinemann.

Turban, E., & Volonino, L. (2010). *Information Technology For Management – Transforming Organizations in the Digital Economy* (7th ed.). Wiley.

Turetken, O. (2008). Is Your Backup IT-Infrastructure in a Safe Location – A Multi-Criteria Approach to Location Analysis for Business Continuity Facilities. *Information Systems Frontiers*, *10*, 375–383. doi:10.1007/s10796-008-9081-8

Turkle, S. (2008). *Always-On/Always-On-You: The Tethered Self. In Handbook of Mobile Communication Studies*. Katz and Castells.

Turnbull, J. (2016). *The art of monitoring*. Academic Press.

Tweedy, D. (2013). *2013 RMIS review*. Retrieved June12, 2016,from http://pdf32.keenbooks.org/pdf/for-now-7_5p6pp.pdf

Van Hove, L. (2016). Testing Melcafes Law: Pitfalls and Possibilities. *Information Economics and Policy*, *37*, 67–76. doi:10.1016/j.infoecopol.2016.09.001

van Zadelhoff, M. (2016). *The Biggest Cybersecurity Threats Are Inside Your Company*. Retrieved 15 May 2017 fromhttps://hbr.org/2016/09/the-biggest-cybersecurity-threats-are-inside-your-company

Vandewater, E. A., Bickham, D. S., Lee, J. H., Cummings, H. M., Wartella, E. A., & Rideout, V. J. (2005). When the television is always on heavy television exposure and young childrens development. *The American Behavioral Scientist*, *48*(5), 562–577. doi:10.1177/0002764204271496

Varga, M. (2010). Challenges of Data Management in Always-On Enterprise Information Systems. In N. Bajgoric (Ed.), *Always-On Enterprise Information Systems for Business Continuance: Technologies for Reliable and Scalable Operations* (pp. 109–128). IGI – Global. doi:10.4018/978-1-60566-723-2.ch007

Veeam Report. (2014). *The Veeam Data Center Availability Report 2014*. Available at: https://www.veeam.com/wp-availability-report-2014.html

Venkatraman, A. (2013). Human error most likely cause of datacentre downtime, finds study. *Computerweekly*. Available at: http://www.computerweekly.com/news/2240179651/Human-error-most-likely-cause-of-datacentre-downtime-finds-study

Verano-Tacoronte, D., & Melián-González, S. (2008). Human resources control systems and performance: The role of uncertainty and risk propensity. *International Journal of Manpower*, *29*(2), 161–187. doi:10.1108/01437720810872712

Vuong, J. (2015). Disaster recovery planning. In *Information Security Curriculum Development Conference 2015* (pp. 1–3). Academic Press.

Wahono, R. S. (2015). A Systematic Literature Review of Software Defect Prediction: Research Trends, Datasets, Methods and Frameworks. *Journal of Software Engineering*, *1*(1), 1–16.

Wankel, L. A., & Blessinger, P. (2013). Inventive Approaches in Higher Education: An Introduction to Using Multimedia Technologies. In In Increasing Student Engagement and Retention using Multimedia Technologies: Video Annotation, Multimedia Applications, Videoconferencing and Transmedia Storytelling (Cutting-edge Technologies in Higher Education, Volume 6 Part F) Emerald Group Publishing Limited, pp.3 – 16.

Wan, S. H. C., & Chan, Y. (2008). Improving service management in campus IT operations. *Campus-Wide Information Systems*, *25*(1), 30–49. doi:10.1108/10650740810849070

Webb, G. R., Tierney, K. J., & Dahlhamer, J. M. (2000). Business and disasters: Empirical patterns and unanswered questions. *Natural Hazards Review*, *1*(2), 83–90. doi:10.1061/(ASCE)1527-6988(2000)1:2(83)

Weinman, J. (2007, August). Is Metcalfe's Law Way Too Optimistic?. *Business Communications Review*.

Weinman, J. (2015, November). Digital Technologies and Competitive Advantage. *Research-Technology Management*, 12-17.

Wester, R. B. (2006). Emergency preparedness, business continuity, and the new normal. In *1st Joint Emergency Preparedness and Response/Robotic and Remote Systems Topical Meeting* (Vol. 2006, pp. 603–609). Academic Press.

Whitworth, P. M. (2006). Continuity of operations plans: Maintaining essential agency functions when disaster strikes. *Journal of Park & Recreation Administration*, *24*(4).

Wiengarten, F., Humphreys, P., Gimenez, C., & McIvor, R. (2016). Risk, risk management practices, and the success of supply chain integration. *International Journal of Production Economics*, *171*, 361–370. doi:10.1016/j.ijpe.2015.03.020

Williams, A. (Ed.). (2016). Monitoring & management with docker & containers (Vol. 5). Academic Press.

Williams, S. (2017). Always On: Managing Online Communities in a 24/7 Society. In Promotional Strategies and New Service Opportunities in Emerging Economies (pp. 314-328). IGI Global.

Williams, A., & Heins, M. H. (1964). *Risk management and insurance*. New York, NY: McGraw-Hill.

Winkler, U., Fritzsche, M., Gilani, W., & Marshall, A. (2010). A Model-Driven Framework for Process-centric Business Continuity Management. *Proceedings of the 2010 Seventh International Conference on the Quality of Information and Communications Technology*, 248-252. doi:10.1109/QUATIC.2010.46

Wolf, R. (2008). The Evolution of Enterprise Risk Management. *The Actuary*. Retrieved January 12, 2017, from https://www.soa.org/Library/Newsletters/The-Actuary-Magazine/2008/June/act-2008-vol5-iss3-wolf.aspx

Wolf, J. (2011). Sustainable Supply Chain Management Integration: A Qualitative Analysis of the German Manufacturing Industry. *Journal of Business Ethics*, *102*(2), 221–235. doi:10.1007/s10551-011-0806-0

Yao, X., Turoff, M., & Hiltz, R. S. (2010). A field trial of a collaborative online scenario creation system for emergency management. In *ISCRAM 2010 - 7th International Conference on Information Systems for Crisis Response and Management: Defining Crisis Management 3.0, Proceedings*. Information Systems for Crisis Response and Management, ISCRAM.

Yin, R. K. (1994). *Case Study Research. Design and Methods* (2nd ed.). Newbury Park, CA: Sage Publications.

Yoshida, K., & Deyle, R. E. (2005). Determinants of small business hazard mitigation. *Natural Hazards Review*, *6*(1), 1–12. doi:10.1061/(ASCE)1527-6988(2005)6:1(1)

Yusuf, Y., & Little, D. (1998). An empirical investigation of enterprise-wide integration of MRPII. *International Journal of Operations & Production Management*, *18*(1), 66–86. doi:10.1108/01443579810192916

Zambon, E., Bolzoni, D., Etalle, S., & Salvato, M. (2007). A model supporting business continuity auditing & planning in information systems. In *Second International Conference on Internet Monitoring and Protection, ICIMP 2007*. Academic Press. doi:10.1109/ICIMP.2007.4

Zhu, Z., Nakata, C., Sivakumar, K., Grewal, D. (2013). Fix It or Leave It? Customer Recovery from Self-service Technology Failures. *Journal of Retailing, 89*, 15–29.

Zobel, C. (2011). Representing perceived tradeoffs in defining disaster resilience. *Decision Support Systems*, *50*(2), 394–403. doi:10.1016/j.dss.2010.10.001

Zsidisin, G. A., Melnyk, S. A., & Ragatz, G. L. (2005). An institutional theory perspective of BCP Planning for purchasing and supply management. *International Journal of Production Research*, *43*(16), 3401–3421. doi:10.1080/00207540500095613

Index

www.ingramcontent.com/pod-product-compliance
Lightning Source LLC
LaVergne TN
LVHW081325300926
849161LV00008B/1880